Majority Leadership in the U.S. House

Majority Leadership in the U.S. House

Barbara Sinclair

The Johns Hopkins University Press

Baltimore and London

© 1983 by The Johns Hopkins University Press
All rights reserved
Printed in the United States of America

The Johns Hopkins University Press, Baltimore, Maryland 21218
The Johns Hopkins Press Ltd., London

Library of Congress Cataloging in Publication Data

Sinclair, Barbara, 1940—
  Majority Leadership in the U.S. House.

  Bibliography: p. 257
  Includes index.
  1. United States. Congress. House—Leadership.
2. Democratic Party (U.S.) I. Title.
JK1411.S56 1983   328.73'0762   83–278
ISBN 0-8018-2934-8
ISBN 0-8018-2933-X

CONTENTS

v

TABLES

PREFACE

AND

ACKNOWLEDGMENTS

In 1977, after he pushed President Carter's energy program through the House of Representatives, Tip O'Neill was hailed as the strongest Speaker since Sam Rayburn. In 1981, after suffering a series of legislative defeats at the hands of President Reagan, O'Neill was labeled weak and ineffective. Building winning coalitions is considered a central function of majority party leadership, and as this turnabout shows, the leadership to a large extent is judged on its coalition-building success.

"Keeping peace in the family" is an equally important, though less publicly visible, party leadership function. As the phrase implies, this function involves the promotion and maintenance of intraparty harmony; it requires that leaders help members satisfy their expectations regarding their roles in the chamber, mitigate intraparty conflicts, and foster cooperative patterns of behavior among members.

This study examines how the current majority party leadership performs these functions and how the leadership's activities are shaped and constrained by the environment in which it works. During the 1970s changes in House rules and norms, high membership turnover, and the rise to prominence of new party-fragmenting issues transformed the environment in which the House majority party leadership operates. The current leaders work in a much less predictable environment than their predecessors did. Because Democrats have controlled the House since 1955, this is perforce a study of Democratic party leadership. Party leadership has not received much attention in the recent literature on Congress (but see Waldman 1980; Dodd 1979; Dodd and Sullivan 1981; Peabody 1976); with the present study, I propose to fill, at least partly, that lacuna. Because leadership activity can only be understood in terms of the context in which leaders function, this is also an examination of the postreform House of Representatives.

Chapter 1 opens with a discussion of the two central majority party leadership functions and the complex interrelationship between them. The need to "keep peace in the family" places limits on the coalition-building strategies that the leadership can use. Winning coalitions must be built repeatedly; consequently, tactics that might be successful in the short run are counterproductive if they exacerbate intraparty conflicts or produce generalized dissatisfaction among the members. Yet the leaders cannot allow the peace-keeping function to lead to immobility. The transformation in the House environment during the 1970s which led to a less predictable House of Representatives has made balancing the two central functions even more difficult.

Although majority party members benefit collectively when their leaders are successful at performing these functions, members also have individual goals, and behavior that furthers the attainment of those goals may work against leadership success. The leaders' influence over the behavior of their members, thus, is a function of the extent to which the leaders can help or hinder members' goal attainment. Introducing strategies used by current leaders, the final section of chapter 1 argues that developing strategies that are consonant with members' goal-directed behavior is central to leadership success.

My analysis of how the current leadership operates begins with chapter 2. The focus is on the Speaker, the majority leader, and, to a lesser extent, the majority whip. Leadership duties specified by rules and tradition as well as the services leaders can, by virtue of their party leadership positions, perform for members provide resources that the leaders can use to carry out their primary functions.

Effective leadership always requires adjusting strategies to the context in which they will be applied. One key to successful leadership in the post-reform House is providing members with opportunities to participate in the legislative process but channeling their participation so that it is beneficial to the party effort. Another is finding means of coping with the uncertainty that the rules and norms changes have created. Chapter 3 examines how, as a component of a strategy to accomplish these ends, the core leaders use the whip system, the Steering and Policy Committee, and the Rules Committee.

The majority party leadership operates in an environment peopled by a broad variety of actors—fellow House members, Senators, administration personnel, and lobbyists—whose behavior can affect leadership success at "keeping peace in the family" and building winning coalitions. Chapter 4 analyzes the relationship between the leadership and these actors: the impact of the behavior of these actors on leadership success; the rate and nature of interaction; and the extent to which, and the ways in which, the leadership attempts to influence the behavior of the actors.

In building winning coalitions at the floor stage, leaders face the problem of making the most effective use of limited resources within a context of high uncertainty. Chapter 5 examines the stages in the coalition-building process and the wide variety of coalition-building techniques used by the leaders. Although some of the rules changes of the 1970s augmented the techniques available, what distinguishes the current leadership's approach to coalition building from its predecessors' is not primarily the specific techniques employed but, rather, the current leadership's active attempt to involve as many Democrats as possible in the coalition-building process.

Abstract examinations of leadership coalition-building efforts necessitate the sacrifice of enlightening contextual detail and tend to convey the somewhat spurious impression that the leadership is always in charge. The case studies of the leadership in action presented in chapters 6 and 7 provide a somewhat different perspective for understanding the current leadership. The impact of the broader political context on strategy and on the likelihood of success is more readily illuminated, making more apparent the tenuousness of the leadership's control and the roots of that tenuousness in time constraints, limited resources, and high uncertainty.

Chapter 8 begins with a summary analysis of the problems leaders face in performing their two principle functions, takes a look at the strategies that the current leadership has developed to cope with these problems, and continues with an assessment of leadership success. Because members' goal-directed behavior may conflict with the requirements of coalition building and party maintenance, successful performance of these central functions depends on leaders being able to influence their members' behavior. Yet since the revolt against Speaker Cannon leadership resources have been insufficient to affect decisively members' goal achievement. The current leaders, in addition, must perform these functions within the highly unpredictable environment of the postreform House. Speculations about the future of leadership in the House of Representatives based on this analysis conclude the chapter.

I began this research in 1978 and 1979 when I served as an American Political Science Association Congressional Fellow in the House majority leader's office. The study is based on participant-observation and on interviews I conducted between 1979 and 1982 with House leaders and members and their staffs as well as informed observers. All unattributed quotations are from interviews I conducted. I owe a major debt to all those who used some of their precious time to talk with me.

Very special thanks are due to Representative Jim Wright and his staff: Craig Raupe, Kathy Mitchell, Barbara Sadoff, John Mack, Dick Olson, Marshall Lynam, Janice Joyner, Beth McNeill, and Paul Driskell. They gave me a home base and much help and friendship throughout this research. Bob Peabody helped me with access and advice. The APSA Congressional Fellowship Program provided me with the opportunity to spend a year working on the Hill, without which this research would not have been possible. Tom Mann, then the program's director, was always helpful. The Academic Senate, University of California, Riverside, supported the research with several intramural grants, and the Dirksen Congressional Leadership Research Center also generously provided some financial support. Steven Smith contributed extremely helpful suggestions for improving the manuscript. I would also like to thank Henry Y. K. Tom, my editor, for his suggestions and his efficiency. To Donna Cooney, who always found a way to get my chapters typed, and to Debbie Webster, who did much of the typing, I am also thankful.

Some of the material in chapter 5 first appeared in my article "The Speaker's Task Force in the Post-Reform House of Representatives," *American Political Science Review* (June 1981), and is reprinted with permission.

Majority Leadership in the U.S. House

1

COALITION

BUILDING

AND PARTY

MAINTENANCE

IN A NEW

ENVIRONMENT

Majority Party Leadership Functions

It is not difficult to understand why the attentive public—including the press—judges the majority party leadership almost exclusively upon its coalition-building success. During the twentieth century the ability of the House of Representatives to legislate has been uncertain. Given the chamber's large and heterogeneous membership, majorities seldom simply materialize; they must be constructed. Political parties have usually provided the basis upon which majorities are constructed, and the majority party leadership is expected to play a central role in the coalition-building process.

Satisfying the expectations of followers and of other significant actors is central to successful leadership. In order to meet those expectations the majority party leadership in the House of Representatives must perform not one but two principal functions. First the leadership is charged with building winning coalitions on major legislation—legislation of importance to the party as a collectivity—and thereby satisfying the legislative output expectations of its membership and of significant actors outside the chamber. Second, the leadership must "keep peace in the family," as the current leaders express it. The heterogeneity of the Democratic party and the often conflicting policy and power goals of members pose constant threats to party coherence. Generalized dissatisfaction among members with the institution and their role within it can also endanger party harmony. "Keeping

1

peace in the family" (also referred to as "party maintenance") dictates that leaders help members satisfy their expectations regarding their individual roles in the chamber; it requires leaders to mitigate intraparty conflicts and foster cooperative patterns of behavior among party members.

A number of other functions have devolved upon the majority party leadership. As chief officer of the House, the Speaker has an institutional responsibility to maintain the reputation of the House as a functioning legislature. The Speaker and the majority leader act as the chief public spokesmen for their party in the House. The party leadership plays a central role in liaison between the House of Representatives and the White House and has a role in the setting of the party's policy priorities, especially when the president is of the other party. It also performs general legislative coordination within the House.

House and party rules and tradition provide the majority party leadership with a variety of tools and resources that can be used in the performance of these functions. The Speaker, as chief officer of the House, presides over the chamber and applies the rules; the position provides him with a variety of appointive powers and a sizeable staff. As leader of his party in the House, he makes appointments to a number of party positions, chairs the party's Steering and Policy Committee, and oversees the work of other party-officers. The majority leader and the whip, who with the Speaker make up the core leadership in the modern House, are not officers of the House; they are party officials and act as lieutenants of the Speaker. The majority leader schedules legislation for floor consideration; he is the chief party spokesman on the House floor. The whip oversees the whip system, which is charged with collecting and disseminating information. Conducting whip polls to determine how members stand on important legislation is the whip system's single most important function.

The relationship between the leadership's two primary functions shapes and constrains the leadership's use of its tools. The need to "keep peace in the family" places limits on employable coalition-building strategies. Winning coalitions must be built repeatedly; consequently, tactics that might exacerbate intraparty conflicts or produce generalized dissatisfaction among members must be eschewed no matter how effective they may be in the short run. The use of such tactics would not only reduce the future success of coalition building but, over the long run, might even endanger the leaders' own positions. Because their success as leaders is defined, to a considerable extent, in terms of their success as coalition builders, the peace-keeping function cannot be allowed to lead to immobility. Yet the necessity of passing legislation that is controversial within the party inevitably strains party harmony.

There is, thus, a tension between the two functions, yet successful performance of one of them can increase the leadership's chances of success at the other. To the extent the leaders can "keep peace," their chances of building winning coalitions in the future are increased, and to the extent leaders are successful at building winning coalitions on bills that satisfy their members' expectations as to legislative outputs, they contribute to "keeping peace in the family."

The environment in which the leaders operate largely determines the extent to which the two functions can be successfully reconciled, and it strongly influences the strategies most likely to be effective. An understanding of the current leadership's style and strategies, then, requires a review of the transformation in the House which occurred during the 1970s.

The House and the Democratic Party in the Postreform Era

Scholars increasingly agree that congressional leadership is best understood from a contextual perspective (Jones 1981; Cooper and Brady 1981). The context or environment shapes and constrains leadership styles and strategies. Rules, the characteristics of the membership, and norms are the most salient aspects of the internal House environment for the leadership. House and party rules distribute resources in the chamber. The size of the party membership is a basic resource. Membership stability and factors such as member goals and reelection needs influence which leadership styles are feasible. Norms affect how resources can be used. To a large extent, the broader political environment determines the House's policy agenda. Whether the issues at the center of controversy cut along or across party lines influences strategy choices and the probability of success.

Rules Changes

The 1970s saw a constellation of rules changes aimed at curbing the power of committee chairmen (See Ornstein 1975; Dodd and Oppenheimer 1977). In the aftermath of the revolt against Speaker Joseph Cannon early in this century, seniority had become the sole criterion for appointment to chairmanships, and as a result chairmanships had become independent positions of power over which the majority party had little control (Fenno 1965). During the 1950s conservative southern Democrats chaired most of the major committees, and they often exercised their power autocratically. Not only did they frequently block legislation desired by more liberal northern Democrats, many also denied junior members the opportunity for meaningful participation. The chairs' almost total control over the organization, staffing, and agenda of their committees made iron-handed tactics possible. Thus Graham Barden, (D-N.C.), conservative chairman of the Education and Labor Committee during the 1950s, blocked progressive legislation through a variety of devices ranging from keeping the committee's staff small and (reportedly) incompetent to simply refusing to hold committee meetings. He tightly managed the subcommittees and denied Adam Clayton Powell (D-N.Y.) a subcommittee chairmanship even though Powell was clearly entitled to one by virtue of seniority.

The Rules Committee, the "traffic cop" that regulates the flow of legislation to the floor, was controlled by a bipartisan conservative coalition and constituted another bottleneck for progressive legislation. Under the direction of its able and extremely conservative chairman, Howard Smith (D-Va.), the committee often blocked bills reported by the substantive committees. In 1960, for example, the Rules Committee killed an aid-to-education bill that had passed both chambers by refusing to send the bill to a conference with the Senate.

Influence in the House, thus, was distributed in a decentralized but highly unequal fashion. As the liberals saw it, the committee chairs' arbitrary power was the problem, thwarting both their policy goals and their desire for meaningful participation. Although frustrated, liberal Democrats could do little to challenge the power of the committee chairs. Throughout most of the 1950s the Democratic margin in the House was narrow and the party was fairly evenly split between liberals and conservatives. The 1958 election dramatically increased the Democratic margin, and most of the new members were northern liberals. Nevertheless, the reformers moved cautiously. The Democratic Study Group, an organization of liberal members which would later spearhead the reforms of the 1970s, was formed, and in 1961 Speaker Sam Rayburn was prevailed upon to move against the Rules Committee. The bitter fight to enlarge the Rules Committee was won, but this proved to be only a partial solution. The leadership majority was often shaky (Oppenheimer 1977).

Its conservative impact on legislation was a major part of the liberals' frustration with the distribution of power in the House; thus their overwhelming legislative success in the 89th Congress (1965-66) temporarily took the steam out of the reform effort. However, it became clear fairly quickly that the basic problems had not been solved. The Vietnam War and the election of a Republican president gave renewed impetus to the reform effort.

The 1970 Reorganization Act, one of the first fruits of this effort, was passed by a coalition of liberal Democrats and Republicans. The act contained a variety of sunshine provisions: it encouraged open committee proceedings and required that all committee roll calls be made public. Other provisions were aimed at safeguarding the rights of minorities (for example, minority members were guaranteed the right to call witnesses at committee hearings) and at enabling members to obtain information on measures before they reached the floor (conference reports were required to be available for three days before a House vote could be taken, and debate on a conference report was to be evenly divided between the majority and the minority). One of the most important changes was the institution of recorded teller votes in the Committee of the Whole House, where bills are amended; prior to the 1970 act, no recorded votes were taken at this crucial stage.

Liberal Democrats had altered their strategy even before the passage of the 1970 Reorganization Act. Throughout the 1960s, as Republicans began winning House seats in the South and Democrats made inroads into previously Republican territory in the North, the center of gravity of the Democratic party moved decidedly to the left. As the liberals' strength increased, they decided to concentrate upon changing party rather than House rules. The committee assignment process and the designation of committee chairs, over which the liberals hoped to gain a measure of control, are within the province of the party.

The crucial step was the revitalization of the party caucus, which for half a century had been inactive, meeting only at the beginning of a new Congress, and then largely to ratify decisions made elsewhere. In 1969, at the beginning of the 91st Congress, liberals won a rule providing for monthly meetings of the caucus at the request of fifty members.

Beginning in 1971 the Democratic Caucus passed a series of rules changes the effect of which was to distribute positions of influence more widely among members and to shift power from full committee chairs to subcommittee chairs. Each member was limited to chairing only one subcommittee, and each subcommittee chair was empowered to hire one professional staff member. The Subcommittee Bill of Rights, passed in 1973, contained provisions to circumscribe the power of the full committee chairs: it removed from full committee chairs the power to select subcommittee chairs and gave it to the Democratic caucus of the committee, which consists of all Democratic members of the committee; it required subcommittees to have fixed jurisdiction and adequate budget and staff; and it mandated that legislation be referred to subcommittee within a fixed time. A rule aimed at the highly centralized Ways and Means Committee required all committees with twenty or more members to establish at least four subcommittees. As a result of a series of rules changes instituted in 1971 and 1973 full committee chairs and the chairmen of Appropriations subcommittees have to be approved by secret ballot in the Democratic Caucus.

The 1970s also saw an immense growth in the staff resources available to members of the House. In 1967 personal staff totaled 4,055; in 1979 that figure stood at 7,067. The number of employees of House committees increased from 702 in 1970 to 1,959 in 1979 (Bibby, Mann, and Ornstein 1980, pp. 69–70). The most junior member is now entitled to hire a staff of at least eighteen.

The reactivated caucus also provided a forum for members whose policy goals were frustrated by committees that did not reflect majority sentiment in the party. The caucus several times instructed the Rules Committee to allow floor votes on specific amendments to tax bills to which floor amendments had previously been barred. One result of such action by the caucus was the repeal of the oil depletion allowance. The early 1970s saw the caucus pass a series of resolutions urging or ordering committees to act on antiwar measures that had been bottled up. But by the late 1970s member leeriness of undermining the committee system led to a decline in caucus legislative activity. Nevertheless, the caucus had been established as a mechanism for calling to account committees unwilling to respond to the wishes of an intense majority of the party.

The rules changes of the 1970s have severely limited the discretion of full committee chairmen. Their power to run their committees has been strictly curtailed and, because they are dependent on the caucus for their positions, they must be responsive to the wishes of the party majority. Subcommittees, on the other hand, have gained considerable autonomy: subcommittee chairs are no longer beholden to the full committee chair for their position, their workload, or their resources. The rule that limits members to chairing only one subcommittee has increased the number of subcommittee chairmen, and that rule combined with the new procedures for choosing subcommittee chairmen has increased the activity level of subcommittees. Because he is chairing only one subcommittee, a member can devote his time to that task; because he is elected by his fellow committee Democrats, he must be active to justify his reelection. The rules changes, in addition, encourage participation by rank-and-file members, participation made more feasible by the increase in such members' staff resources. These changes have made the environment in which the party leaders operate less predictable. The number of significant actors is larger. There is more taking place, and it is taking place in more arenas.

Some of the rules changes of the 1970s, however, augmented the resources of the party leadership. The power to make committee assignments was taken from the Democrats on Ways and Means and given to the Steering and Policy Committee, which the Speaker chairs and to which he appoints a number of members. Rules Committee nominations were made the prerogative of the Speaker. In addition, the Speaker has been granted increased power over the referral of bills; in those cases in which a bill is referred to more than one committee, he can set time limits on the committees for reporting the bill out.

Membership Changes

The success of the reform movement in the House is largely attributable to changes that took place beginning in 1958 in the composition of the Democratic membership. Liberal and relatively junior northern Democrats working through the Democratic Study Group spearheaded the reform effort, and after 1958 their numbers grew both in absolute terms and as a proportion of the Democratic membership. The close party balance that prevailed from 1953 to 1958 was destroyed by the 1958 election; since then Democrats have held a majority of at least 55 percent, and the margin has usually been considerably greater. The increase in Democratic strength came among northern Democrats, while the numbers of southern Democrats declined both as a proportion of the total House membership and as a proportion of their party. From 40 percent during the period from 1953 to 1958, the proportion of the Democratic membership held by southern Democrats dropped to about 33 percent in the years 1959 to 1964, to 30 percent in the 1965 to 1974 period, and to only slightly more than 25 percent during the 1975 to 1982 period.*

During the 1970s, then, the Democratic House leadership had sizeable, and increasingly northern, majorities. The average number of Democrats in the 94th through 96th congresses was 286. The 1980 election reduced the size of the Democratic majority to 243 (55.9 percent), but it did not appreciably increase the proportion of the membership from the South (26.7 percent).

Membership turnover—intraparty as well as interparty—in the mid and late 1970s was, however, far from an unmixed blessing for the leadership. Such turnover has been very high by post–World War II standards. The number of Democratic freshmen and the proportion of Democratic members who were freshmen were both unusually high in the 94th, 95th, and 96th congresses. The seventy-five freshmen elected in 1974 in the wake of Watergate constituted slightly more than one-quarter of the Democratic membership during the 94th Congress. Forty-two Democratic freshmen were elected to the 96th Congress. And the forty-seven member class elected to the 95th Congress was larger than any Democratic freshmen class between 1960 and 1972, except for the 89th Congress class which was elected in the 1964 landslide. The result of this high turnover has been an increasingly junior Democratic membership. In the 94th Congress, 44 percent of the Democrats were serving their first, second, or third term; that figure rose to 51 percent in the 95th, and to 53 percent in the 96th. In contrast, between 1961 and 1974 the mean percentage of first, second, or third termers was only 31 percent; at its highest in this period, in the 89th Congress, the percentage reached 42 percent. Only twenty-two Democratic freshmen were

*The regional categorization used throughout the study is: New England: Conn., Maine, Mass., N.H., R.I., Vt.; Middle Atlantic: Del., N.J., N.Y., Pa.; East North Central: Ill., Ind., Mich., Ohio, Wis.; West North Central: Iowa, Kans., Minn., Mo., Nebr., N.Dak., S.Dak.; South: Ala., Ark., Fla., Ga., La., Miss., N.C., S.C., Tex., Va.; Border: Ky., Md., Okla., Tenn., W.Va.; Mountain: Ariz., Colo., Idaho, Nev., N.Mex., Utah, Wyo.; Pacific: Alaska, Calif., Hawaii, Oreg., Wash. The northeastern region includes the New England and the Middle Atlantic states.

brought in by the 1980 election, but the Democratic membership of the 97th Congress was nevertheless quite junior: 42 percent of Democrats were serving their first, second, or third term.

The sheer number of newcomers presents a problem for the leadership since the rules now make full participation by the most junior member possible. Furthermore, these junior northern Democrats are somewhat less loyal to party than are their senior colleagues (see Sinclair 1981).

Norms Changes

The huge Democratic freshmen class elected in 1974 has often been portrayed in the press as the instigator of change. Actually, many of the rules changes were already in place before the 1974 election. In the deposing of several committee chairs, the most dramatic event of the reform process, the 1974 freshmen did play an important role, but as foot soldiers not as generals. In January 1975 the Democratic Caucus stripped three very senior members—F. Edward Hebert, Wright Patman, and Bob Poage—of their chairmanships. Although the vote was by secret ballot, the freshmen are assumed to have supplied the margin of victory. This use of the new caucus rules put even the least perceptive chairs on notice that they had to be responsive to the party majority if they wished to retain their positions.

Although the reform effort was led primarily by northern liberals who had entered the House during the 1960s, the high membership turnover in the 1970s had a strong influence on the actual effects of the rules changes. By and large, these new members were young; their formative political experiences had taken place in the turbulent 1960s and they entered the House during a period of challenge to the power structure. Furthermore, many of the large 1974 Democratic freshmen class were elected from previously Republican districts.

These members were not inclined, nor could they afford politically, to wait before attempting to make their mark in the House. Norms of apprenticeship and of deference to senior members, already weakened during the 1960s, received a final blow. New members actively participate in committee and on the floor, feeling no need to refrain from speaking and offering amendments even during their first months in office. The norm dictating that House members specialize in the work of their committees still holds to a considerable extent, but the extensive participation of very junior members inevitably means that less expertise is brought to bear at the committee stage.

A variety of sunshine provisions (the opening up of committee mark-ups, for example) encourage junior members to participate actively and sometimes to grandstand. Those members from marginal districts especially seem to feel that no opportunity for publicity can be passed up. Self-advertising activities, including everything from daily press releases to personal crusades on issues such as ethics, have increased, and publicity frequently is gained at the expense of the institution. Thus the sense of institutional patriotism has been severely weakened.

A contest over a major subcommittee chairmanship which took place at the beginning of the 96th Congress (1979–80) illustrates some of these changes in norms which have accompanied the rules changes. Prior to the reforms, committee chairmen selected subcommitte chairmen, most frequently on the basis of seniority. The present system provides that members bid for subcommittee chairmanships in order of full committee seniority. The bidder must then receive a majority affirmative vote of the Democratic members of the committee. If he does not, the bidding process continues until someone does receive a majority. This procedure was based on the presumption that seniority would and should usually be followed in the granting of subcommittee chairmanships but that some mechanism for circumventing seniority in extraordinary cases should be available.

In January 1979 Henry Waxman (D-Ca.), a member of the 1974 class, won the chairmanship of the Health and Environment Subcommittee of the Interstate and Foreign Commerce Committee over Richardson Preyer (D-N.C.), who was entitled to the position on the basis of seniority. Preyer is a moderate southerner and a highly respected member of the House; thus this was not one of those extraordinary circumstances at which the new procedure was aimed. No claims were made that Preyer was ideologically out of step with the Democratic majority or that as chairman he would act in an arbitrary and unresponsive fashion. Waxman's victory under these circumstances shows the severe weakening of the seniority norm. Even highly respected senior members cannot count on the deference that senority alone brought in the past. The selection to the chairmanship of this extremely prestigious subcommittee of a member with only four years of service also indicates a lesser emphasis on expertise, certainly of expertise gained by long service on the committee.

Although such challenges are exceptional, the combination of the rules changes and high turnover has led to members assuming subcommittee chairmanships early in their House careers (see Loomis 1982). Members' personal inclinations and their reelection needs have prompted a high rate of subcommittee activity and a large flow of legislation. Such activity has been made possible by the autonomy subcommittees have won from the full committee in terms of agenda and staffing.

The norms and rules changes of the 1970s have lessened the prestige of the committees and undermined the norm of reciprocity among committees. Previously, there existed a strong presumption in favor of the committee's bill. "Go with the committee on the floor" was the watchword; "the committee has exhaustively examined the matter and has brought its expertise to bear." For example, Wilbur Mills (D-Ark.), one of the most skillful of the chairmen of the 1960s, brought his tax bills to the floor under a closed rule that allowed no amendments. His substantive and political expertise, combined with the tendency to "trust the committee," made it possible for Mills to persuade the House to grant him closed rules and then to pass his bills unchanged. The reciprocity norm is weaker now and there is a greater tendency to "mark-up" bills on the floor. Younger members are simply not willing to defer to the committee.

The recorded teller vote has also stimulated the offering of amendments on the floor and the acceptance of those opposed by the committee majority. When a member's position on amendments in the Committee of the Whole was not recorded, supporting the committee's position was often the easiest course for him to take. Now the amending process can be used to make a variety of political points, and members, especially those from marginal districts, are acutely aware that their vote may be used against them in the next campaign. Consequently, few members will automatically support the committee's position.

The number of recorded votes grew many-fold during the 1970s. During the 91st Congress (1969–70), the last before the institution of the recorded teller vote, the House took 433 recorded votes; during the 95th Congress (1977–78), 1540 recorded votes were taken. As the number of roll calls increases so do the difficulties committees encounter in protecting their bills on the floor.

New Issues and New Voting Alignments

Changes in the issues at the center of controversy in the 1970s produced more fluid and thus less predictable voting alignments (see Sinclair 1981). Energy, environmental and consumer issues, and foreign and defense policy questions split not just North from South in the Democratic party; they also frequently divided northern Democrats. By the late 1970s persistent high inflation began to affect debate on a wide variety of social welfare and economic policy questions, and by the early 1980s it had transformed that debate.

An examination of the shape of House voting alignments from the 1950s through the 1970s indicates that the current party leadership must cope with a membership that is less predictable in voting response. Examining voting behavior within issue areas requires a schema that allows us to classify most of the roll calls taken. Aage Clausen (1973) developed a useful issue categorization in his work on the congresses of the 1950s and early 1960s, and I have shown the categorization to be applicable for a much longer period (see Sinclair 1982). The four policy categories or domains of Clausen's which will be used here are government management of the economy, social welfare, civil liberties, and international involvement. The government management category centers on legislation dealing with the economy and the nation's resources, such as business regulation, public works, conservation and environmental legislation, energy legislation, monetary and fiscal policy, and the overall level of governmental spending. In contrast, the social welfare domain includes legislation designed to aid the individual more directly, such as aid to education, public housing, and labor legislation. The civil liberties category includes black civil rights and such issues as subversive activities regulation and federal criminal justice procedures. The international involvement domain includes all nondomestic policy questions.

For an issue classification to be useful, not only must it make substantive sense, but the votes included in a given category must elicit similar voting alignments. After roll calls were categorized into Clausen's issue domains, those that evoked similar alignments were selected (see Sinclair 1977). A large proportion of the roll calls met the test for inclusion into the resulting issue scale or dimension. Each congressman was then given a score on each issue dimension in each of the congresses he served. In most cases, the score is simply the percentage of the roll calls included in the dimension on which he took a position that would popularly be called liberal. For example, a high score on the social welfare dimension indicates the congressman voted in favor of establishing and expanding various social welfare programs.

The Domestic Issue Dimensions

House Democratic leaders of the 1950s and 1960s had to contend with a party split along North-South lines. That division is evident in each of the three domestic issue areas, but its depth varied (see table 1.1). The leadership could count on support from northern Democrats in all three areas; on the government management of the economy dimension, southern Democrats provided considerable support, although appreciably less than their northern party colleagues. The split was deeper on social welfare issues, where southern Democrats were actually less supportive than Republicans from the northeastern states. On the civil liberties dimension, southern Democrats provided essentially no support, while Republicans, especially those from the Northeast, were somewhat supportive.

The 1970s saw a change in alignments in all three domestic issue areas. On the social welfare and civil liberties dimensions, northern Democratic support decreased slightly and southern Democratic support increased appreciably. Republicans who during the 1950s and 1960s had provided significant support on the civil liberties dimension, now provided less than did southern Democrats.

The transformation of southern politics accounts for the increased southern support on social welfare and civil liberties. The increase in black voting brought about by the Voting Rights Act and growing Republican competition resulted in more and more southern Democrats needing black votes for

Table 1.1

DOMESTIC POLICY SUPPORT SCORES
(By Party and Region)

Years	Democrats			Republicans		
	All	North[a]	South[a]	All	Northeast	Other
Government management						
1953–68	85.3	91.9	73.3	15.3	19.3	13.4
1969–76	70.5	83.1	45.3	24.6	39.2	19.5
1977–78	72.3	83.9	47.2	24.1	41.0	19.4
Social welfare						
1953–72	75.1	94.1	40.3[b]	33.1	49.4	25.5
1973–76	79.6	91.0	55.0	32.4	52.2	26.0
1977–78	78.3	89.4	52.1	27.2	46.9	21.7
Civil liberties						
1955–72	53.9	83.3	9.9	46.1	58.2	43.8[c]
1973–76	63.6	78.1	33.3	31.3	45.3	32.9
1977–78	64.7	77.4	36.5	21.4	35.9	20.8

[a] Border Democrats are not included in the North or the South.

[b] The 88th Congress score is excluded. It is abnormally high and thus obscures the pattern.

[c] Southern Republicans are excluded from the civil liberties scores.

election, and many senior members responded by modifying their voting behavior. In addition, many of the members first elected in the 1970s were more moderate than their predecessors had been.

For the current party leadership, voting trends in these two issue areas are basically favorable. Although the support levels of northern Democrats have slipped since the 1960s, those of southern Democrats have increased significantly. The current leaders can expect more votes from southerners than their predecessors could, but southerners quite clearly are not reliable supporters in these issue areas.

In the government management of the economy area, trends during the 1970s were much less favorable for the party leadership. Despite the regional split within the Democratic party in the late 1960s, voting coalitions on government management issues remained party-based. Northern Democrats were highly supportive and the mean support score of southern Democrats was considerably closer to that of their northern party colleagues than to that of the most supportive group of Republicans. The first year of the Nixon administration, 1969, marked an abrupt change in voting alignments that persisted throughout the 1970s. The regional split within each party deepened; the support of Democrats from the South fell sharply and that of northeastern Republicans increased. During the 1970s southern Democrats were barely more supportive on the government management dimension than northeastern Republicans. Democrats from the border states, who during the 1950s and 1960s had tended to be almost as supportive as northern Democrats, were significantly less supportive, although they still scored considerably higher than southern Democrats. Furthermore, the mean support score of northern Democrats decreased; northern Democrats were no longer as cohesive as they had been in the 1950s and 1960s.

These alignment changes can be traced to a shift in the issues at the center of controversy. During the 1970s environmental and consumer protection legislation became increasingly central elements of the government management agenda. The Arab oil embargo thrust energy policy to the center of controversy. The unprecedented peacetime inflation that plagued the economy during the 1970s altered the debate on spending policy, and the new congressional budget process, which provided a forum for such debate, accentuated the change.

This new agenda led to a change in voting alignments. Environmental and consumer protection legislation had its greatest appeal to the affluent in the industrialized areas (Harris 1973, pp. 99-118). In industrializing areas, elites and often the general population as well found such regulations a barrier. When the debate was phrased in "environmental protection versus jobs" terms, labor also found itself in opposition. Energy policy pitted producer against consumer interests. Thus northeastern Republicans, representing affluent constitutents in a heavily industrialized and non-oil-producing area, moved toward the Democratic pole on the government management dimension while southern Democrats, representing an oil-producing and a still-industrializing area, moved to the Republican pole. Northern Democrats found their usual unity on the government management dimension strained as environmental legislation divided their constituents, and their level of support dropped.

International Involvement

Developments in the international involvement area during the 1970s were even more troublesome for the leadership. From 1952 through 1968, foreign aid dominated the international involvement agenda in the House. The foreign policy consensus that had kept other issues off the voting agenda began to break down in the mid-1960s, but the House leadership during Lyndon Johnson's presidency kept most anti-Vietnam War measures from coming to the floor. By 1969 the war had transformed the international involvement agenda. Assumptions that had been widely accepted were questioned, and previously noncontroversial decisions provoked heated conflict. Opposition to the Vietnam War led many to reappraise the direction of U.S. foreign and defense policy more generally, as the size of the military budget, the need for a wide variety of expensive and deadly new weapons systems, and U.S. aid to repressive regimes were brought into question.

From 1969 to 1976 two distinct clusters of international involvement roll calls appeared in each Congress. One consisted mostly of roll calls on foreign aid bills—primarily votes on "across the board" cuts and on passage. The other included numerous votes that were directly related to the Vietnam War but also roll calls on cutting Department of Defense appropriations, on cutting funds for a wide variety of weapons systems (the antiballistic missile, nerve gas, and B-1 bomber are examples), on barring aid to Chile and other dictatorships, on overseas troop cuts, on prohibiting the importation of Rhodesian chrome, and on prohibiting the Ford administration from becoming involved in Angola. This dimension is here labeled foreign and defense policy reorientation (see Clausen and Van Horn 1977). Certainly those members who supported these departures were challenging basic precepts of American foreign and defense policy.

Voting alignments on the traditional international involvement dimension did change in the 1970s (see table 1.2), but the change was primarily due to the change in partisan control of the presidency.* The international involvement dimension splits both parties along regional lines, but all segments are more responsive to presidents of their own party than they are to opposition presidents. The 95th Congress, the first of the Jimmy Carter presidency, saw a continuation of this pattern. Northeastern Republicans and those from the interior dropped in support to about the level they maintained during the Kennedy-Johnson years. Both northern and southern Democrats increased their support, but in a development with ominous implication for the president and the leadership, northern Democratic support remained well below the high level it had attained in the Kennedy-Johnson years. During the 95th Congress northern Democrats, traditionally the mainstay of a Democratic president's support on foreign aid, split on the international involvement dimension. The intense debate on other aspects of foreign and defense policy apparently led some northern Democrats to question the value of the foreign aid program

The foreign and defense policy reorientation dimension split, as can be seen in table 1.2, not just North and South in the Democratic party but also the northern Democrats. Those members committed to a reorientation of foreign and defense policy, almost all of whom were northern Democrats, did not alter their course when a Democratic president was elected—the reorientation dimension did not disappear. Carter's policy was not in total conflict with these members' views as the Nixon-Ford policy have been and

---

*The voting response of Pacific Republicans on the traditional international involvement dimension underwent a secular change during the period under discussions. At the beginning of the period they voted very much like northeasterners; by the end of the period they were as unsupportive as interior Republicans. Because this secular trend tends to obsure the administration-related pattern, the scores of Pacific Republicans on the aid dimension have been excluded from this discussion.

Table 1.2

INTERNATIONAL INVOLVEMENT SUPPORT SCORES
(By Party and Region)

Years	Democrats			Republicans		
	All	North[a]	South[a]	All	Northeast	Other[b]
Aid						
1953–60	69.0	88.3	41.2	60.8	87.3	41.0
1961–68	77.1	92.2	47.2	39.6	63.5	27.9
1969–76	63.9	78.9	36.2	51.8	73.4	43.5
1977–78	70.1	82.8	44.3	39.8	62.2	33.7
Reorientation						
1969–76	49.3	66.3	18.1	18.4	29.0	15.0
1977–78	54.1	67.9	24.9	18.7	32.0	15.0
Hard line						
1977–78	62.4	74.9	35.7	23.4	38.1	19.1

[a] Border Democrats are not included in the North or the South.

[b] Pacific Republicans are excluded from the aid scores.

these members supported Carter when they agreed with him. But when their views and administration policy were in conflict, they felt free to oppose the president. Quite clearly, the vigorous debate on a whole series of questions that had been considered beyond debate before the Vietnam War represents a fundamental change in the centers of controversy, one with which both relatively soft-line Democratic presidents and hard-line Republican presidents will have to contend.

As the reorientation dimension represented a challenge from the left to the hard-line foreign and defense policy of Republican presidents, Carter's attempt to incorporate some elements of the new perspective into his foreign policy brought with it a change in the debate. A scale representing a hard-line challenge to Carter's foreign policy appears in the 95th Congress. Prominent are votes on amendments restricting U.S. aid to Communist or left-leaning countries and attempts to restrict the president's discretion with respect to the Panama Canal Treaty and the withdrawal of U.S. troops from Korea. Southern Democrats and northeastern Republicans were a part of the hard-line attack on the Carter policy (see table 1.2). Northern Democrats were split; their support of Carter's policies against attack from the right was considerably lower than their support on the foreign aid scale, which itself was significantly below the support northern Democrats gave Kennedy and Johnson on foreign aid.

Support Predictability

This analysis shows that voting behavior changed and suggests that it became less predictable during the 1970s. The dimension scores, however, group roll calls of widely varying importance and so do not allow us to address questions about support predictability directly. The problems faced by the leaders are illuminated through an examination of key votes taken during the 95th Congress (1977–78), the first of the current leadership team. For this purpose roll calls considered crucial by the president, the party leadership, and/or key Democratic constituencies were selected in seven areas: energy, foreign and defense policy, budget, debt limit increases, labor, social security, and economic policy (see Sinclair 1981). For each member the proportion of the votes in each area on which the member supported the Democratic party leadership was computed. Then, using these supported scores on the seven indexes, members can be classified by support reliability. The House membership was divided into seven categories, ranging from consistently strong supporters to consistently strong opponents with middle categories indicating unreliability or erratic support.*

The relationship between this support categorization and party-regional group membership can be seen in table 1.3. Only 17 of 278 Democrats fall into the three unsupportive groupings, and of these 12 are southerners. Thus the number of consistent Democratic opponents is small. One-half of the border Democrats and close to two-thirds of southern Democrats, however, fall into the middle, relatively unsupportive and unpredictable, category and what is more surprising, so do one-fifth of northern Democrats. The group of highly reliable supporters consists almost entirely of northern Democrats; but more important than the composition of the group is its size: only 34 House Democrats supported the leadership on 80 percent or more of the roll calls included in each of the seven key vote indexes. Fewer than one-fifth of northern Democrats are highly reliable supporters over the whole range of issues under study.

A closer examination of northern Democratic support allows us to draw some conclusions concerning the locus of the increased unpredictability. As can be seen in table 1.4, senior members are more reliably supportive than

---

*Those members whose support score is 80 percent or greater on all seven indexes are classified as highly reliable supporters. On the other end of the scale are those who scored below 20 percent on all seven. Members who scored 50 percent or higher on all seven indexes and 80 percent on at least five of the seven are the next most supportive group. Again, a comparable group at the opposite end of the scale are those who scored below 50 percent on all and below 20 percent on at least five of the seven. Toward the supportive end of the continuum but clearly less reliable than the previously defined groupings are the members who scored 50 percent or greater on all but one scale and 80 percent or greater on at least three of the seven. The comparable group of relatively unreliable opponents are those who scored below 50 percent on all but one index and below 20 percent on at least three of the seven. Those members whose pattern of support fit into none of these categories constitute a middle group whose voting behavior is even more unpredictable.

Table 1.3

SUPPORT RELIABILITY IN THE 95TH HOUSE OF REPRESENTATIVES
(By Party and Region)

Group	Support							
	High							
	%	No.	%	No.	%	No.	%	No.
Northern Democrats	17.7	32	42.0	76	18.8	34	19.9	36
Border Democrats	4.2	1	8.3	2	29.2	7	50.0	12
Southern Democrats	1.4	1	8.2	6	9.6	7	64.6	47
Northeastern Republicans	0	0	0	0	0	0	48.4	15
Other Republicans	0	0	0	0	0	0	6.7	7
All	8.2	34	20.3	84	11.6	48	28.3	117

Group	Support					
					Low	
	%	No.	%	No.	%	No.
Northern Democrats	.6	1	0	0	1.1	2
Border Democrats	4.2	1	4.2	1	0	0
Southern Democrats	8.2	6	5.5	4	2.7	2
Northeastern Republicans	16.1	5	16.1	5	19.4	6
Other Republicans	25.7	27	27.6	29	40.0	42
All	9.7	40	9.4	39	12.6	52

junior members; almost 30 percent of northern Democrats first elected in the 1940s and 1950s fall into the highly supportive group, while only 6.3 percent of the 95th Congress freshmen do. On the other end of the support continuum, there is a clear difference between those first elected before 1974 and the 94th and 95th freshman classes; a much larger proportion of the latter fall into the middle, relatively unpredictable, support category. (The right-most column in table 1.4 combines the four lowest support categories from table 1.3. Thus it includes both relatively unpredictable members and low supporters. However, since only 3 of 181 northern Democrats are low supporters, the members included are overwhelmingly from the middle, unpredictable, category and are referred to as such in the discussion.)

Those junior members elected from districts previously held by Republicans are particularly troublesome to the party leadership. When northern

Table 1.4

EFFECT OF SENIORITY ON
SUPPORT RELIABILITY AMONG NORTHERN DEMOCRATS

Those First Elected in	Support							
	High						Low[a]	
	%	No.	%	No.	%	No.	%	No.
1950s or earlier	29.2	7	45.8	11	20.8	5	4.2	1
1960s	22.7	10	52.3	23	11.4	5	13.7	6
1970 and 1972	17.4	4	56.5	13	17.4	4	8.6	2
1974	15.5	9	31.0	18	24.1	14	29.3	17
1976	6.3	2	34.4	11	18.8	6	40.6	13

[a] The lowest category here consists of the four lowest support categories in table 1.3

Democrats first elected in 1970 or later are divided into those who won seats previously held by Republicans and those who succeeded Democrats, quite strong differences in support patterns appear. Democratic members holding previously Republican seats, many of whom were first elected in the 1974 landslide, are much more likely to fall into the middle less predictable, categories: 40 percent of them fall into the middle category or below, while only 16.1 percent of other junior Democrats do.

Support is related to seniority among southern Democrats too. If we compare those first elected in 1970 or earlier with those who entered the House in 1972 or later, we find that the preponderance of both groups fall into the middle, unpredictable, category (65.8 percent of the former, 62.5 percent of the latter), However, slightly over one-fifth of the more senior group fall into the three basically non-supportive categories in contrast to little more than one-tenth of the less senior group. About 25 percent of the less senior members qualify for the three supportive categories; only 13.1 percent of the more senior members do.

In its coalition-building efforts, then, the Democratic House leadership confronts a relatively unpredictable party membership. Northern Democrats can no longer be relied on to provide a solid block of support. Junior members, especially those elected from previously Republican districts, defect from the party position fairly frequently. The leaders must pick up a large proportion of northern Democrats to win a House vote; they can accomplish this, but northern Democratic support is not automatically theirs.

The changes in the southern component of the Democratic House membership present opportunities for the leadership but also contribute to the uncertainty of the coalition-building process. Southern Democrats cannot be written off as unpersuasible, and junior southern members in particular are a potential source of leadership support. The increase in southern support on social welfare and civil liberties issues is due in considerable part to the election of more supportive members beginning in 1972. Yet even the most supportive of the new members does not fall into the highly reliable category. A fair number of southern votes on most high priority roll calls are obtainable, but the leadership must work for each of them.

The cohesion of the minority as well as that of the majority party affects the difficulty of coalition building. How much help can the leadership expect from Republicans? As can be seen in table 1.3, no Republicans fall toward the Democratic end of the support continuum and but a few fall in the middle category. Furthermore, if Republicans are divided into those first elected before 1970 and those first elected during the 1970s, a considerably larger proportion of junior members than senior members fall into the lowest support group. Thus 40.2 percent of junior as opposed to 27.8 percent of senior Republicans provided support for the Democratic position less than 20 percent of the time on all seven indexes. Two-thirds of the junior but only one-half of the senior Republicans fall into the two lowest support categories. Republicans who first entered the House in the 1970s, then, are more likely than members first elected earlier to oppose strongly the Democratic position across the whole range of issues. Consequently, the Democratic House leadership increasingly has to rely solely on its own party members for majorities.

Impact on Party Leadership

Because of the changes of the 1970s, the Democratic leadership is faced with considerable uncertainty in its attempts to build winning coalitions. According to a top leader, "The democratization of the House has proceeded so far that all kinds of things can come percolating up from below, and that can cause problems for the leadership." The high level of subcommittee activity and the decrease in the full committee chairs' control over subcommittees present information-gathering problems for the majority party leadership. With the dispersion of influence has come the need to touch a larger number of bases and the uncertainty over whether one has touched all the necessary ones. According to Majority Leader Jim Wright:

> The leadership's task must have been infinitely less complicated in the days of Mr. Rayburn and Mr. McCormack. In Mr. Rayburn's day, about all a majority leader or Speaker needed to do in order to get his program adopted was to deal effectively with perhaps 12 very senior committee chairmen. They, in turn, could be expected to influence their committees and their subcommittee chairmen whom they, in those days, appointed. . . . Well, now that situation is quite considerably different. There are, I think, 153 subcommittees. The full committee chairmen are not inviolable in their own precincts. They are not the great powers that they once were. They are dependent upon their own members for their election and for the support of their subcommittees for the program. And so, the leadership sometimes has to go beyond the committee chairmen

and deal with the subcommittee chairmen. We always try to work with the person who will have the responsibility of managing a bill on the floor. Increasingly, that is the subcommitte chair's appointment. . . . [Therefore] we have to deal with a great many more people than was the case in Mr. Rayburn's day or Mr. McCormack's day. (Quoted in Deering and Smith 1980 p.1)

The large membership turnover of the 1970s presents problems for the leadership which go beyond these members' high level of activity and their tendency toward independence. The sheer number of new members handicaps the leadership because the better the leaders know a member, the more likely their efforts at persuasion are to be successful. If, as occurred during the 1970s, each election brings in a large number of freshmen, developing the sort of personal relationships that provide the basis for effective persuasion becomes difficult and time consuming.

The House floor has become a more important and less predictable decision-making arena. A longtime observer contends that "there is more of a tendency now, if a committee has difficulty reaching a consensus, to throw it onto the floor of the House and have it resolved by floor amendments. There are some committees that just sort of throw up their hands and say, 'Let the members decide.' Lots of controversial amendments are brought to the floor that used to be decided in committee. Perhaps committees found it easier to reach a consensus when you didn't have as much public participation in the process. Also perhaps the issues are more complex."

Certainly the combination of the recorded teller vote and the decline of intercommittee reciprocity has severely heightened unpredictability at the floor stage. Since junior status, party affiliation, or lack of expertise no longer bars members from offering amendments, amendments can originate anywhere; it is impossible to anticipate all the amendments that may be offered. According to Morris Udall, (D-Arz.), the House has become a "fast breeder reactor" for amendments: "Every morning when I come to my office, I find that there are 20 new amendments. We dispose of 20 or 25 amendments and it breeds 20 more amendments" *(Congressional Quarterly Weekly Report,* 12 May 1978, p. 877).

As a record vote must be called upon request by twenty-five members (until 1979 the number was twenty), almost any member can force a vote. Many members simply do not believe that they should defer to the committee majority, and even those who might be inclined to do so can be faced with a politically difficult situation by the public nature of these votes. Republicans and dissident Democrats have become adept at fashioning amendments with considerable constituency appeal. Votes that a clever opponent "back home" can represent as favoring reparations to Vietnam, "giving away" the Panama Canal, or supporting federally funded legal aid for homosexuals present a ticklish choice to the Democrat who would like to support the leadership.

The large number of amendments offered to many major bills strains the leadership's resources and increases the probability that the committee majority and the leader will be "ambushed" on the floor. "We are in the process of moving from a time in the history of the House when committees had too much power, and we are moving to a point where the floor itself becomes a large, unwieldy committee," according to Paul Simon (D-Ill.). "We are not doing the job of legislating as we should. We are legislating by whim" (*Congressional Quarterly Weekly Report,* 12 May 1978, p. 878).

The heightened level of floor activity is even more of a problem than it might be otherwise because of the prominence of new issues that fragment the Democratic party. The leadership cannot count on solid support from Northern Democrats as it could on most issues during the 1960s. On the other hand, the southern Democratic contingent in the House became more heterogenous during the 1970s as the race issue declined in saliency in the South and somewhat more "nationally oriented" Democrats were elected. When the party leadership attempts to build winning coalitions, there are few Democrats who can be written off completely and few who can be counted on to be loyal across the board.

The transformation of the House during the past decade has also complicated the party maintenance function. When the issues at the center of controversy divide the party, peace-keeping becomes more difficult. The rules and norms of the postreform House have multiplied opportunities for party members to come into conflict with one another. Norms such as intercommittee reciprocity and deference to senior members, which served as a restraint on conflicts over power and policy, have been severely weakened. The shift of influence to the subcommittee level as well as the rise to prominence of issues that cut across traditional committee jurisdictions have increased the frequency of jurisdictional conflicts.

The postreform environment not only has complicated the coalition-building and peace-keeping functions but has also exacerbated the problems of reconciling the two functions. The uncertainty arising from widespread participation makes coalition building a more complex enterprise; yet member expectations about their roles in the chamber are such that any leadership efforts to restrain participation would be highly detrimental to party maintenance. As a consequence of the changes of the 1970s, then, the current party leaders operate in an environment that is much less predictable than the one their predecessors knew. On the other hand, some of the rules changes did augment the resources the leadership commands, and the decline in the powers of the committee chairmen makes them less formidable competitors for influence in the chamber. The challenge the leadership faces is that of using its still limited resources effectively to build coalitions and to "keep peace in the family" within an extremely fluid and unpredictable environment.

Member Goals and
Leadership Influence

■■■■■■■■■■■■■■■ Majority party members benefit collectively when their leadership is successful at building winning coalitions and "keeping peace in the family." The party's legislative record depends on successful coalition building; such success also contributes to the maintenance of the power of the House in the governmental system. A minimum level of party coherence is necessary for the party to organize the House, and organizing the House provides great benefits to party members in the form of chairmanships of committees and subcommittees. Intraparty harmony also contributes to coalition-building success and makes the members' jobs easier and more pleasant.

Members' collective interest in leadership success does not necessarily result in individual behavior conducive to that outcome. Members also have individual goals, and behavior that furthers the attainment of those individual goals may work against leadership success. Because leadership success is a collective good, any one member's actions will have only a small impact upon its realization and as a consequence, when there is a conflict, an individual member will be more likely to choose the behavior that will further his individual goals at the expense of leadership success. The leadership, by performing its primary functions, is supplying a collective good to its membership, but it cannot assume that its members will freely act in such a way as to further coalition-building success or intraparty harmony.

Leaders' potential for influence over their members' behavior depends on their potential impact on member goal achievement. The more leaders can help or hurt members in attaining their individual goals, the greater their potential influence. Their actual influence depends on their willingness to use whatever resources they have and their skill in doing so. Successful coalition building and party maintenance are a function not only of the leadership's influence but also of the extent to which members' goal-directed behavior uninfluenced by the leadership is consonant with leadership-desired behavior. Influence and success, thus, are not synonymous. Both, however, are related to the goals of members and to the behavior patterns involved in attaining those goals within the given environment. An understanding of majority party leadership thus requires an analysis of member goals, of the behavior of members in pursuit of those goals, and of the extent to which the leaders can influence the attainment of those goals by members.

The goals of House members, like those of other human beings, are undoubtedly multiple and diverse, so building a framework for analysis requires acceptance of some simplifying assumptions. Following Fenno (1973) and Kingdon (1973, 1977), we shall assume that reelection, intra-Washington influence, and good public policy are the primary goals of

House members. Different members of course place different relative weights on the three goals. A junior member elected by a narrow margin, for example, will emphasize reelection more than will a senior member who has a history of landslide victories.

The Reelection Goal

What patterns of behavior does the reelection goal entail? Although our knowledge of congressional elections is more limited than our knowledge of presidential elections, the 1978 Center for Political Studies election study indicates that high favorable name recognition is critical (see Mann and Wolfinger 1980; Hinckley 1980). Establishing and maintaining such recognition requires vast amounts of district-related activity such as effective casework and projects—everything from obtaining funds for the proverbial new post office to obtaining federal grants for local governments. In addition, members believe that they must keep their overall voting record in line with constituency sentiment and that, on issues highly salient to the constituency, voting the constituency is by far the safest course (Fenno 1978; Kingdon 1973).

The 1978 study showed that although most voters recognize their congressman, they possess little specific information about him. In light of this, why are House members so concerned about the impact of their Washington behavior—especially their votes—on the constituency? Why do most of them believe that good casework and a heavy schedule of local appearances, while important, are not enough? The 1978 study strongly suggests that the high reelection rate of incumbent members is due in considerable part to the weakness of their challengers, who are much less likely to be recognized by voters. Jacobson and Kernell (1981) argue persuasively that the quality of the challenger and of his challenge is a function of the perceived probability of his defeating the incumbent. Good challengers—those with political experience, for example—are more likely to run when the incumbent is perceived as weak; similarly, financial backers who supply the large amount of money needed to defeat an incumbent are more likely to be found for races in which the incumbent is seen as beatable. The district elites who have to deal with the congressman are unlikely to support a challenger unless they perceive that he has a high probability of winning.

The congressman's reelection-directed behavior, then, is aimed not only at developing and maintaining favorable name recognition among the mass constituency but also at discouraging strong challengers by appearing to be unbeatable. Careful attention to the district, maintenance of a high voting participation rate, and voting the district are all elements of a strategy aimed at depriving potential challengers of good campaign issues. Keeping constituency elites reasonably satisfied through the provision of services and policy payoffs can deprive potential challengers of a basis of support.

There are a number of ways the party leaders can aid their members in their quest for reelection, but for most members most of the time the leadership's help is only marginally significant in this regard. The leaders can help members with campaign funds, but incumbents generally can raise as much money as they need without such help. The leaders can speak for a member in his district and by so doing raise the member's status among the attentive public there. The leadership can help a member obtain a committee assignment of use to his district; however since once a member gets an assignment he seldom loses it, this can only be given once, and furthermore, the competition for many constituency-service committees is not intense. The leaders can sometimes help a member get projects or grants for his district by using their influence with the administration. They can also help a member to secure passage of minor but locally important legislation. The leadership can provide information to members which may prevent them from making mistakes; it can help by keeping no-win issues from reaching the floor; it can use its control over legislative scheduling to help members maintain a high voting participation rate.

Thus the leadership's ability to influence the reelection chances of its members, although not negligible, is usually marginal. Furthermore, the leaders are severely constrained in their ability to withhold their help. Success at building winning coalitions is in part a function of the size of the majority party, and since leaders have absolutely no control over nominations, withholding help, if it had any effect, would only increase the chances of the Republican challenger. From the leaders' point of view, almost any Democrat is preferable to a Republican, as even the most uncooperative Democrat at least votes with his party in organizing the House. The need to "keep peace in the family" also places limits upon the leadership. A systematic withholding of all favors from members who only erratically support the leadership would be perceived as unfair and would strain party harmony, since most such members believe they are only doing what they must to insure reelection.

The party leadership's marginal influence over the reelection chances of the party's members is not new to the postreform era. The situation faced by members as they seek reelection had changed, however. Members now command much greater resources for serving the district. Staffs, office budgets, access to sophisticated technology like computers, and the number of paid trips home have all greatly increased. As party organizations have declined, the local elites on whom the congressman depends for support are less likely to be party-based, and as a result, current members may see their reelection as even more dependent on their own efforts and less so on the party's record than members in the 1950s and the 1960s did. The importunings members get from non-party-based local elites are less likely to reinforce party regularity. Consequently, reelection-directed behavior is more likely than previously to conflict with leadership-desired behavior.

The Power Goal

In the prereform House a member attained intra-Washington influence through an institutional leadership position on a committee or in the party hierarchy. Seniority determined the first; party leaders, to a large extent, controlled the second. Committee-based influence is still important, and as rules changes have increased the importance of subcommittee chairmanships, the number of influential positions has increased. Changes in the House have also made the outsider role a viable one for members of the House: it is now possible for a member to become influential within the Washington community as a spokesman for a national policy coalition—a route previously restricted to senators.

Party leaders can help those members who choose traditional routes to influence. The leadership has more influence over committee assignments than it did in the prereform days, and since competition for assignments to the most influential committees is intense, the leadership's support or opposition can be decisive. The number of such desirable positions is, however, limited, and once a member attains a committee assignment he is considered entitled to retain it. Over the distribution of committee and subcommittee chairmanships, the leadership has little real control. Although committee chairmen are now nominated by the Steering and Policy Committee and approved by the full caucus, only under extraordinary circumstances is seniority not followed. The new procedure does give the leadership leverage it did not have previously in that committee chairmen are aware that they must be responsive to the Democratic membership. Subcommittee chairmen are chosen by the Democratic caucus of the committee in a process in which the leadership has no official role. The leaders appoint deputy and at-large whips and some members of the Steering and Policy Committee. These positions confer some influence on their holders and so provide a resource to the leadership. There are various other ways the leaders can single out a member—by appointing him to chair the Committee of the Whole or to head a legislative task force, for example. Because of the leaders' prestige appointments such as these do enhance a member's standing in the chamber.

To a considerable extent the influence of a committee or subcommittee chairman depends on his ability to pass his legislation intact, and the leadership can provide important aid in that regard. It can help a committee leader get a rule, schedule the legislation on a favorable day, provide a whip check, engage in persuasion. With the decline in intercommittee reciprocity, the floor has become a much more important decision-making arena; consequently, the help the leadership can provide has also become more important. The one subcommittee chairmanship per member rule combined with high membership turnover has resulted in a number of junior, and thus inexperienced, subcommittee chairmen who are especially likely to need leadership help when managing legislation on the floor.

Those members who seek intra-Washington influence through an outsider strategy are largely beyond the leadership's control. There is little the leaders can do to affect their attainment of that goal. The vast majority of House members, however, still seek influence by more traditional routes, and the leadership's resources are relevant for their goal attainment.

The leadership's use of these resources to influence member's behavior, however, is constrained by a variety of considerations. In making assignments to the choice committees, norms concerning regional balance and fair representation of various segments of the party act as constraints. A single-minded attempt to use such assignments to ensure loyalty would be perceived as unfair, would probably fail, and would certainly strain party harmony. Norms also limit the leadership's discretion in the appointment of whips and Steering and Policy Committee members, though to a lesser extent. However, inclusion of members with ties to all sections of the party is important for successful coalition building.

The leaders have considerable resources they can use to help or hinder legislation at the floor stage, yet their discretion in the use of these resources is severely constrained. Building majority coalitions to pass major legislation is their job; they cannot withhold their help from the committee or subcommittee chairman just because he is often uncooperative. On lesser legislation the leaders have more leeway, but the desire to help or teach a lesson to a chairman is only one of many factors they must consider in deciding how deeply they will become involved.

The Policy Goal

For those members who want to participate in the making of good public policy, the right committee assignment and an institutional position of influence on the committee are important. Although the leaders can help a member get a desired committee assignment, the resulting leverage for the leadership is limited, and in the allotment of subcommittee chairmanships, the leaders have no formal role.

The policy-oriented member is interested not only in having an impact in committee, but also in seeing his policy preferences translated into law. Consequently leadership help on a bill at the post-committee stage can contribute significantly to such member's goal attainment. The greater importance of the House floor as a decision-making arena has increased the value of the resources the leadership possesses for influencing floor activity. Active leadership support greatly improves a controversial bill's probability of passage. If the leaders agree with a policy-oriented member on what is good (and politically feasible) public policy, they contribute significantly to the member's goal attainment in the course of doing their job. If there is substantial disagreement, the leadership, in doing its job, frustrates the member's goals.

By and large the leadership can affect an individual member's goal achievement in only a peripheral or sporadic rather than a central and continuous manner. The goal toward which the leadership can make the most significant contribution is good public policy, and if a consensus on policy exists within the party, the leaders can aid their members in achieving their policy goal. Furthermore, if the consensus has its origins in the members' constituencies, if the members are receiving strong and congruent policy signals from their districts, the leaders, by facilitating the passage of responsive legislation, also aid in their members' reelection. When such a constituency-based consensus exists, the leadership has the ability to affect members' goal achievement and consequently their behavior, and members behavior uninfluenced by the leadership is likely to be consonant with leadership preferences. Building winning coalitions and "keeping peace in the family" will be relatively easy. The leadership's potential for influence, thus, tends to be greatest when its exercise is least necessary to success.

A constituency-based consensus of both strength and breadth such as existed during the New Deal and the 89th Congress is rare. More typically, a substantial proportion of majority party members agree on some core tenets but disagree on many issues. During the late 1970s and early 1980s the Democratic core of agreement was shrinking under the impact of seemingly intractable economic problems. In performing their leadership functions, the current leaders are faced with a far from united party and a limited ability to affect member behavior through influence on member goal achievement.

Leadership Strategies:
An Introduction

■■■■■■■■■   The revolt against Speaker Cannon in 1910 severely limited the majority party leadership's resources for affecting a member's ability to attain his goals, and although the 1970s saw some augmentation of leadership resources, leadership influence today is seldom decisive to a member's goal attainment. In terms of the functions they are expected to perform and their limited resources for doing so, the current leaders face a situation that is not very different from that faced by all majority party leaderships since Cannon.

What has changed is the House environment. The rules now allow, and norms dictate, high rates of participation by members both in committee and on the floor. Although member goals have not changed, the behavior patterns members perceive as most effective toward goal attainment have.

At both the committee stage and the floor stage, there are more significant actors than there were in the prereform era. The current leaders, consequently, operate in a much less predictable environment than their predecessors did. Furthermore, any attempt by the leadership to decrease uncertainty by dampening broad participation would directly conflict with member goal-directed behavior.

Sam Rayburn, the most highly regarded Speaker of the prereform era, used a highly personalized leadership style: he made little use of formal leadership structures; he utilized an informal network of colleagues as his primary source of information; and he relied on personal negotiation with a few key actors in coalition building. He was heavily engaged in doing favors for members, again on a personal and informal basis. Rayburn believed that this leadership style helped to maintain "peace in the family" by providing as few forums as possible in which antagonistic elements in the party could confront each other directly. Norms of apprenticeship and deference to senior members also contributed to party maintenance.

Change in the House has made the Rayburn strategy obsolete. In a highly unpredictable environment more formal and more systematic ways of gathering information are necessary, and a strategy based on personal negotiation with a few key actors is obviously untenable in a House with wide participation.

The current leaders' response to this new environment displays three major thrusts. First, the leaders use positive inducements rather than negative sanctions; they are heavily engaged in the provision of services to members. Second, the leadership employs its formal powers and its influence to structure the choice situation. Third, the leadership attempts to include as many Democrats as possible in the coalition-building process.

Speaker O'Neill strongly believes that the carrot is more effective than the stick, and current leadership is heavily involved in providing services to its members. Some House Democrats believe the Speaker does not make enough use of negative sanctions, but he in fact does not possess sufficient resources to affect decisively the goal attainment of members. Consequently use of the stick is likely to have a negative impact on party maintenance without significantly increasing the chances of success in coalition building.

All Speakers since Cannon have lacked negative sanctions for effectively coercing individual members and thus have had to rely on positive inducements. The service orientation of the current leadership extends beyond simply doing favors for individual members: the present leadership is much more involved in providing services to the Democratic membership collectively than its predecessors were. Because of new rules and norms, rank-and-file satisfaction or dissatisfaction is more important than it used to be, as almost any member can cause problems for the leadership. By providing services, the leaders contribute to party maintenance and, as a by-product, gain information vital to the performance of both of their primary functions.

The coercive strategies the leaders use are ones that coerce the membership collectively, not individually. The leadership often can and does use its resources to structure the choice situation to the advantage of the outcome it favors. Its employment of carefully constructed rules for floor consideration of important bills is an example. Such strategies require member acquiescence, whether it is overt or tacit. This limits their applicability, but members do not perceive their use as unreasonably coercive; consequently, the party maintenance function is not adversely affected.

The attempt to include as many members as possible in the coalition-building process—the strategy of inclusion—consists of expanding and using the formal leadership structures and of bringing other Democratic members into the process on an ad hoc basis. In the new House environment the core leadership is too small to undertake the task of successful coalition building alone; including other members in the process provides the leadership with the assistance it needs. The strategy of inclusion also allows the leaders to satisfy members' expectations that they will be able to take a significant part in the legislative process and thus contributes to "keeping peace in the family."

CHAPTER 2

THE CORE LEADERSHIP: TASKS AND RESOURCES

The Development of Leadership Offices

The Speaker, the majority leader, and the majority whip form the core of the majority party leadership in the modern House of Representatives. Of these offices, the one mentioned in the Constitution and the only one that is an office of the House is the Speakership. In Article I, the Constitution provides that "The House of Representatives shall choose their Speaker and other officers." Because the Constitutional Convention did not debate the nature of the office, we do not know what the framers envisioned. Mary Follett argues persuasively that the Speaker was intended to be a political leader, not simply an impartial moderator (1974, pp. 25–26). The early Speakers, according to Follett, were "keen guardians of party interest" but not "real party leaders" (1974, p. 69). Henry Clay, who served six terms as Speaker between 1811 and 1825, was the leader of his party and established the position of the Speaker as a legislative leader (Follett 1974, p. 71). "As a presiding officer Clay from the first showed that he considered himself not the umpire but the leader of the House: his object was clearly and expressly to govern the House as far as possible. . . . He made no attempt to disguise the fact that he was a political officer" (Follett 1974, pp. 71–72). Most of the Speakers between 1825 and the Civil War did interpret the office as a political one, but not all were leaders of their party or faction. The political turmoil surrounding the slavery issue frequently made choosing a Speaker difficult, with the consequence that "second-rate men" or "tools in the hands of the real leaders" were sometimes chosen

(Follett 1974, p. 96). Since the Civil War the Speaker has been considered and has almost always in fact been the leader of his party in the House.

The Speaker's powers have varied widely over time. Between 1890 and 1910 the Speakership was an extremely potent office. The Speaker appointed the members and chairmen of all committees and was himself the chairman of the Rules Committee. Yet, no matter how powerful the office, the Speaker has never been able to thwart an intense majority for a significant period of time. He is elected by his party colleagues and his powers depend on the House membership, which can change the rules. Speaker Joseph Cannon's use of his immense resources to frustrate the progressives within his own party led to the bipartisan revolt of 1910 which stripped the Speakership of much of its power. Certainly since the revolt, the majority party leadership has shared influence within the chamber.

During the nineteenth century, the chairman of the Ways and Means Committee was usually considered the majority floor leader because his committee handled so much of the major legislation. Occasionally the Speaker chose a trusted lieutenant or his leading intraparty rival to serve as majority leader. Sereno Payne (R-N.Y.) in 1899 became the first officially designated majority leader and at the same time chairman of the Ways and Means Committee. The offices remained cojoined until 1919, when they were separated, and the majority leader now gives up his committee positions upon assuming the party office (Ripley 1967, pp. 24–25; Galloway 1961, pp. 107–8).

The whip also became an officially designated position at about the turn of the century (Ripley 1967, p. 33). The Democratic whip system first developed in the early 1930s, when it consisted of the chief whip and a number of assistant whips, each of whom was responsible for a regional group of party members. In recent years it has expanded even further. It now includes the majority whip, a chief deputy whip, four deputy whips, regional whips elected from nineteen zones, and fifteen appointed at-large whips.

Leadership Selection

The full membership of the House formally elects the Speaker. In reality each of the two party contingents selects a nominee for Speaker at the beginning of each Congress, and the majority party's candidate is elected by a straight party-line vote.

The Democratic Caucus, as the organization of all House Democrats is known, selects its candidate for Speaker at the organizing caucus meetings in December of election years. No incumbent Speaker has been denied renomination while his party remained in the majority. Usually sitting Speakers face no opposition within their party and are routinely renominated. Since the 1930s Democrats have elevated their majority leader to the Speakership when that office became vacant as a result of retirement or death (see Peabody 1976).

Thomas P. "Tip" O'Neill, Jr., of Massachusetts became Speaker in 1977. O'Neill was first elected to the House in 1952; he represents a Boston district and is a New Deal liberal. He began his ascent up the leadership ladder when he was appointed majority whip in 1971. Majority Leader Hale Boggs was killed in an airplane crash in 1972 and O'Neill was easily elected to replace him in that position. After Carl Albert's retirement as Speaker, O'Neill moved up without opposition in the caucus. A large, white-haired man with all the proverbial charm of the Irish, O'Neill is immensely popular with the Democratic membership. According to a fellow leader, " 'Tip' can charm the pants off people."

Since 1911 the Democratic caucus has chosen its majority leader, and by the 1970s automatic promotion from whip to majority leader appeared to have become the rule. In 1976, however, a spirited four-way contest for the position developed (see Oppenheimer and Peabody 1977). John McFall, the whip, was tainted by scandal and was knocked out in the first round of voting. On the final round, Jim Wright of Fort Worth, Texas, defeated Phillip Burton of California by one vote. Rumors that Burton would challenge Wright in 1978 persisted for over a year. Wright solidified his position, however, and was routinely reelected in 1978, 1980, and 1982.

Jim Wright began his House career in 1955. Before his election as majority leader he had served for several years as a deputy whip whose task was persuading southern Democrats to support the leadership. A political moderate, Wright was seen as providing ideological balance to the leadership team. His oratorical skills and the respect he commands among the Democratic membership have proved to be of equal importance to his effectiveness as majority leader.

The Democratic whip is appointed, not elected. Technically the choice of the majority leader, he is actually selected by the Speaker. In 1976 O'Neill appointed John Brademas, an Indiana liberal, to the position. After Brademas's electoral defeat in the 1980 election, O'Neill chose Thomas Foley of Washington, who had just completed two terms as chairman of the Democratic Caucus.

The current leadership team is in several respects typical of twentieth century Democratic leaderships. All of the leaders are senior members of the House; Tom Foley, the most junior, was first elected in 1964. Lengthy service in the House appears to be a necessary but certainly not a sufficient condition for ascent into the top leadership. The team is regionally diverse; both North and South are represented. The three top leaders differ somewhat ideologically yet all are in the mainstream of the Democratic party. The leadership selection processes generally produce a team that collectively has ties to the major segments of the party but is not so diverse ideologically as to preclude a close working relationship.

The Job of the Speaker

▆▆▆▆▆▆▆▆▆▆▆▆▆ The Speaker wears two hats: he is an officer of the House and the leader of his party in the chamber. The two roles are neither clearly separable nor of equal importance. The Speakership is predominantly a partisan position; within the limits of fairness, he is expected to use the resources provided by the first role to help him perform the second.

Officer of the House

In his capacity as an officer of the House, the Speaker is the chamber's presiding officer and is charged with a variety of administrative tasks. The Speaker either presides over the House himself or appoints the presiding officer. Despite the accretion of rules, precedents, and traditions that act as constraints, the position of presiding officer of the House is a powerful one. As Floyd Riddick has pointed out, "Tradition and unwritten law require that the Speaker apply the rules of the House consistently, yet in the twilight zone a large area exists where he may exercise great discrimination and where he has many opportunities to apply the rules to his party's advantage" (quoted in *Congressional Quarterly Guide to the Congress*, p. 129). In light of this discretion, the choice of an appropriate presiding officer to act in the Speaker's stead is vital, and only majority party members are selected. When the Speaker finds it necessary to appoint a Speaker pro tempore he goes down the leadership hierarchy, asking the majority leader first, then the whip, and so on. The Speaker never presides over the Committee of the Whole. Since it is in Committee of the Whole that bills are amended, great care goes into the selection of the presiding officer when important bills are scheduled.

A parliamentarian and two assistant parliamentarians aid the Speaker in discharging his duties as presiding officer. The office of parliamentarian is nonpartisan in the sense that a change in party control of the chamber does not necessarily lead to a change in personnel. The parliamentarians advise the committees and individual members of both parties as well as the majority party leadership. Nevertheless, the parliamentarians owe their first duty to the Speaker; their job is to help him accomplish his aims within the rules. Since the House rules are immensely complicated, the Speaker's access to the parliamentarian's expertise becomes itself an important resource.

The parliamentarian also assists the Speaker in selecting members to preside over the Committee of the Whole. Lists of members, arranged by type of bill under consideration when they presided, are maintained. When a controversial bill is scheduled, the parliamentarian will often present the Speaker with a list of recommendations from which to make his choice. Political factors are kept in mind: "We don't want a chairman who will have to make a ruling which is politically embarrassing to himself." The choice of presiding officer is most crucial when a bill is both controversial and new in approach. According to a participant, "There are five or six outstanding presiding officers and the Speaker tries to use those on the really tough bills—those on which there are no precedents." On minor bills, the Speaker often selects junior members to preside. This way, the Speaker singles out a member and gives him some visibility in the chamber. As O'Neill has said, "Men get pride out of the prestige of handling the Committee of the Whole, being named the Speaker of the day" (Malbin 1977, p. 942).

The Speaker can replace the presiding officer at any time. In late September 1980 the House was involved in routine business and a junior member was in the chair. In a surprise move the Republicans made use of an obscure rule that allows any member of the Rules Committee to call up a resolution cleared by the committee seven days after it has been reported. The resolution called up contained a waiver of the Budget Act, so that if the previous question were to be defeated, as Republicans were urging, the Senate budget resolution could have been offered as a germane amendment. The purpose of the maneuver was to embarrass the Democrats during the election period. As soon as Republican Rules Committee member Trent Lott made the motion, the presiding junior member was replaced by Dan Rostenkowski, then chief deputy whip and an experienced presiding officer.

Among his limited powers, the presiding officer has some discretion in the length of recorded votes. Before the installation of the electronic voting system, roll call votes ordinarily took thirty minutes and could easily be stretched to an hour. Electronic voting has reduced but not eliminated the leeway. Members must be given fifteen minutes to vote, but the presiding officer can declare the vote over as soon as the fifteen minutes have expired—or allow some extra time. In the spring of 1979 a bill raising the debt limit came up for a vote. The bill had already failed once and a major effort had been mounted to pass it on the second try. As time ran out, the leadership was ahead by two votes. O'Neill's gavel fell instantly. Members were not given the opportunity, as they often are, to change their votes. In a situation where the leadership is trailing in votes the presiding officer will allow a vote to go on considerably beyond the fifteen minutes to give the leadership time to switch some votes.

The Speaker is charged with referring bills to committee. With the institution of multiple referral in the mid-1970s, this has become more than a routine task. When a bill is referred to more than one committee, the Speaker is empowered to set a deadline for reporting. From the 94th Congress through the first session of the 96th, 3,856 measures were referred to more than one committee (Oleszek 1980, p. 7). The large number of multiple referrals means that the opportunity to set time limits arises frequently, and on important legislation it is often used. A deadline prevents a hostile subcommittee or committee from "bottling up" a bill. Furthermore, multiple referral can be used to change an unfavorable balance of forces by bringing into the process committees more sympathetic to the leadership's viewpoint. Yet multiple referral can also slow down the legislative process and create headaches for the leadership (Oleszek 1980). Nevertheless, the procedure does provide the Speaker with useful new strategic options.

In his administrative capacity the Speaker is in charge of allocating space on the House side of the Capitol. A room in the Capitol is universally desired; it is both a convenience and a status symbol. Speaker Rayburn, it was reported, used this "perk" extensively and in a personal way. O'Neill, in contrast, has eschewed doing so; the task has been delegated to an aide. Some observers believe this is a mistake on O'Neill's part; but given the limited space available, using its allocation politically does involve pitfalls.

Provider of Services to Members and Information Gatherer

Keeping members satisfied, always a significant leadership function, has taken on added importance with the House reforms that increased the visibility and clout of even junior members. Leadership services to members, in which the Speaker himself is very much involved, take a variety of forms. As O'Neill says, he commands a lot of "little odds and ends" he can use as favors for members (Malbin 1977, p. 942). The less predictable environment in which the leadership operates has made information gathering more difficult and more vital. In addition to contributing to "keeping peace in the family" and to accumulating credits that can be used in coalition building, many of the services the leaders perform provide important information to the leaders as a by-product.

For providing services and information gathering, few resources available to the Speaker surpass staff. Leadership staffs have grown significantly in the last two decades. D.B. Hardeman, a longtime Rayburn staffer, reports that at the end of his tenure as Speaker, Rayburn employed only eight people. This included both leadership and constituency office staff. In 1981 O'Neill's Washington staff totalled seventeen, of whom thirteen worked in the Speaker's rooms or the Speaker's office in the Capitol. Neither the parliamentarians and their staff nor the Steering and Policy Committee staff are included among the seventeen.

Personal staff on the Hill often have rather ambiguously defined jobs; they are expected to be generalists who can "pinch hit" where necessary. This is probably even more the case for professional employees of the leaders than for those of rank-and-file members. Staff located in a leadership office do not necessarily spend all their time on leadership work; nor do those located in the personal office necessarily confine themselves to the leaders' constituency concerns. Consequently, it is not possible to determine exactly how many aides leaders have working in leadership matters at a given time. Nevertheless, the increase in leadership staff resources has been dramatic.

According to a senior O'Neill aide, "This [leadership office] is a service organization" (Malbin 1977, p. 941). Providing services to members consumes a great deal of the Speaker's time and that of his aides. Because the Speaker has more influence with the administration than rank-and-file members do, he receives numerous requests for help. As O'Neill explained, "We're happy to try to open the door for [members], having been in the town for so many years and knowing so many people. We do know where a lot of bodies are and we do know how to advise people" (Malbin 1977, p. 942). One of the Speaker's senior aides handles the Speaker's patronage and deals with the administration on jobs and projects. During the Carter presidency a large part of this aide's job was helping members who had not been successful in their approaches to the administration.

The Democratic leadership, of course, has better access to and influence with a Democratic than with a Republican administration, but even when Republicans control the White House, the Speaker's power to get a hearing is much greater than that of the ordinary Democratic member, and many people in the agencies know that, regardless of the president's party, maintaining good relations with the House leadership is important. Nevertheless, a shift in White House control to the opposition party severely reduces the number and significance of the favors the leadership can provide its members. Furthermore, if the Republican administration is skillful, the Democratic House leaders will find administration favors used against them.

The Speaker is charged with making numerous appointments to boards and commissions. Often this involves simply securing for them the positions members want and finding people to take appointments, if necessary. The more desirable positions provide the Speaker with an opportunity to accumulate credits with members. The Speaker also uses his appointive powers to compensate members. For example, shortly after Phillip Burton was defeated in his race for majority leader, O'Neill appointed him to the Interparliamentary Union. Although the two positions are obviously not comparable, the Burton appointment was a gracious gesture, especially since most participants believe O'Neill was pleased that Wright defeated Burton. The appointment of Jerry Patterson to chair the select committee on committees at the beginning of the 96th Congress was also, in part, a compensation. Patterson had desired an appointment to Rules, and the California Democratic delegation had supported him, but O'Neill chose another Californian. In the use of his appointive powers, then, the Speaker contributes to "keeping peace in the family."

Members make numerous and varied minor requests of the Speaker. An important constituent wants to meet the Speaker and perhaps have his picture taken with him. A member wants to make certain physical alterations that require the Speaker's approval as head of the House Office Building Commission. A member wants the Speaker to sign a letter or make a call on his behalf. Often such matters can be handled at the staff level: "Eighty percent of the time I do it without even telling him, sign his name to a letter or make a call. You've got to know when you've got to ask him or bring it to his attention." Other requests do require the Speaker's personal attention. An aide provided one example of such a request: "_____ just walked in here. The Appropriations Committee is about to cut out some kind of weapon that's important to him. Maybe they manufacture it in his district. I don't know, but it's usually the case. So 'Tip' could speak to some members of the Appropriations Committee to keep the weapon in. That happens fairly often." The Speaker's intervention on behalf of a member does not assure success, but his attempts build up credits for him with members. An aide explained:

> "Tip" can't assure it, but he can talk to some people. Now, some of those people he talks to, even his friends on Appropriations, might say, " 'Tip,' you don't want to ask me this; it's a stupid request, you know this thing ought to be cut out." And "Tip" will say, "the guy asked me to ask you." So he really hasn't done anything, maybe it *will* make a difference, and they ask. They want to use his powers, members do, to get things for their own districts or their amendments on the floor; they ask him all the time. He doesn't always do them; they may think he does. He may be effective and he may not be when you ask him. But they like him to try.

The Speaker frequently acts as a mediator of conflicts among Democrats. "He monitors the conflict until the parties work it out," a member noted (Cohen 1978b, p. 1385). "He works to put out fires all the time," an aide said. Such mediation is peace-keeping in its most direct form. It involves, as one leader put it:

> Trying to mollify members who are angry with other members, trying to keep dangerous rifts from developing within the party. Sometimes getting people together of opposite viewpoints and letting them talk their problems out in a way that lets each understand that the other has a problem. Sometimes you can come to a compromise. Sometimes it's a question of committee jurisdictions. The average citizen would be utterly amazed at the extent to which members of committees are jealous about the jurisdictional domains of their committees. They hate for that to be invaded by any other committee. And sometimes "keeping peace in the family" involves that kind of an operation, where you get someone from another committee and try to bring him along in an affirmative way with something you're trying to do that came out of the other committee.

During the first nine months of the Reagan administration acrimony within the Democratic party ran unusually high. Liberals chafed over conservatives whose defections they saw as betrayals; the authorizing committtes were upset at the Appropriations Committee; the Budget Committee was the target of more than its usual share of hostility. In all of this the Speaker and the rest of the leadership acted as mediators. Sometimes they worked out satisfactory agreements, but even when no agreement was possible, the Speaker prevented a complete breakdown in relationships through innumerable meetings with the mutually antagonistic parties.

The leaders consider frequent one-on-one contact with their membership vital. Speaker O'Neill calls it "listening to confession." According to an aide, "He plays the role of confessor or whipping boy for members. If they are unhappy about almost anything, not just with the House but with what the Senate or the Administration has done, they come and complain to him. It serves as a vehicle for the expression of their frustrations or as a catharsis." Playing the "father confessor" role is a service that the Speaker provides to the membership, one that serves to defuse tensions and direct resentments away from the leadership. As such it contributes to "keeping peace in the family". "He listens to their problems. It's not necessary and often not possible to do anything about their problems," a senior aide in another leadership office explained. "Listening is what's crucial. This should *not* be thought of as wasting time."

The Speaker's accessability to members serves an informational function as well, as this statement by an aide implies: "The Speaker will see any member. He's accessible and approachable. New members are surprised that they don't need an appointment. If he's in the office too much, the Speaker gets itchy. He'll say, 'I should be on the floor or in the cloak room finding out what's going on.' " In the House, as in all institutions, information is a vital precondition to influence. Sam Rayburn as Speaker relied heavily on an informal network to provide him with necessary information. The Board of Education where news was swapped and bourbon and branch consumed was adequate to its time. The current leaders, of course, maintain networks of friends and acquaintances which serve as information sources, and their many informal conversations with members who seek them out are another important source.

Because of the wide dispersion of influence and the high rate of subcommittee activity, the current leadership cannot rely solely on informal information channels. Leadership staff have increasingly become the eyes and ears of the leaders. A high-ranking Speaker's aide described his job as "keeping the Speaker appraised of what's going on legislatively—what's problematic, who are the problems, what's likely to embarrass us down the road, what's likely to be valuable politically down the road." Gathering information is at least a peripheral part of the job of all leadership staff. The increase in the size of these staffs, consequently, represents an important augmentation of leadership resources.

The present leadership does a great deal of speaking on behalf of Democratic members in their districts. Speaker O'Neill and Majority Leader Wright make numerous trips each year. This activity seems to have been expected of the majority leader for quite some time, but O'Neill is more of a traveler than were previous Speakers, visiting the districts of thirty to forty Democrats each year (Fenno 1981, p. 5.). He customarily appears at members' fund-raisers. Such visits constitute a relatively important favor, for the Speaker's appearance is likely to raise the status of the member among his politically attentive constituents and, because the Speaker is a good draw, the member is likely to raise more money.

For the Speaker, such visits have a two-fold payoff. Of course he hopes the members thus benefited will be be grateful, but spending some time in a member's district also provides him with information that can be useful in the realm of persuasion. As a leadership aide explained, these trips provide a "feel" for the member's political situation: "If a guy tells 'Tip' 'I can't go with you on this one. It will hurt me in the district,' 'Tip' can say, 'Aw come on, they love you back home. You can do anything you want to,'—or he knows the guy does face a tough reelection fight and shouldn't be pushed."

The present Speaker's service orientation has multiple payoffs. By doing favors he accumulates "chits" that can be used in coalition building. Although he does not demand a quid pro quo for such help, most members do feel some obligation to reciprocate. By "listening to confession" and by mediating conflicts he contributes to party maintenance. And in the process the Speaker picks up information vital to the successful performance of both of these primary leadership functions. "The nature [of leadership] is knowing what makes a member tick, how far you can go with him," explained a senior Speaker's aide (Malbin 1977, p. 941).

Spokesman for
the House Democratic Party

In his dual role as chief officer of the House and leader of his party in the chamber, the Speaker is often called upon to act as spokesman for his party and for the House. A senior aide explained: "[The press] call me all the time to get the Speaker's viewpoint and also to find out what's happening and how the leadership feels, its position. A thousand other questions." The Speaker holds a short press conference each day the House is in session. He can use his spokesman position to focus attention, to communicate the intensity of his views to the membership and the administration (a statement spoken in public and published in the Washington newspapers conveys more commitment than one communicated in private), and to put pressure on members. A committee majority that does not comply when the Speaker states at a press conference that he "hopes, believes, and expects" a committee to report out a certain bill in the near future is directly rebuffing the Speaker.

During Democratic administrations the Speaker can use his spokesman role simply as another tool in the coalition-building process. When the

White House is in Republican hands, however, House Democrats expect a broader interpretation of the role; they expect the Speaker to communicate Democratic positions not only to the Washington community but also to the public at large. This expectation was especially intense during the early part of the Reagan presidency when House Democrats believed that their serious concerns about the Reagan program were not receiving adequate media attention. The Speaker responded by increasing his media contacts and appearing frequently on the morning news shows and the Sunday interview programs. No one can compete with the president in commanding public attention, however. Furthermore, congressional leaders are least able to compete when they need to most—when the president is highly popular. O'Neill's inability to meet his members' expectations resulted in considerable dissatisfaction.

The tasks that have devolved upon the leadership, then, provide resources the leaders can use in performing their primary functions. If the leaders are unable to carry out those tasks in a way that meets member expectations, however, they become liabilities rather than assets. O'Neill is fond of saying that as Speaker he possesses no weapons. Neither he nor any Speaker since Cannon has commanded resources sufficient to affect decisively most members' chances of attaining their goals. Yet the current Speaker does possess valuable resources. His powers and duties as an officer of the House are an important basis of influence. So too are the favors he can do for members by virtue of his party leadership position. Keenly aware of the limitations of his resources, the Speaker is leery of using negative sanctions. Because of changes in the House during the 1970s, O'Neill believes that the Rayburn one-man-show style of leadership is no longer viable. Consequently he makes extensive use of the other core leaders and of other members, as well.

The Job of the Majority Leader

First and foremost, the majority leader is the Speaker's lieutenant. "The Speaker ultimately has to be the leader of the House," Jim Wright has said (Cohen 1978a, p. 712). The majority leader "must work *with* the Speaker, in a supportive role, and never against him" (Wright 1976). The job of the majority leader therefore depends heavily on the Speaker's notion of what it should be. "In the 1950s Rayburn *was* the leadership," according to a longtime House staffer. "McCormick's role was limited to announcing the program when the Rules Committee gave them a program." The current Speaker, operating in a very different House, entrusts significant responsibility to the majority leader.

Certain duties by tradition devolve on the majority leader. He is responsible for scheduling legislation for floor consideration, he acts as the party's floor leader, and he is expected to take the lead on issues that are important to the party but that are politically too risky for the Speaker to handle. The majority leader's sizeable staff help him discharge these duties. In mid-1981 eight employees worked in the majority leader's office in the Capitol, only two of whom were strictly clerical. As is the case with all leadership staff, an important aspect of the job of the majority leader's professional employees is information gathering. A senior aide explained: "It would be very hard to write a job description of [my job]. The only thing I could say would be the senior staff is the eyes and ears of the leadership. You're giving them the information that they've got to have and you already know what their prejudices are, and what their inclinations are. And [you say], 'You'd better watch it, here's what ____'s about to do, or ____'s going to do this afternoon.' You just pick this up by gossip."

Scheduler

Control over scheduling is probably the most significant power of the majority leadership. When a bill is scheduled can make the difference between victory and defeat. In addition, because members believe maintaining a high voting participation rate to be important, scheduling intimately affects every member's Washington work life. As the frequency of recorded teller votes in the Committee of the Whole has increased, the impact of scheduling is greater now than it was when such votes were unrecorded.

Since the leadership has an interest in satisfying the expectations of members and of significant outside actors, both of whom are affected by scheduling decisions, these decisions involve a number of not always compatible considerations. The leadership tries to maintain a smooth flow of legislation so that the House accomplishes its work and meets a variety of deadlines and it attempts to accommodate the floor managers and the membership at large. Strategic considerations become paramount on major legislation when passage is perceived to be in doubt.

Little legislation is ready for floor consideration early in the session, especially if it is the first session of a Congress. If the House is not in recess, it must meet at least every four days, so an aide of the majority leader will "seine" the committees, looking for legislation to put on the floor. The leaders try to avoid pro forma sessions, preferring to do business every day the House meets. According to a participant, "This is a matter of image. We don't want the press to report the House didn't do anything, that we set a record of 3.7 seconds in session."

Committee staffs vary greatly in knowledge of and attention to scheduling questions. Some staff directors call the majority leader's office as soon as their committee has reported a bill. According to an aide, "_____ at Foreign Affairs and _____, the second a bill is reported, *the second,* they'll call over here and I'll know what's doing." Others "think you get scheduled by magic." An aide said: "_____ Committee is an example. You've got an older guy who's the staff director; he doesn't pay any attention; he doesn't monitor his subcommittees closely. We have to call them. They may have twenty bills they're about to report and he doesn't even call." Because of such problems, the majority leader's staff go through the calendars every morning to check what has been reported. The aides also work closely with the Rules Committee staff director, who sends copies of all letters requesting rules to the majority leader's office.

Early in the session scheduling decisions are made primarily by staff. As the committees begin to report out legislation, though, the majority leader's office is deluged with requests for floor time, and at this point the leaders become heavily involved. Prospective floor managers vigorously lobby for floor time. An aide gave an example: "_____ comes down and he'll say, 'Jim, do you realize what you're doing? We just must get this Department of Energy bill on; its so vital' and so forth—all the big nuclear stuff. Then [someone else] will say, 'All right, I just have to assume that the leadership thinks that nuclear bombs are more important than children.' "

The leadership tries to accommodate the floor manager by scheduling his bill at a time he finds convenient. Early in the session that is relatively easy, but later it can conflict with the need to maintain a smooth flow of legislation to the floor. "You just have to balance off everybody's prejudices," an aide explained. "Half the committees up here don't want to work on Friday. So you have to sometimes lean on them." A floor manager can pull his bill from the schedule at any time, but most of them learn quickly that to do so frivolously is costly. A participant explained:

> If the chairman doesn't want to bring his bill up, there's nobody to handle it. That's that—the chairman's boss. He doesn't do it very often. Now _____ did us that way one time on a Thursday. He did it arbitrarily because he really wanted to go home. That's the only reason. He didn't say that, but that's why he pulled it. We put it on again within a week and he pulled it again. We had put it on a Friday, just to zing him a little bit, so he pulled it. Then we kind of passed the word to the staff, "All right, you've had two runs at it, it's going to be a cold day in hell when you get back on. Now, goddamn it, we got a lot of these things that are terribly important and you've done us that way twice."
> So, that bill finally passed in September. This was March. In September it finally got through. A less important bill never would have gotten through.

In terms of accommodating the floor manager, the most common problem is too much legislation and too little time. Late in the session there is a tendency to placate floor managers by overscheduling. A competent floor manager knows that if his bill is the fourth of four controversial bills scheduled for one day, there is little chance it will be reached. Floor managers believe, however, that getting it onto the printed schedule establishes the presumption that their bill will eventually reach the floor, so there is considerable pressure to overschedule. As a result, the printed schedule comes to bear little resemblance to what is actually taken up. This form of accommodating floor managers thus adversely affects the membership at large.

Deadlines impose another set of constraints on the House schedule. In accordance with the Budget Act, the first budget resolution is to be approved by 15 May; much of June is usually devoted to appropriations bills; the deadline for approval of the second budget resolution is 15 September. These and other nondiscretionary items increase the competition for the remaining time.

The desire to accommodate floor managers, the necessity of meeting various deadlines, the difficulty of predicting how much floor time a given measure will take, and the dictates of strategic scheduling give rise to an extremely complex process. The majority leader's office may prepare up to twelve tentative schedules (called "tentatives") before a final schedule is announced. Throughout the process the majority leader's staff stay in contact with the Speaker's staff—although the majority leader is charged with scheduling, the Speaker has the final say. A senior O'Neill aide exercises general oversight over the schedule, and the amount of consultation between the aide and the staff of the majority leader increases as the session progresses. According to a majority leader's aide, "You clear more [decisions] towards the end. You just almost have to live with them as you get down towards the end." Late in the session scheduling decisions bear more weight. The aide continued:

> We clearly have three more weeks' work to do in three days now. So anything you do, you're affecting something that's either highly privileged or has been promised faithfully that we'd get done. So any time I move at all on anything, change anything at all, it has implications that are serious enough they oughtn't to be done purely at a staff level. If we insist on doing foreign aid, we're not going to do the Department of Defense authorization act. If we insist on doing rationing and all three of these appropriations, then I think that the disability compensation amendments or the export administration is in trouble.

A special telephone system connecting the offices of the majority leader, the Speaker, The Rules Committee, and the majority whip facilitates communication among these offices. The depression of a button on a specially equipped telephone puts a person in any of these offices in immediate contact with a person in any of the others. Such a system makes it difficult for members to play leaders off against one another. An aide explained; "You can tell if someone's upset with you. You can tell what they're going to do. They have one appeal beyond us, that's the Speaker. I press the button and I've got him. They have to dial and there ain't any way they can get him before I can. And I say, 'You're going to get a call from _____ and he's all shook and so stick with me. I've got a real good reason why I told him what I did.' And so when they get [the Speaker], he'll just 'on the one hand, on the other' them and won't do it. So it's really useful.''

Lobbying on scheduling extends beyond members and senior committee staff to include the White House and interest groups. The leadership expects lobbying from a Democratic administration but insists that it be kept within certain bounds. "When Carter first was elected," an aide recalled, the administration made scheduling requests "all the time. The bill would be scheduled and they'd call in a panic and say, 'You've got to pull that bill.' Until we taught them a lesson two or three times and just said, 'We don't tell you when you can meet on a given subject or discuss it privately and you don't do our scheduling.'. . . Once we've scheduled it, the White House can't pull it. Then we can accede to it occasionally, but they can't come up here and tell us to do it." Administration requests that are short of demands are not considered illegitimate. The aide continued:

> Oh, they lean on us. They lobby all the time, and there's no problem with that because the leadership is almost always hand in glove with them, almost always. Even on the rare occasions when they're not, there will be somebody in the leadership for it and so you go along. The bill creating a department of education is a good example. They lobbied very thick and fast and kept trying to get us to move it up closer to be sure and get it on. We finally did. But you don't mind that. It's the call from OMB [Office of Management and Budget] or somebody else in the administration saying, "You can't do that," or "It's got to be pulled." And they don't do that anymore. They sometimes call and say, "Please don't," or "Can't you do something about it?" in which case we'll say, "Well, you call the chairman of that subcommittee; we'll call him too and maybe we can talk him out of it." Rather than us pulling it arbitrarily, which we could do.

Interest group representatives call the majority leader's office constantly for information about scheduling, and quite frequently to lobby. Lobbyists sometimes request that a bill be delayed to give them more time for persuasion, but they often want assurance that a bill will be scheduled. The National Education Association lobbied vigorously on the scheduling of the Department of Education bill. No one in the leadership and few other members were enthusiastic about the bill, and everyone knew it would occupy an immense amount of floor time. In this case, however, it was the administration's, not the NEA's pressure, that finally persuaded the leadership to schedule the bill. Interest group lobbying that is too insistent is considered to be illegitimate meddling in the internal business of the House.

Despite its frequency, direct interest group lobbying has a relatively minor impact on scheduling. Internal House considerations, administration requests, and broad-gauge political concerns allow little leeway for attending to interest group wishes not consonant with them. Lobbying may increase the probability of a minor bill reaching the floor because it indicates the existence of an interested constituency. On major bills of interest to an essential Democratic constituency such as labor, the group's representatives and the leadership will work together closely, so that such lobbying is usually unnecessary. The common situs picketing bill brought to the floor in the 95th Congress at the behest of the AFL-CIO, represents a partial exception. House leadership had opposed scheduling the bill because it believed (correctly) that the bill would not pass.

The minority party plays no formal and little actual role in House scheduling. The minority leader may occasionally make a request of the Speaker, and the Speaker may or may not accede, although he will be sympathetic to minor requests related to meeting times if they are not made frequently. In early 1981 the Democratic leadership made an agreement with the minority concerning the scheduling of President Reagan's priority economic legislation (see chapter 4). Political considerations led the Democratic leadership to adopt this extremely unusual course. Given the president's popularity, the leadership was concerned that the Democratic party in the House not be perceived as obstructionist. Furthermore, as the Senate was under Republican control, Senate action could force the leadership's hand.

As a congressional session progresses, scheduling becomes not only politically but also technically more complex. Estimating floor time for a bill is both critical to the integrity of the schedule and extremely difficult. A participant explained how such estimates are made:

> The staff director will say, "All right, we reported this damn thing and it's CETA and it's going to be mean." And then you'll say, "All right, we've got a helluva week; I don't think we can get you on there that week. How about the following week?" and once you start negotiating with them, then you start asking them the critical questions: How long is it going to take? How many amendments are there going to be? How much time do you need? At that stage, he's got you hooked, so then he'll start lying. He'll say, "Well, I tell you what, if we can get two hours, we can wind this thing up. It's just not that bad." Well, you just automatically add two more hours to it; it's a four-hour bill; that means it's over a half-day bill. So you just do some mental adjustment. Then you'll go talk to somebody else who knows about the bill or you hear from the minority and you readjust. It's not a four-hour bill; it's a nine-hour bill or it's just a dog or they're really going to filibuster it. And then the Speaker is apprised of that.

Accommodating the work, travel, and speaking plans of the general membership involves predictability in scheduling. Members want to know as far in advance as possible when the House will be in session so they can make their calendar. When he became Speaker, O'Neill adopted an Obey Commission recommendation that has immensely increased predictability. In January a schedule of Washington work periods and district work periods for the year is made up. Except for the adjournment date, which is given as a target, the House follows this schedule closely. In this way members can make out-of-town commitments without fear of missing an important vote. To a large extent the Obey Commission schedule of daily House meeting times is followed, and this, too, makes it easier for members to plan their own time. Those members senior enough to remember the old system are pleased by the change. "In the fourteen years I've been here, it's the best job of scheduling," one said. "Under Albert and McCormack, it was much less predictable in terms of when the House was in session. We might work fifteen minutes one day and a chairman who thought he couldn't pass his bill would pull it off the floor and they wouldn't have a backup. The next day we might work until one o'clock in the morning." Early in the session, the leadership will not schedule votes on Mondays and Fridays so those members who want to visit their district can do so without missing roll calls. The leaders never spring surprises by bringing up a bill without warning.

Copies of the schedule for the following week are distributed at the Thursday morning whip meeting. The majority leader or, if he is not available, another leadership figure announces the schedule on the floor, usually on Thursday afternoon. A printed copy is sent by the whip's office to all Democrats. Once the schedule is disseminated the leadership does not change it capriciously, but adhering to it religiously is not always possible, especially later in the session. Conference reports, which may be brought up at any time, may have to be added; bills may take longer than estimated; a whip count may show unexpected trouble and action on the bill may consequently be postponed; a bill may run into unanticipated trouble on the floor and be pulled off before it is completed.

In deciding what legislation to bring up when, the leadership also tries to accommodate the membership, so that Democrats have "something positive to go home with." An aide explained how one scheduling decision was made prior to the August 1979 recess: "The House—especially the Democrats—looked bad when it rejected the president's original [gas rationing] plan. Passing something was necessary so members could say they responded to the energy crisis. We didn't try to finish the foreign aid appropriations. It would have taken a lot of floor time and no one can go home and brag about passing a foreign aid bill." Accommodating members by substantive scheduling decisions also involves keeping some issues from reaching the floor. Measures that present many Democrats with a no-win situation and that the leadership either opposes or believes have no chance of passing the Senate are kept off the floor whenever possible. Two leading examples are busing and gun control. On the latter, a participant explained: "Right now Rodino's got it and he's sitting on it, and if it got out of his committee by some miracle, well, we'd have to depend upon the Rules Committee holding it for awhile and mucking it around and eventually the Speaker would try to keep it off the floor because that would wind up defeating an awful lot of good Democrats."

Strategic scheduling is discussed later in this book, when coalition-building strategies are analyzed. On major controversial legislation, strategic considerations override all others. As the leadership's scheduling flexibility is a critical tool for affecting floor success, it must be protected even though that sometimes decreases predictability. The following exchange illustrates leadership scheduling control and the leaders' care to maintain their flexibility.

> Mr. BAUMAN [R-Md.]. Mr. Speaker, I wanted to inquire of the gentlemen from Texas (Mr. Wright) whether the gentlemen is sure that the debt limit increase bill will come up on Monday and not on Tuesday or, possibly, later today. . . .
> Mr. WRIGHT. Mr. Speaker, the plan is to bring it before the House on Monday, and it will be brought on Monday unless it is changed.
> Mr. BAUMAN. And I think that depends upon whether or not the first quorum call shows the gentlemen have the votes to pass it.
> Mr. WRIGHT. Mr. Speaker, I congratulate the gentlemen from Maryland on the astuteness of his observation. (*Congressional Record*, 96th Cong., 1st sess., 29 March 1979, vol. 125, p. 1842)

Floor Leader

As floor leader, Jim Wright is responsible for seeing that business flows smoothly on the floor. Because of the multitude of demands made on his time, he usually delegates the task of "guarding the floor" to senior staff. Particularly when the House is scheduled to take up a number of different measures in quick succession, an aide stays on the floor. The parliamentarian and the presiding officer, of course, know the order of business and have lists of members to recognize. If the person who is supposed to be recognized is not on the floor, the majority leader or his staff must go into action. In one case, a bill was called up and the subcommittee chairman who was managing the bill was not on the floor. A majority leader's aide called him "frantically" from the cloakroom and then had to find someone to fill in until he arrived. According to the rules, anyone from the committee would do; the only committee member immediately available was a freshman who did not even serve on the subcommittee that had written the bill, but he was pressed into service and "stumbled along for five or ten minutes until the subcommittee chairman showed up."

The floor leadership must also sense incipient problems and attempt to do something about them before they become major. The majority leader is available to his colleagues, and during roll calls he circulates among them and can often pick up early signs of trouble. Of course the minority is often the source of problems. During the 95th and 96th congresses three Republicans, Robert Bauman, John Ashbrook (Ohio), and John Rousselot (Ca.), frequently seemed to be the minority's actual floor leaders. A skillful parliamentarian, Bauman especially was frequently a thorn in the leadership's side. Because these members held no official leadership positions, O'Neill and Wright did not want to give them recognition by dealing with them directly, so senior staff had to find out what these Republicans were up to. An aide explained: "Conversation with Bauman or Ashbrook or Rousselot, the 'gadflies,' as we call them, and they are the effective leadership on that side, we talk to them a lot. I'll talk with one or more of them almost every day to get a feeling for what they think about one given thing. The fact is, as far as real consultation, it almost never goes on, but you do all you can to keep them from throwing the monkey wrenches into the gears. If they can, you know they will. And if you can get wind of something, you can go over and kind of maybe pull the teeth of the problem before it happens. Wright himself, almost never. The Speaker, almost never."

The floor leader's job also entails making speeches on the floor on major legislation and making leadership motions. To be sure, Wright is a consummate orator; but as important as the style and substance of his speeches is the fact that he as majority leader speaks. A speech by the majority leader puts the imprimatur of the leadership upon the legislation; it indicates not only the leadership's position but also its commitment. Wright tries to limit his involvement so as "not to wear out my welcome"; nevertheless, his job requires that he make frequent floor speeches. From 1977 through 1980 he averaged forty major floor statements a year in his capacity as floor leader (not including announcements of the schedule and other routine matters.) A motion or an amendment offered by the majority leader carries a clear leadership imprimatur. For example, he always offers the motion to adopt the rules of the House at the beginning of a Congress. At times he offers an amendment to signal the Democratic membership that the leadership's full weight is behind it (for examples, see chapters 5, 6, and 7).

Doer of the "Dirty Jobs

The division of labor between the Speaker and the majority leader is determined in part by their House constituencies. "Geographic splits are still strong," a participant explained. "If you had a Speaker from Massachusetts and a majority leader from New York, you'd just have one hell of a time bringing it off. Albert was very dependent upon 'Tip' to help him with the northerners and easterners, and 'Tip' is very dependent upon Wright to help him with the border states, the southerners, the westerners."

To remain leaders, of course, the leaders have to be reelected by their districts. Because the character of a member's constituency does place some constraints upon what he can do, even if he is a leader, the leadership seeks a regional balance within the team. The majority leader is expected to take the lead "when the Speaker knows something must be done but can't do it himself." Majority leader John McCormack of Massachusetts played a key role on civil rights issues because Speaker Rayburn, a Texan, could not afford politically to be "out in front" on the issue. During the 95th Congress disagreements arose constantly between the House and the Senate on medicaid funding of abortions. Speaker O'Neill, a Catholic from a heavily Catholic district, had to keep his distance from the issue, so Majority Leader Wright was charged with working out compromises. "I don't enjoy this. But I know that 'Tip' can't politically and I can," explained Wright. On another occasion, when Carter asked Congress to lift the ban on aid to Turkey, "the leadership had to support the president, 'Tip' was clear on that. But 'Tip' didn't want to upset Brademas [who is of Greek extraction] or his own Greek constituents, so 'Tip' didn't want to take the lead." The task, thus, devolved on Wright. Another time, after O'Neill had agreed to speak at a fund-raiser for an eastern Democrat, the member was arrested on a morals charge. O'Neill believed that politically he could not appear but that the leadership should show support for the member, who is well liked. The majority leader was asked to go in his stead. Wright did so, and his appearance solidified his support among eastern Democrats.

Being willing, when necessary, to take politically risky action is a part of leadership. The leaders cannot persuade their members to do so if they themselves are unwilling to set an example. All the leaders must take risks occasionally, but as the second man in the heirarchy, the majority leader most often finds himself the "point man." During the 95th Congress the leadership used all its resources to pass Carter's energy program. Wright vigorously argued on the floor against deregulation, not a popular position in his Texas district. A participant explained, "Jim Wright wouldn't have been out front on this if he'd been Speaker. He would have delegated it."

Provider of Favors for Members

Like the Speaker, the majority leader wields extensive influence so that he can help members in a variety of ways. By doing favors, he builds up capital that can be used in persuasion and contributes to party maintenance. In addition, most majority leaders eventually run for Speaker, and the services they provide members aid them in building the support necessary to capture the position.

The leadership tasks delegated to him provide the majority leader with a basis for doing favors for members. Both prospective floor managers and other members make numerous requests with regard to scheduling: "They want a bill scheduled, or they want to postpone bringing a bill to the floor. . . . Somebody will be saying, 'Look, for God's sake, don't schedule that bill for Monday, it'll kill me. I've got to be here for that vote. And I have long since been committed to attend the annual meeting of my chamber of commerce in my town. It's very important. But if I'm not there to vote on that bill, it just really embarrasses me deeply at home.' So you know, maybe I will be able to get that bill changed. Put off until Tuesday instead of Monday, for sufficient cause."

The electronic voting system makes any member's vote on any issue immediately known to the other members. Because the majority leader's position is taken as the leadership position, both how and when he votes can influence others. Members will frequently ask Wright to vote early during the fifteen-minute roll call. An aide said, "They may ask him, 'Would you please be in the well [in front of the House chamber] and would you please vote early? I know you're for me and I know you don't want to speak on it, it's too hairy for you, but would you please vote early? And be in the well.' " Alternatively, members who know Wright will vote against their position may ask that he do so as unobstrusively as possible: "They may say, 'I know you've got to vote this way, but would you stay out of it?' So Wright will just stay down here till the last minute and slip up there and walk on the floor and vote and slip right back out and nobody will ever know he just voted one way and it was clear that the leadership wasn't taking a major role in it."

Committee and subcommittee chairmen frequently ask the majority leader to speak on behalf of their bill or against an amendment. "I try to do that with some discrimination because if I did it every time, on every bill, soon it wouldn't mean anything when I went to the floor to speak," Wright explained. "That's just a decision I have to make individually, and I don't have any rule of thumb except to speak only when the bill is important, or the amendment is important and when our position may be in jeopardy."

Discretion is also required when the majority leader considers bestowing favors through the other leadership tasks he performs. Obviously, he cannot change the schedule to help one member if such a change would seriously inconvenience other members or endanger the passage of important legislation. Helping a member by casting a vote early or late is constrained by the majority leader's need to maintain the party position. Nevertheless, within the constraints imposed by the coalition-building function, he can use his scheduling and floor leadership roles to aid individual members. By so doing, he builds up "chits" which can be used for coalition building in the future, and contributes to "keeping peace in the family."

Like the Speaker, the majority leader has greater access to the administration than do rank-and-file members. He gets numerous requests for help from members. A senior aide explained the situation during the Carter presidency:

[We get such requests] frequently. They'll say, "I can't even get the sons of bitches to answer my calls," or "I can't get anything out of DOT. Would you guys, I hate to ask you, but would you get Jim to lean on Brock Adams or lean on the liaison people at the White House for me? I'll call them one more time, but I don't think I've even got their attention." And it's relatively simple. Many times, I'll do no more than call the office of Frank Moore and just tell him, "Frank, I don't want to take any of your time, but goddamn it, answer ____'s phone call. He's been after you and it's important to us, and he's getting a little bit peeved at you." So, he'll answer it immediately.

Because the position of majority leader carries considerable prestige, members frequently ask Wright to meet influential constituents. The majority leader is invited to attend and sometimes speak at Democratic members' fund-raisers in Washington and attends as many as he can, and he also travels a great deal on behalf of members. In his first eighteen months as majority leader, Wright visited eighty-three congressional districts (Cohen 1978a, p. 713). Wright has also aided members with direct campaign contributions. In 1978 the Jim Wright Majority Congress Committee raised $300,000, most of which was given to Democratic House candidates (Cohen 1978a, p. 714). Because he himself had a tough reelection race in 1980, Wright was not able to give as much to colleagues, but he did make some contributions.

A majority leader's assistance—or lack of it—is seldom critical to a member's career success. Yet, its effect is far from negligible. By a skillful use of his resources the majority leader can build up a reservoir of good will that directly contributes to "keeping peace in the family" and also prepares the ground for effective coalition building.

The Whip and the Rest of the Inner Circle

A large part of the majority whip's job entails overseeing the whip system's extensive information-gathering and disseminating efforts. The whip supervises the conducting of whip polls to ascertain how Democratic members stand on measures the leadership considers important. Such polls provide the information on which subsequent tactical decisions are based.

In addition, as part of the core leadership group, the whip serves as an advisor to the Speaker and participates in leadership decision making. Although formally appointed by the majority leader, the whip is actually the Speaker's choice. While political considerations such as regional balance play a role in his choice, the Speaker chooses a member with whom he has a comfortable and close relationship. John Brademas, whip in the 95th and 96th congresses, was an O'Neill protégé; the close personal relationship of Brademas and O'Neill made for an effective working relationship. Tom Foley, who became whip at the beginning of the 97th Congress, had been a member of the leadership in the two previous congresses by virtue of his position as chairman of the Democratic Caucus.

The chief deputy whip and the chairman of the Democratic Caucus complete the inner circle. The chief deputy whip is the majority leader's choice. In 1977 Wright selected Dan Rostenkowski of Illinois, who had managed Wright's successful campaign for majority leader. An astute politician with ties to big city members, Rostenkowski is also close to O'Neill. At the beginning of the 97th Congress, when Rostenkowski became chairman of the

Ways and Means Committee, Bill Alexander of Arkansas was selected as chief deputy whip. Alexander had served as one of the three deputy whips and has ties to conservative southern Democrats, a group that had increased in importance because of the narrower Democratic majority in the 97th Congress. Gillis Long of Louisiana replaced Tom Foley as caucus chairman in 1981. A political moderate and an extremely popular member, he, like his predecessor, is "on the same wave length as the Speaker and the majority leader."

The members of the inner circle see each other frequently at meetings. All of them except the caucus chairman attend the weekly whip meetings; all are members of the Steering and Policy Committee, which meets about twice a month; all usually attended the biweekly White House breakfasts during the Carter administration and the occasional meetings with the Senate leadership. In addition, there is a daily leadership meeting prior to the Speaker's press conference. These meetings, which include a large number of aides, usually last only fifteen minutes. Nevertheless, they provide the leaders with an opportunity for general information sharing and consultation. "This provides a daily opportunity to touch base, talk about what's coming up today," noted one leader. Sensitive strategic decisions are discussed at special meetings or at informal, even chance, get-togethers. A great deal of the consultation among the leaders is highly informal. The Speaker may call the majority leader and ask him to come up to the Speaker's rooms for a moment; various of the leaders may talk on the floor or run into each other in the halls. A good deal of coordination occurs, as a senior aide said, "by osmosis." In 1981 the leaders broke with the tradition of informality; they decided that responding effectively to the new Republican administration required greater coordination and they instituted weekly leadership meetings.

Successful performance of the leadership's two primary functions requires that the inner circle include members with ties to all segments of the party. The resulting diversity can lead to intraleadership disagreements. The members of the inner circle represent different districts and bring different perspectives to their tasks. Consequently, cooperation among them is not always complete. The inner circle's collective interest in party maintenance and coalition-building success, however, serves to keep such frictions under control. By and large, the working relationship is smooth.

The inner circle, then, consists of five people of whom the Speaker is definitely the boss, with the majority leader serving as second in command. This group, however, is far too small to carry out alone all the tasks necessary for successful coalition building in the postreform House. Chapter 3 describes the extended leadership circle upon which the core leaders depend for help.

THE

EXTENDED

LEADERSHIP

CIRCLE

The Whip System

███████████████ The whip system, supervised by the majority whip, expanded significantly in both size and function during the 1970s. It carries on an extensive effort in information collection and dissemination and is centrally involved in the politics of persuasion.

Evolution of the Whip System

A whip system in the Democratic party consisting of a chief whip and a number of assistant whips first arose in the early 1930s. Each of the assistant whips was chosen by and was responsible for the members of one geographical area or zone—New England, for example. In the 1950s, Speaker Sam Rayburn, who preferred a very informal leadership style, made little use of the whip system or even of the chief whip. Carl Albert, who became majority whip in 1955, was assigned so few responsibilities that his aide got bored and asked for a transfer to the district office. As one senior staffer notes, "Rayburn ran the whole thing out of his back pocket." And when the position of deputy whip was created in 1955, for Hale Boggs, who had wanted to be whip, a senior aide explained, "Boggs's consolation prize was the deputy whip [position]. No staff, no nothing, just a paper job. But Albert didn't have anything to do, so Boggs had double nothing to do."

As Speaker during the 1960s, John McCormack made more use of the whip system than Rayburn had, although by later standards the level of activity was not impressive (Ripley 1969, p. 212). To a large extent the White House liaison staff performed the vote-counting function during the Kennedy and Johnson administrations. In the 1970s the whip system expanded as the number of whips appointed by the leadership increased. The deputy whip position was divided into two positions in 1970. In 1972 the position of chief deputy whip was created and the number of deputy whips grew to three. Three new appointive positions, called at-large whips, were added in 1975. Women, blacks, and freshmen were demanding inclusion in the whip system, and these new positions were created in response (Dodd 1979, p. 31). When Tip O'Neill became Speaker in 1977, he increased the number of at-large whips to ten. In 1981 a fourth deputy whip position was created and the number of at-large whips rose to fifteen.

A variety of idiosyncratic factors played a role in this expansion; so too did the leadership's needs in a changed environment (Dodd 1979). Democratic loss of the White House in 1968 deprived the House leadership of services previously provided by the administration liaison staffs. Sharp policy disagreements between the president and congressional Democrats demonstrated the need for more organized leadership efforts, while rules and norms changes in the House increased the leadership's need for assistance.

In the 1960s the zone whips were charged with both obtaining vote counts and persuading their colleagues to support the leadership position (Ripley 1969, p. 199). Yet because they are chosen by the members of their zones, their loyalty to party and to the leadership is sometimes minimal. The increasingly upredictable environment of the 1970s compounded the problem of unsupportive whips who do not engage in persuasion because it increased the leadership's need for a loyal group of assistants to aid in persuasion efforts. The more uncertain environment has also made it necessary to conduct whip polls more frequently. Ripley reports that seventeen completed polls were conducted in 1962 and 1963 (1969, p. 212). In contrast, fifty-three were taken during the 93d Congress (1973–74) (Dodd 1979, p. 39). According to the chief staffer in the whip's office, approximately eighty polls were conducted during the 95th Congress and about the same number were taken during the 96th Congress.

Appointed and Elected Whips:
The Division of Labor

This heavy work load combined with the loyalty problem necessitated a division of labor. The elected zone whips conduct the initial count; most of the other whips, who are appointed by the leadership, act as an arm of the leadership in persuasion efforts. Many participants believe this division of functions has increased the efficiency of the counting operation: "The whip system is a very efficient, well-run counting house, and it produces very reliable counts, which are a key tool in making decisions. Some people have the view that it ought to be more of a lobbying operation. It ought to be less of a reflection of the grass-roots sentiment and more of a vehicle for conveying views down the line. I don't think the two functions can be combined effectively. You can't get an honest count if the counters are themselves instruments of persuasion."

Whips themselves perceive a difference in the responsibilities of the appointed and the elected whips. Most of the appointed whips believe they owe some responsibility to the leadership, while elected whips owe their allegiance to their zone members. Not surprisingly, elected whips from the more conservative regions perceive the sharpest distinction between the two types of whips. One of them said, "As I see it, the zone whips are really elected to represent the members in the Democratic whip zones, whereas the appointed whips are essentially appointed to represent the leadership and so I perceive a substantial difference in my responsibilities as an elected zone whip and somebody like _____, who's an appointed whip, for example. I think that when he accepts a position that comes from the leadership, that's sort of where he owes his responsibility in that position."

Although most of the appointed whips are loyalists who are heavily involved in persuasion, a few are not. In appointing at-large whips, party leaders seek regional balance and try to accommodate influential members who request the position. A conservative member explained that he had asked for the appointment after serving as a zone whip from the beginning of his congressional career: "So when Jim Wright was elected majority leader, I said, 'Jim, I've always been on the whip organization but I didn't run for zone whip this time, but I would like some way of being able to sit in on those meetings just frankly to keep informed.' " Asked if he was involved in persuasion efforts, this member replied, "If it's something the leadership feels real keen about, I do talk to people and let them know the leadership feels strong about this legislation." He saw his role primarily as a provider of information, but this, too, is of value to the leadership. As a staffer explained, even those who do not get involved in persuasion efforts, "*do* serve as information conduits and, if you can persuade them, they may have an effect on the people close to them."

All whips fulfill the function of conveying information to and from the leadership. Most of the whips questioned mentioned this as a central part of the job. "I see the job as providing liaison between the Democratic leadership and the members," a zone whip said. "I think primarily what the members in my zone expect of me is to be kept as informed as possible about what the legislative schedule is going to be, what major issues they can expect to be faced with, and essentially what the leadership position on those issues is going to be," another zone whip commented. An appointed whip said: "We try to keep our people, the people who we sort of identify with, informed of the leadership's position on things—what they'd like, what we're seeking, what we're trying to do. Not only on policy, but also on scheduling and programming. . . . We pick up static from our people and relay it to the leadership, so they know what's going on, but we also pick up information from the leadership and convey it back. It's a two-way conduit."

The deputy whips involve themselves in persuasion but serve in other ways as well. One deputy whip described his job:

Well, it's the feeler for the Speaker and the majority leader, really. I think if
the majority leader or the Speaker wants something to develop on the floor
. . . from the membership, we go out there as the whips to start the development of the thought. That's one facet of the job. Another facet of the job is
you're kind of the complaint post. They come and complain to you and then
you reflect what the membership is saying to the leadership, principally because
members are a little reserved about going face to face with a Jim Wright or a
Tip O'Neill, so they'll complain to that lower eschelon. I tell the Speaker
what's going on, what's happening, what the members are saying.

The Whip Meetings

The whips meet weekly when the House is in session. For both leaders
and whips, information exchange is the single most important function
served by the meetings. In addition, the meetings serve a safety valve function by allowing the expression of rank-and-file complaints directly to the
leadership and provide the leaders with a forum for persuasion efforts and
morale building. Because, on almost any given legislative battle, some
whips oppose the leadership position, sensitive strategic questions are seldom discussed.

When Hale Boggs initiated these meetings during the 1960s, neither the
Speaker nor the majority leader attended. The current leaders, O'Neill and
Wright, always attend. The meetings convene at nine o'clock on Thursday
mornings in the majority whip's office. The majority leader announces the
schedule for the following week and copies of it are distributed. The leaders
answer questions about scheduling and adjournment time. They frequently
report on meetings they have had with the president and other administration officials. They may explain how they see the political situation. The
majority whip often urges members to complete their whip checks.

Controversial legislation is often discussed, with the leaders or a whip
who serves on the committee of origin explaining the issues. On particularly
important and complicated measures, the floor manager may be brought in
to brief the whips. During the 1981 budget and tax fight, for example, the
chairmen of the Budget and Ways and Means committees frequently attended to keep members up to date on developments on those major pieces of
legislation. If a complex parliamentary situation is expected, a careful explanation is offered to those present. In one case, after hearing a lengthy explanation of an exceeding complicated situation, one whip asked the floor
manager simply to vote early so that others could follow his lead.

Whips frequently ask questions about how much controversy to expect
on a bill and how long debate is likely to last. Since almost every committee
is represented in these meetings, the leadership will ask the whip on the committee of origin to answer questions about particular bills. At one meeting a
Banking Committee member told his fellow whips that the Housing and
Community Development Act of 1979 was not large and so probably would

not prove to be highly controversial. A member of Armed Services reported that the Department of Defense Authorization would probably take longer than usual because draft registration was at issue. Sometimes the leaders will ask the whips for information. For example, a Ways and Means member was asked by the leadership how long he thought debate on the Trade Agreements Act would take. Although by statute twenty hours of debate are allowed, the floor manager had assured the leadership it would take only two. The whip replied, "There's no way of predicting. It's a very complicated document and if members have really gone into it, debate might take a long time." Another whip said, "Let's hope they haven't," and everyone laughed.

Members sometimes lobby for their legislation in responding to such questions. They emphasize intracommittee consensus if they can: "It really has no controversial features. The subcommittee was unanimous." A hard sell can be employed if it is done with humor. A whip who was floor manager of a bill scheduled for that afternoon said, "There are three things I want you to do. One, vote with me on all amendments; two, vote against _____ on all amendments; three, vote for the bill [on final passage]. (Laughter) We can't rewrite this bill on the floor. We've done everything we can to get people on board. You should know that on the really good amendments we've put [a committee Republican's] name to get Republican support."

The meetings also give the whips an opportunity to ask more general questions, to make suggestions, and to voice complaints. For example, during the spring of 1979 members expressed concern about the president's attitude toward patronage versus civil service for census workers. Democrats, especially those representing poorer districts, were concerned that traditional patronage positions, placed under civil service by Ford just before he left office, might not be reconverted by Carter. Not only do members see such jobs as being of some value in poor area, they also feared an undercount in the 1980 census would result if census workers were not from the local community. The leaders set up a series of meetings with administration officials and eventually resolved the problem. During consideration of the budget resolution a whip complained that the leadership was not sticking to the schedule: "People are getting annoyed. We're going on till 6:30 when you said we'd adjourn by 5:30." A leader replied, "Budget is a special situation. After this, we'll stick with the schedule." At the same meeting a California whip warned the leadership that they would probably lose thirty Californians on the gas rationing bill. Another member wanted assurance that the votes scheduled for the following Monday would not be put over until Tuesday. His large eastern state had a primary on Tuesday and the members had to be at home but did not want to miss a number of roll calls. He was assured that the schedule that had been arranged to accommodate this large delegation would not be changed.

In early 1979, as a balance-the-budget mood was sweeping the country and the leadership was trying to pass a debt limit increase, whips urged the leadership to provide members with an opportunity to vote for a balanced budget. A southern whip said, "Can we assure our people they will have a meaningful vote on a balanced budget? It would be a lot easier to persuade them on the debt limit if I can tell them that." The leaders explained some of the problems involved and the sort of proposals they found unacceptable but also said that work on a responsible proposal was underway. As a vote on an antibusing constitutional amendment approached, members vulnerable on the issue urged the Speaker to provide some protection for them. The amendment had been discharged from the Judiciary Committee—a procedure that allows for one hour of debate on the floor. A number of whips were arguing in the meeting that "that's no way of amending the Constitution." A southerner said, "All these arguments about procedure are not going to be convincing to the people back home. I signed the discharge petition but I'm going to vote against it. I've already told [a whip active in the opposition effort] that. But it would help a lot if maybe the Speaker and Rodino would hold a press conference announcing full-scale hearings. People around here may know about that but people out in the country don't." Another southern whip concurred: "I didn't sign the petition and don't intend to vote for it. I don't intend to reinvent this issue—inflict it upon my constituency again. But something like such a press conference would be helpful, especially with the Republican sections of my district." At a whip meeting during the budget mark-up period a member from an inner city district asked about the "rape of urban programs" in the Budget Committee, and several others expressed deep concern. A leader requested that they wait until the Budget Committee finished its work: "Then you can take a look at it; it may not be as bad as it looks now. Don't prejudge." Another whip asked if leadership strategy was to pass the resolution with Republican help. Both the Speaker and the majority leader assured him it was not.

Complaints about the Carter administration were often aired. A whip said he had heard the president intended to run against Congress. "I ran as a Carter Democrat and have tried to support Carter. But the administration liaison people never come to see me. With the president, its a one-way street," he complained. The leadership promised to talk to the president about running against Congress. Another member complained, "The president sends us Panama, SALT, Rhodesia. Every time I've been to the White House it's been about foreign affairs. If he doesn't start worrying about domestic policy, especially energy and inflation, he won't be reelected." A leader replied, "We can criticize the president in a meeting like this, but kicking the hell out of him in the press is wrong."

During the first half of 1981, when the Democratic party was sustaining a series of defeats at the hands of the Reagan administration, the whip meetings were especially intense. The whips were "bitching and moaning and screaming and yelling," a regular attender said. Party strategy was repeat-edly debated. "Also," a staffer explained, "you have everyone from Rangel to Montgomery there. Although it wasn't *ad hominem*, the liberals were asking how long the conservatives would be allowed to get away with defecting without any sanctions. There was considerable implicit and explicit criticism of the leadership, although, again, it wasn't personal."

Because the regional whips collectively are representative of the diversity of the party, the whip meetings provide the leadership with invaluable infor-mation. The rumors and member gripes which the leadership hears can pro-vide an early warning of trouble. Furthermore, by offering members an op-portunity to confront the leadership directly with their complaints, the meetings often defuse dissatisfaction.

The leaders also find the meetings useful for conveying information to their membership. A number of the zone whips write up a summary of the major points covered in the meeting and send it, along with a copy of the tentative schedule, to all members in their zone. Information that is particu-larly critical spreads quickly even without this formal procedure.

The leadership, in addition, uses the meetings for persuasion and to build morale. Generally, the leaders' exhortations to support the party position are fairly low key: "I hope we'll all stick together on that"; "I hope you'll vote for the bill and urge all your friends to do so." Sometimes, however, stronger language will be used, as on the Panama legislation, when a leader said, "This one will separate the men from the boys. The whips are sup-posed to have some spine and help others have some spine."

In the whip meetings, as elesewhere, leadership persuasion often involves minimizing the electoral risks of supporting the leadership position. On the Panama legislation, a leader said that the electoral risk of voting for the leg-islation had been greatly exaggerated. Members should remember that a lot of oil goes through the canal to the Northeast, he pointed out, and that the repercussions of not passing the legislation would take a lot of explaining. Regarding the antibusing constitutional amendment, a leader admitted, "A fellow can get hurt on that." He continued, "But when you lose support with a part of your district on something like this, you usually pick up sup-port with another."

Appeals to "gut" party loyalty—to preventing the Republicans from beating the Democrats—are frequent. In discussing the foreign aid bill a leader said, "There are lots of amendments and all are mischievous. Try to encourage our brothers to screw up their courage and resist. The Republic-ans are just trying to embarrass us."

The leaders are generous in their thanks for and praise of whips' efforts: "I really want to thank you for the manner in which you've been able to hold this thing [the budget resolution] together"; "I want to say a word of appreciation to the whips for the tremendous job you've done"; "I certain-ly want to tell you how much I appreciate your efforts on Panama—it wasn't easy." Thanks, praise, and exhortation are sometimes combined. In the midst of the debate on the budget resolution a leader told the whips:

> Yesterday afternoon whipping on this, I'm happy to say we finally started acting like a party. People were supporting programs they might not really like very much because they knew they were important to other members and necessary to hold the coalition together. Some people came up and asked me if I'd support an amendment increasing funding for a program of which I'm prime sponsor. Even though I'd otherwise be favorable, I told them I couldn't because if I did, how could I tell others not to support amendments? We were finally acting like a national party, not like a bunch of warring regional tribes.

The weekly whip meetings aid in building solidarity. The atmosphere is one of camaraderie; there is a good deal of laughter and joking. The in-group feeling nurtures an "us against them" attitude toward the Republicans. A member's report that the Republicans were "split all to hell" on budget strategy was greeted with vigorous applause.

For the members who serve as whips, attending the meetings is the primary payoff. The opportunity to express their view to the leadership directly and regularly is highly valued. So, too, is the information they receive. According to one whip, "The Thursday morning meetings are probably the best damn meetings I go to all week. Information is the payoff. That's my payment for being whip."

Taking a Whip Count

A central function of the whip system is conducting whip polls to determine the voting intentions of Democrats on major legislation. The initial count provides the information necessary for an effectively targeted persuasion effort. "A whip count is never really completed," a participant explained. "It's a rolling process of turning names over, of counting and persuading. A process, not an event."

The whip system conducts a whip poll only on instruction from the Speaker, who is usually responding to a request from the committee chairman. "It's [the chairman's] feel whether he thinks that he can get the bill through on his own or he needs help from the leadership," a senior aide explained. If he does not receive a request for a poll on a high-priority bill, the Speaker may order a count and give the floor manager the results. A Speaker-initiated poll is rare, however, because chairmen almost always ask for polls on major legislation.

More frequently a poll is requested which the leadership considers unnecessary. A participant cautioned:

> You have to be very careful of that. It's hard to tell a chairman no. In fact, you never do. But it's true that you have a nervous Nellie who is afraid, so he wants a whip count, but you have to worry that you don't overdo the whip sys-

tem. Because if you're asking a new question every day, you're going to wear out the system and the credibility, and the members are going to get irritated. So what will happen is we'll do the whip count but without much enthusiasm. To do it unenthusiastically would be just for the whip staff member to call the whip contact and just say, "We're doing a poll and let us know how your members feel." And then you don't follow up.

Once the decision to conduct a poll has been made, the question or questions to be asked must be determined. Because the floor manager is assumed to be more familar with the bill than anyone else, he plays a lead role in question writing. "You can't expect to be able to count every conceivable problem that can arise. You have to rely pretty much on the judgment of the committee as to what they think their principal problem is, whether it's an amendment or the passage of a bill or adoption of the rule, or whatever," a participant explained. So identifying the key problems and writing the questions has become a critical part of the process. The number of questions must be kept small to avoid overtaxing either the whips doing the polling or the members being polled. Yet, because of the high level of amending activity on the House floor, a number of crucial votes can often be anticipated. Consequently, choosing the votes to ask about and phrasing questions broadly enough to yield information on voting response in a variety of circumstances—but not so broadly that the responses are meaningless—has become increasingly important.

When the decision on what to ask has been made, a senior aide in the majority whip's office will write the actual question. "Normally, they say what they want us to count and I write the question," he offered, "and I think it's very important not to load the question. Sometimes people want us to ask a loaded question like, Will you vote against the nasty, rotten X bill or X amendment? That doesn't do you any good." The majority whip's office transmits the written questions to the regional whips, who are charged with polling the members in their zones. A hand-carried memorandum conveys necessary information and instructions to each of the zone whips: "The House in the near future or the House on such and such a day will consider HR whatever it is. The bill does this. Please ask members in your zone the following question: Will you vote for HR xyz? We need responses by such and such a time. A whip advisory on the bill is attached." The whips are then supposed to talk with each member in their zone, using information provided in the memorandum to explain the bill if necessary, and report their results to the whip's office.

Often, however, the task of conducting the poll is delegated to staff. "A lot of this is staff to staff, I know that, it's not supposed to be, but it is," an aide of the chief whip said. "And there's very little we can do about it at the zone whip level." The use of staff to conduct whip polls has long been a problem for the leadership, which occasionally asks the whips to conduct a poll personally. Usually, however, the leadership relies on the appointed whips to refine the count. The result of the initial poll is a division of Democrats into support categories: right, leaning right, undecided, leaning wrong, wrong, absent, and not contacted. Democrats not listed as voting "right" as well as any whose reported support for the leadership position "looks strange" will be apportioned among the appointed whips. Their job at this stage is both to obtain an accurate reading of their assignees' voting intentions and to persuade.

Because a number of subsequent strategy decisions depend on these results, the accuracy of the whip poll is critical. Participants interviewed seemed quite satisfied with the accuracy of the polls. Indeed, one junior whip noted, "We can turn it around boom, boom, boom, this fast and give you a decent count and be within a few votes." The whip counts on the key roll calls in 1981 reportedly were accurate to within one vote. The accuracy of the counts is dependent on the in-House nature of the whip operation. Members are more apt to tell colleagues of their intentions than they are interest group representatives. "There are a lot of ways a member can give the impression he might go with a group without actually commiting himself," one leader stated. "He can say, 'You have a good point, I hadn't thought about that,' or 'I'll try to help you.' He may not want to say, 'Hell no, I won't vote with you.' After all, the bill may never get to the floor. But they will tell their colleagues."

Working the Door

In addition to overseeing the counting procedure, the majority whip is responsible for informing members of the party position as they enter the chamber to vote on roll calls of importance to the party. He stands at the door facing the Library of Congress, through which most Democrats enter, while deputy or at-large whips may be assigned to other doors. When does the whip "work the door"? A senior aide explained, "You go on 'feel'. You know which are the important amendments. Sometimes the floor manager will ask him to."

As members stream into the chamber, the whip signals thumbs up or thumbs down, loudly says, "Aye vote" or "Nay vote," and adds a brief phrase that telegraphs something about the issue. A leader explained, "When you are working the door on an unexpected amendment, you have to compress into a quick slogan why members should vote against it. 'The committee or the leadership wants a "no" vote' is enough for some members. You get to know who those are. With others you need more." Because numerous unanticipated amendments are frequently offered, because members are seldom inclined simply to follow the leadership, and because of the time constraint, effectively working the door is an art of considerable importance. An appointed whip who frequently performs the job described the skill it demands: "You get to have a pretty good feel of how you can talk to somebody. Each person's personality is a little different. You can throw a little bit of a joke into one and a snide comment into another one. You're only going to get four or five words. Your have to do it just right, in order to reach someone." The whip used as an example a conservative Republican's amendment to delete from an appropriations bill all funds for the United States Metric Conversion Board. "I work the door that Brademas usually works," he said. "And guys came in and I found that with those who enjoy a little sense of humor, I'd say 'It's just a communist plot, vote "no." ' And you know, it worked fine. They enjoyed it and they kept voting 'no.' It just worked fine."

Disseminating Information

The majority whip's office has become an information-disseminating center (see Dodd 1979). A whip packet containing the projected floor schedule for the week and, when they are available, copies of scheduled bills and committee reports is sent to all Democratic members over the weekend. In 1973 the newly appointed whip John McFall initiated the whip advisory, a one-page summary of the content and legislative history of and amendments expected to be offered to a bill scheduled for floor action. An advisory is prepared and is sent to all Democratic members prior to floor consideration of every scheduled bill, resolution, and conference report.

Over time, a routine procedure for preparing advisories has developed in which the committee of origin sends a draft to the majority whip's office, where staff review it for clarity, accuracy, and length. The whip's staff determine whether all the important and controversial matters are covered and consult with the committee staff about any changes. As a staffer said, "You must have the advisory in a form agreed to by the committee. You can't have the committee chairman disown it on the floor. The committee has got to be 'on board.' " Yet the whip's staff strongly believe that the "accuracy of the advisories must be impeccable, . . . otherwise the leadership loses credence." Consequently, the whip staff must sometimes persuade the committee staff to take out "propaganda" and to include unpalatable details such as cost estimates.

In 1980 the advisories were supplemented by whip-grams, which are prepared for those bills on which the leadership expects to encounter trouble. A staffer gave this explanation for the institution of the whip-gram: "There's a major information problem around here that the whip's office is trying to handle. It is tough to pass information around here because staffs get in the way and members are so busy. Partly it's illegitimate. Some claim they just don't get the party position. If so, they must live in a hermetically sealed world. The whip-gram is a partial response." Whip-grams are shorter and more partisan than advisories and, according to one staffer, "They give debate points that the members can use to defend themselves back home. This is crucial." In addition, they clearly state the leadership's position. A September 1980 whip-gram on a bill to increase the United States' contribution to the International Monetary Fund concluded, "The Leadership urges Democratic Members to support the bill, and to resist efforts by the Republican right-wing to encumber this program with silly and destructive amendments."

The whip's office periodically prepares and disseminates other information that it believes will be of use to the membership. For example, analyses of complicated and controversial issues are frequently prepared: "Each gives the answer to a politically difficult question—a Democratic answer. [The issue papers] are some attempt to counter the splintering in Democrats' positions—a modest attempt to keep people together on the issues." Before recesses and adjournments the whip's office sends every Democrat a package of materials to use when speaking in his district. These "recess packets" include a legislative checklist of the achievements of the Congress, various whip issue papers that discuss selected issues and accomplishments in more detail, and speech cards that summarize the major points of the issue papers.

In 1981 the majority whip's office began to put together a weekly leadership information pack consisting of selected clippings from newspapers and magazines as well as highlights from the Speaker's press conference. The clippings were chosen with an eye toward bolstering sagging Democratic morale and providing debate points favorable to the leadership's position. Articles concerning the doubts of leading businessmen over the administration's economic program and a poll that registered a decline in Reagan's popularity, for example, were given prominent play. As a whip staffer indicated, it was the political situation that dictated the substitution of the leadership information pack for the recess packet: "We'd had the recess packets, which listed the bills passed and the accomplishments of the Democratic Congress. That hasn't been possible this year because there have been so few bills—everything has been budget—and because the bills that have passed could hardly be considered accomplishments by Democrats. Also the disagreements about strategy [among Democrats] have made writing anything difficult."

Staffers in the whip's office contend that the expansion of these information services was a response to the growing independence of the House membership in the 1970s. Members, no longer willing to follow blindly the lead of the committee majority and the party leadership, insisted on knowing the details of issues they were voting on. Another factor was the success of the Democratic Study Group's information system. By the early 1970s that group's information dissemination activities had become sufficiently extensive and useful to members that many joined the group solely to avail themselves of its information services. Although the leadership and the Democratic Study Group tend to agree on legislation, the monopoly the

DSG was developing in terms of providing digestible information to members was a potential threat to the leadership, which responded by increasing its own activites in that area.

The present information dissemination services of the whip's office are vital for successful leadership. Of course the leadership hopes that members will be grateful for the services provided, but at least as important is increased leadership control over information. The credibility of the whip advisories depends on a relatively evenhanded, objective presentation of the material. Nevertheless, the advisories, as well as the other material sent out by the whip's office, are prepared under the aegis of the leadership and certainly do not slight material favorable to its position.

The Steering and Policy Committee

House Democrats created a Steering Committee in 1933. Although it continued in existence until 1956, it never played a significant role in setting party policy. Sam Rayburn was Speaker during much of this period, and his leadership style was highly personalized. The committee's last chairman explained its lack of function: "Mr. Sam decided what will be done" (Ripley 1967, p. 47). In 1962, at the behest of liberals, the committee was reestablished, but again it was simply a paper entity, seldom meeting and having no legislative or political impact (Ripley 1967, p. 47). The reform wave of the 1970s led to a revitalization of the committee. In 1973 the old committee was replaced with a new Steering and Policy Committee, which in late 1974 was made the committee on committees, assuring it a role of real significance. The committee also provides a forum for political and legislative discussion and sometimes endorses legislation prior to House floor action.

From the 93d through the 96th Congress the committee consisted of twenty-four members. The Speaker (who serves as chairman), the majority leader (vice-chairman), the caucus chairman (second vice-chairman), and the majority whip are ex officio members. Twelve members are elected from geographical zones and the Speaker appoints the remaining eight members. Appointed and elected members may serve no more than two consecutive full terms. Late in 1980 the secretary of the caucus and the chairmen of the four most important committees (Appropriations, Budget, Rules, and Ways and Means) joined the committee as ex officio members. The chairman of the campaign committee and the chief deputy whip were included as nonvoting members. Bill Alexander, the new chief deputy whip, had previously served four years on the committee as a Speaker's appointee and thus according to the rules could not be reappointed as a full member.

Committee on Committees

In the aftermath of the revolt against Cannon, the Democrats on the Ways and Means Committee took over the task of assigning Democrats to committees. Although he was able to influence the committee, the Speaker was not a member and took no formal part in its deliberations. In 1973 the Speaker, the majority leader, and the caucus chairman were placed on the committee on committees, and the following year the committee on committees' function was shifted to the Steering and Policy Committee.

Since the Speaker now chairs the committee on committees and appoints a number of its members, leadership influence over committee assignments has been enhanced considerably. The leaders can use their influence to do favors by helping members get coveted assignments, but more important is the leadership's potential for shaping committees so they will be friendly to its views.

Although the leaders can exert considerable influence on the committee's decisions, they cannot dictate. Voting is by secret ballot. The elected members are charged with protecting the interests of the Democrats in their zones, and many of the other members feel a similar responsibility . A deputy whip said: "Now [on committee assignments] you become a little more parochial because your state delegation has a right to have a fair representation on the committees. Nobody quarrels with that. . . . It's part of the game."

Throughout the period between the election and the time committee assignments are made (usually in mid-January), freshmen and those continuing members who wish to change assignments make their preferences known to members of the Steering and Policy Committee. All such Democrats must communicate with their zone representative; many also visit or write the leaders. The leadership offices maintain lists of requests which are periodically updated; their early access to this information aids them in gauging the strategic situation they will face at assignment time.

When the Steering and Policy Committee meets for this purpose, members sit around large tables set up in a U-shape and the party leadership sits at the curved end. The most sought-after committees are taken up first because once assignments to them are made, slots on other committees open up. In 1979, for example, Ways and Means, Appropriations, and Budget were filled the first day, and positions on the Commerce Committee were assigned at the beginning of the second. When nominations are opened, the regional representatives make their nominations first, followed by the other members. The representatives usually say a few words about their nominees, whose names are written on a blackboard.

A complex voting system by which only one nominee is selected on a given ballot was instituted in 1979. On each ballot, members must vote for the number of nominees which matches the number of slots still to be filled. To win, a nominee must receive both a majority and more votes than any other nominee. If on a given ballot two nominees receive a majority and are tied, the next ballot serves as a runoff between the two. Thus the number of ballots required to fill all the vacancies on a committee is equal to or greater than the number of vacancies. In 1979, for example, ten ballots were required to fill five Ways and Means vacancies. Although the procedure is cumbersome, it allows the selectors "to get a look at the ideological and geographical make-up of the committee" at each stage. It was this feature that led to its adoption.

The leadership pursues a number of not always complementary goals in the committee assignment process. In keeping with tradition and its own service orientation, the leadership attempts to accommodate members by giving them assignments they have requested (see Gertzog 1976; Shepsle 1978). The leaders place a great deal of importance on putting together a slate the membership at large considers fair. For one thing, a slate perceived by any sizeable segment of the party to be seriously biased would exacerbate intraparty conflicts; for another, the slate must be approved by the caucus. Each of the leaders also tries to obtain good assignments for the members from his own state, believing this to be his responsibility. Each leader's success in obtaining good assignments for his state colleagues fortifies his reputation because there is an expectation within the Washington community that he will do so and because appearing powerful is an important component of influence. The leaders also attempt to shape committees, especially those most important to the leadership, through the assignment process. "We tried to put reasonable people on the [important] committees," a leader explained. "Some members who wanted new assignments didn't get what they wanted. Members who never go with the leadership—never help out. It's not only [the other leaders] and I who did this. The other Steering and Policy members—the elected ones—feel the same way."

Freshmen congressmen, members and observers agree, are much better treated than they once were. O'Neill tells of an incident that occurred when he was a freshman in the 83d Congress. One of his classmates, John Moss of Sacramento, received only one assignment, and it was to the District of Columbia Committee. Moss no doubt was horrified when the Sacramento papers headlined the story "Moss Elected to D.C. City Council." The other freshmen, O'Neill says, did not fare much better. Changes in the House have led to the current favorable situation for freshmen. "Because the subcommittees are so important and the general change in the locus of power in the House, Steering and Policy is both more careful of and more accommodating to freshmen," a participant explained. "The guy may be a subcommittee chairman in two or four years."

Committee assignment decisions are collectively made and reflect a number of diverse factors, such as trading of support, the nominee's (and the nominator's) popularity, geographical representation, and party loyalty.

One committee member averred, "Jockeying around between members of the Steering and Policy Committee for their respective candidates becomes the most important factor."

The nominating speeches as well as the letters that members requesting assignments send to the leadership indicate which arguments members believe most effective. According to one participant, the most frequently mentioned argument in the nominating speeches is that the member needs the position because of his political situation. One freshman who replaced a Republican asked to be assigned to the committee his predecessor had been on—a committee that was of direct interest to the district. This freshman had informed every member of Steering and Policy of the political importance of the assignment to him, and that factor was mentioned again in the nominating speech as a reminder. The second most frequent argument noted by this participant was that the member's zone had not fared well. A member will indicate, "You owe me one." If the requestor is a senior member that will be brought up, and any special expertise the nominee has will as a matter of course be mentioned. A Steering and Policy Committee member summarized the arguments that are made on behalf of a nominee:

> Background, training, district. Those are the common arguments we all make. Here's an example. I'm trying to get _____, the newest member of my delegation, on the Energy Committee. Now, in doing that, I tell them that he was chairman of the Energy Committee in the state legislature, that's his specialty, that's his background, his law practice dealt with that, he'd fit right in, we don't have anyone from [his state] on that committee. Those are arguments I make. Then I go around trying to make as many commitments and to try to convince people that it's in their interest and our interest to put him there. It boils down to how many votes you get. A lot of times it's trade-offs. I'll help you get this person if you help me with this one. I mean it's all done within the confines of the fact that these people should all be qualified. But there is, quite frankly, a lot of politicking going on.

For positions on the Appropriations, Ways and Means, and Budget Committees, similar arguments are made but party loyalty is more strongly emphasized. Of the process in 1979 one participant said, "Generally, loyalty to the leadership and to the principles of the Democratic party was stressed much more than in the past—certainly more than four years ago. Members seem to have realized that this would be the case. The letters sent to the leadership asking for support for committee positions tended to stress loyalty explicitly." During the 1979 deliberations several leaders brought in indexes of party loyalty, and at the request of members these were written on the blackboard next to the nominees' names. Loyalty scores entered into the voting again in 1981. The participants agreed that party loyalty is considered in the making of assignments, especially to the key committees. "While the leadership was reluctant to put together a slate for the important committees out of fear that they would end up making angry more than they satisfy, there was, I think, more consideration of party loyalty than had been the case, at least in the previous Congress," one participant reported. Another indicated that loyalty can be a tie-breaking factor: "The skillfulness of the zone representative is very important. Whether the applicant's region is properly represented on the committee, the applicant's popularity, his reputation, is very important. Within that, in the last year or two, there's been a lot more attention to the applicant's faithfulness to party positions. Whenever there's a tough contest, people will bring up the level of party support." Some members nevertheless believe that not enough emphasis is placed on party loyalty. "Loyalty is considered, but not enough," one member said. "Some people who take chances to stick with the leadership aren't getting rewarded." Another complained that the impact of specific assignments on the reliability of the committee as a whole was not sufficiently considered: "I think it's very important that you look at the structure of the committee. . . . We really ought to have a committee that represents all segments of thinking *and*, if you're running the House, you ought to have a committee that in a pinch is going to end up on your side of the ledger. That isn't done at all."

Because the leaders themselves pursue multiple goals and because they do not control the assignment process, the loyalty criterion does not dominate all others. When other considerations dictate the choice for an important assignment of someone who has demonstrated low party loyalty, however, promises of support are sometimes extracted from the nominee. In 1979 one such member received the assignment he had requested only after he promised the Steering and Policy Committee that he would support the leadership when he was needed and that he certainly would not be a party to bottling up legislation in committee. After the Gramm debacle, however, the leadership is likely to place less reliance on such promises. In 1981, despite strong opposition from a number of Steering and Policy Committee members, Phil Gramm, a very conservative Texan, was placed on the Budget Committee. Gramm had promised to support the Budget Committee's position on the House floor, and Jim Wright had strongly supported him for the slot. It was a "victory" Wright was to regret bitterly. Not only did Gramm vote against the committee majority on the floor, he also cosponsored the Republican substitutes to the budget resolution and the reconciliation bill (see chapter 6).

Data on committee requests and assignments in the 96th Congress provide a basis for judging how well the leadership's aims were met. Accommodating member requests is one goal that is largely achieved. Of the forty-two freshmen, thirty-seven (88 percent) received at least one of their requested committees; twenty-nine (69 percent) received a requested exclusive or major committee assignment, and of these twenty-five (59.5 percent) received their first or only choice. Returning members who requested either a change in or an additional committee assignment fared less well. Of the forty-two incumbent members who made such requests, fifteen (35.7 percent) were accommodated. The committees requested account for the lower success rate: thirty-seven requests were for Budget, Appropriations, or Ways and Means assignments. Of the twenty freshmen requests for these three committees, seven (35 percent) were granted. In order to accommodate nominees, sometimes the size of a committee is increased—something only the majority party can do. In 1979 three members told the Speaker that an assignment to Public Works was crucial to their political survival and he agreed to create the necessary new slots.

The data indicate that party loyalty is given considerable weight in making assignments to the Budget, Appropriations, and Ways and Means committees. Nineteen incumbent members requested the Budget Committee; the mean party unity score of those assigned was 81.8 percent; of those passed over, 72.8 percent. (Ninety-fifth Congress *Congressional Quarterly* party unity scores, adjusted to disregard absences, are used.) The four Steering and Policy Committee choices of incumbent members for the Appropriations Committee had a mean party unity score of 65.9 percent, while the mean score of the five requestors not assigned was 54.4 percent. Ways and Means assignments were the exception in the 96th Congress. The three incumbents selected by the Steering and Policy Committee as a group scored slightly lower than six not selected (65 percent versus 68.9 percent). A conflict among leadership goals accounts for this deviation from the pattern. Two of the nominees had high party support scores (84 percent mean); the third, Sam Hall of Texas, a very low score (26.8 percent). Despite opposition from some in the inner leadership circle the majority leader believed he had to support his state colleague, and he prevailed in the Steering and Policy Committee. In the Democratic Caucus, however, Hall was defeated by a much more supportive southerner.

Because the 1980 elections resulted in a more conservative Democratic House membership, party maintenance required greater accommodation of conservatives in the committee assignment process. The forty-seven-member Conservative Democratic Forum, a group of mostly southern House Democrats, was formed in part to press for better assignments for conservatives. These members knew that their bargaining position had improved significantly with the decrease in the size of the Democratic party. The leadership did respond to the conservatives' pressure, but to a large extent it did so in a way that preserved mainstream Democratic control over the most important committees. Three new conservatives were placed on the Budget Committee, for example, but two of them supported the Democratic position within the committee, and, in 1981, the Democratic budget resolution was voted out by a comfortable seventeen to thirteen vote.

Accommodating members in the committee assignment process is important for keeping "peace in the family." Assuring that the members assigned to the critical committees are, at least as a group, reasonably reliable is important to coalition-building success. By and large the leadership has managed to accomplish both objectives, but balancing the two can be a tricky enterprise and a transitory accomplishment.

Other Steering and Policy
Committee Functions

After the committee assignment process has been completed, the Steering and Policy Committee meets at irregular intervals, averaging twice each month, depending upon need. Some meetings are devoted to guest speakers —administration officials, interest group representatives, and independent experts. During the first three months of the 96th Congress, for example, the administration sent Health, Education, and Welfare Secretary Joseph Califano to speak on national health insurance; Bob Strauss, the special trade representative, on the trade agreement; and economic advisors Alfred Kahn and Charles Schultz, on inflation. Although attendance at these meetings is sometimes low, members find them useful: "The Speaker's been very good at this. He'll get George Meany and so on from the AFL-CIO to let us know how they stand on things generally. Within the last two or three weeks, we had the Business Roundtable—the top industrial business people in America. . . . To me it's a treasured opportunity to have these people at a meeting on an informal basis where you can ask questions without fear of exposing your ignorance."

The use of Steering and Policy as a forum for speakers began during Carl Albert's tenure as Speaker. The functions of the committee have been considerably extended by Speaker O'Neill. Today Steering and Policy serves as a forum for wide-ranging discussion and as a "consultative body." "Anything is fair game for discussion in Steering and Policy," a member commented. "I would say Tip O'Neill has used the Steering and Policy group very broadly to advise him on a lot of things, to backstop a great many things that he thought ought to be done. And as a forum for expressing both direction and frustration about this place." Steering and Policy is often briefed on important legislation by committee chairmen. This serves a number of useful functions as one member made clear:

> I think the greater effect of Steering and Policy is the fourm which it provides. On policy matters, I think the greatest value is the meeting, the discussion itself. This will enable the committee chairman to get a pretty good idea of the kind of opposition and response and support that he's going to get on the floor. Don't forget they're from all over the country—they're sort of a microcosm. They get a lot of questions raised. They get questions raised sometimes, I know, for which they haven't got a ready answer. Well, that's fine, that gives them an opportunity to prepare the answer. To that extent, it's a good practice run, dry run for them. . . . Of course, there can be an endorsement, but I think probably the greatest thing is the educational opportunity. The committee

chairman gets educated in what the House is going to feel like, and, maybe more importantly, a representative section of the House gets a pretty informal, direct, almost one-on-one explanation of the legislation.

Most frequently the committee discusses legislation shortly before it is scheduled for floor consideration but sometimes discussion begins at a much earlier stage. An exchange of views, a member commented, "helps the leadership to realize what the thinking of the members is. And also it causes some members to start talking it over with their own associates and colleagues. It's part of the eductional process, I think, and part of the formulative process sometimes." The Steering and Policy Committee, then, in the words of a close observer, is "one more tool by which the leadership gets the word out and the word back. It's another communication tool." As a center of information exchange it is useful both to the leadership and to the members who serve on it.

A new function of the committee under O'Neill is that of endorsing legislation. During the 95th Congress the Steering and Policy Committee endorsed seventeen bills and resolutions, including common situs picketing legislation, budget resolutions, strip mining, ethics legislation, the Hatch act revision, and the Humphrey-Hawkins bill. There were fewer endorsements during the 96th Congress in large part because of the change in the political atmosphere. The budget-balancing mood precluded action on new social programs; budgetary matters increasingly dominated the domestic policy agenda. The committee took positions on various budget resolutions and endorsed the welfare reform bill and the synthetic fuels bill. The decrease in endorsements may also have been due to the belief of members that only measures central to the party program should be endorsed and that endorsements may have been made too freely in the past. One member said, "We do not cheapen the Steering and Policy endorsements by putting it on everything. In fact, we don't use it unless we're trying to demonstrate that we really mean it. . . . The only policy there is, is that you don't do it unless it's important. And I'd say also probably you don't do it unless there's at least some concern about getting it through."

The Speaker has never been refused an endorsement he requested of the committee. Voting is usually by voice, and members who disagree with the leadership's position keep quiet. ("They just slink off into darkness," a member reported.) As a result endorsements can be reported as unanimous. That an endorsement does not necessarily signify a true intraparty consensus seems to lessen their impact; nevertheless, members believe they have an effect (see chapter 5).

By expanding the functions of the Steering and Policy Committee, O'Neill has made membership in it, and consequently his appointive powers, more valuable. Committee members meet with the leadership frequently; they discuss, and to some extent participate in the formulation of, legislative strategy. Members thus drawn into the leadership circle, O'Neill believes, develop some understanding of the leadership's problems and, frequently, a stake in the leadership's success. This is one element of O'Neill's strategy of inclusion.

Despite the increased role of the committee, some members as well as people close to the Speaker favor an even greater role. One member commented, "It ought to be taking more of a policy role—deciding what we will consider in the House and the direction we as a party will take." Another participant envisioned the role Steering and Policy could play in this way: "It should anticipate problems which will divide the party and come up with creative compromises. It should anticipate the brunt of Republican attacks and come up with a counter strategy. It should develop creative answers to national problems. Essentially, it should act as a domestic council to the Speaker."

The inclusion as ex officio members of the chairmen of the four key committee increases the possibility that the Steering and Policy Committee can play such a role. O'Neill's appointment of three conservatives after the 1980 election was in part a response to the conservatives' demands, but may also have signaled the Speaker's intention to move toward using Steering and Policy as a forum for working out intraparty compromises. Certainly the committee can function as a true policy committee only if it is reasonably representative of the party—which, when it is smaller, has a more significant conservative segment. At an early 1981 Steering and Policy Committee meeting, O'Neill told the members that he wanted things thrashed out in the committee, that he wanted to hear what the problems were, that he did not want conservatives to keep quiet during meetings and then vote against the party on the floor.

The extraordinary political atmosphere of the first year of the Reagan presidency, however, worked against a further development of the role of the Steering and Policy Committee. Regarding the inclusion of the chairmen of the four key committees, a leadership aide said: "I think the effects have not fully expressed themselves. It's certainly more useful when you have an economics discussion to be sure that present will be the chairman of the Ways and Means Committee, chairman of the Budget Committee, chairman of the Appropriations Committee, chairman of the Rules Committee. On the other hand, the Steering Committee itself has been a victim of the acrimony. Particularly as some of the members of the Steering and Policy Committee have defected on major issues. It's hard to know how it's going." One leader expressed his frustration with the conservatives' behavior:

The reasons [for the expansion of the committee] were to make it a more broadly representative group, to acknowledge the fact that chairmen of those four committees are indeed members of the House leadership and then to give a little broader representation in general. The conservatives had been complaining that they didn't have enough members on Steering and Policy. The Speaker said, "We'll appoint two or three more of you to that committee." We did.

The irony of it is that we did this in an attempt to accommodate the conservative wing and to bring it into the family, and the next thing we discover was that they're deserting the family as soon as the family is under seige from the landlord. They go and join the landlord.

Given the depth of the split in the Democratic party and the inability of the committee to resolve or even camouflage it, the role of the Steering and Policy Committee actually decreased during 1981. It continued, of course, to fill committee assignments and to meet with a variety of invited guests. It also discussed legislation, but it did not play a role of importance in the three big legislative battles of the year. Thus the concentration of legislative attention on bills that irreconcilably split the party militated against the Steering and Policy Committee assuming a greater policy role in 1981. Under these circumstances the committee's heterogeneous membership, which is necessary for party maintenance, made it incapable of playing a significant role in the coalition-building process.

Steering and Policy Committee Staff

The staff of the Steering and Policy Committee in effect works for the Speaker. That staff has grown slowly but steadily since the mid-1970s, and by mid-1981 it consisted of eight professionals and two secretaries. Information gathering is one of the major functions of this group of people. As one staffer said, "Speaker McCormack used to say that the only surprises he wanted were on his birthday. That's our job: to make sure the leadership is not surprised."

The Steering and Policy staff have divided the legislative committees among them, so that each staffer has responsibility for monitoring a number of committees. This division of labor is not always strictly followed but is adjusted depending on the activity level of the various committees. Important bills are closely tracked and potential problems are brought to the leaders' attention. "You hoist the red flags," a staffer said. Thus, among their other functions, the staff serve as an early-warning system concerning legislation in committee. The staff also prepare periodic reports on the status of various bills and provide check lists of legislation that must be passed—authorizations that are expiring, for example. "Just for the leadership we have got to keep a complete list of all bills in every one of our committees and where they are," a staff explained. "A background, how the bill originated, what the bill does, and what the issues are." In addition, the staff sometimes prepare reports on how Democratic members voted on legislation of special interest to the Speaker. Voting behavior on budget resolutions, for example, is carefully scrutinized.

The Steering and Policy staff, then, serve as additional eyes and ears for the leadership. The increased activity at the subcommittee level has made this more formal information-gathering effort necessary. These aides are not, however, simply information conduits. At the instruction of the Speaker, they get involved in working out problems, not just reporting them. A staffer described his job this way:

> A Speaker, if he really wants to run the House—and Tip O'Neill really wants to—he'll hire people like me and put them in a political position. A lot of our work, 90 percent of it, involves politics. We do our politicking on the floor, in the committee, in the office, and we're essentially the Speaker's men when we do this. People are well aware of that and we make them well aware of that so that they know what I'm saying comes from the Speaker's office, and this is his thinking. And it makes for a smoother transition with legislation and we get a lot of the political problems ironed out before you even go to the floor, and it's a good system.

The Rules Committee

■■■■■■■■■■■■■■■■ In the past century the relationship between the party leadership and the Rules Committee has come almost full circle. Speakers in the latter part of the nineteeth century developed the Rules Committee into a powerful instrument for controlling the flow of legislation to the floor. During that period the committee, then chaired by the Speaker, began to make use of special orders or rules that permitted legislation to be taken up out of order and governed the amount of debate and, sometimes, the number of the amendments allowed. These rules soon became the primary route by which major legislation reached the floor.

Joseph Cannon used the power of the Rules Committee to thwart the legislative aims of progressives. When insurgent Republicans and Democrats combined to strip the Speaker of what they believed to be arbitrary powers, they removed him from the Rules Committee. Without the Speaker as a member, the committee became a potential base of influence independent of the party leadership. From the late 1930s until 1961 the committee was dominated by a bipartisan conservative majority and was often at odds with the Democratic leadership, sometimes blocking legislation desired by the leadership and a majority of Democrats and frequently extracting substantive concessions as the price for granting a rule. The Speaker was forced to bargain with the committee, but his resources for doing so were limited. Thus the leadership's control over floor scheduling, perhaps its most potent tool, was incomplete during this period.

When John Kennedy was elected president in 1960 Speaker Rayburn decided the Rules Committee had to be reined in, for if it was not the Kennedy program would be doomed from the beginning. Of the suggestions he considered, Rayburn chose the one he believed would do the least violence to House norms. His proposal to enlarge the committee by three members won on the floor after a bitter fight, by a vote of 217 to 212. Even though Rayburn in effect chose the new Democratic members of Rules, the leadership majority was often shaky. Howard Smith remained chairman through 1966, and, given the powers of that position, conservatives where still able to make trouble for the party leadership. After Smith was defeated in the 1966 primary the equally conservative William Colmer became chairman. Colmer, however, was forced to accept written rules for the committee which limited his power. As Democratic positions on the committee opened up, Speakers used their informal influence over these appointments to make the committee more reliable. By the early 1970s the Rules Committee was no longer an independent obstructionist force; it generally gave the leadership what it wanted (Oppenheimer 1981).

At the beginning of the 94th Congress the Democratic Caucus passed a major rules change that solidified the Speaker's control over the committee. The Speaker was empowered to name all Democratic Rules Committee members, his appointments subject only to ratification by the caucus. Furthermore, the Speaker's nominating powers apply to incumbent as well as new members—he can remove Democratic members from the committee. Although the Speaker has not, and in the foreseeable future probably will not, strike anyone from the committee, he has both guarded and used with great care his prerogative of naming new members. When Andy Young of Georgia left the committee at the beginning of the 95th Congress, O'Neill named Shirley Chisholm of New York to replace him, even though southerners laid claim to the position on the basis of region. At the beginning of the 96th Congress O'Neill stated publicly that he considered state delegation endorsements of potential Rules nominees illegitimate and would consider such endorsements a strike against the member so endorsed (Speaker's press conference, 18 January 1979). Thus O'Neill not only is making sure that the members appointed are people on whom he can depend, but is also guarding against the development of norms constricting the Speaker's discretion.

The "Traffic Cop" Function

The Speaker's control over committee membership, combined with other changes that took place in the House in the 1970s, produced a Rules Committee that is, in the words of O'Neill, "A strong right arm to the leadership" (Malbin 1977, p. 942). When the Rules Committee denies a rule request, it does so with the full acquiescence of the leadership. Speaking of one of the rare instances in which leadership demands were not met by the committee, one participant said, "What makes it so notable is the fact that it is so incredibly unusual. Normally the Rules Committee is an almost unerring predictor of the leadership's preferences." A cooperative Rules Committee is essential if the leadership is to make full use of its scheduling powers. Throughout the 1970s the committee has been cooperative, but the nature of the relationship between leadership and committee has depended on the committee chairman. One described the evolution of the relationship:

I think that the committee has gone through two distinct transformations. Up through Judge Smith, of course, you have the classic "graveyard of legislation" where the thing was utterly beyond the reach of the leadership, and was really the tool by which the old conservative-Republican coalition governed the House at odds with the leadership. And in Colmer's last period and then under Madden and Delaney [the relationship changed]. Madden and Delaney were both fairly supportive of the leadership and, to put it bluntly, I think came to the chairmanship too old to really become independent forces if they'd chosen to. And I think that there's a transition that's going on now. I don't think that Bolling was inclined from day one to just reshape the Rules Committee to his own ideas, but there has been very subtly a transformation going on where the Rules Committee is more steadfastly reliable in terms of the leadership, but in a more consultative way.

Under all recent chairmen, contact between the leadership and the committee at the staff level has been frequent. During the 95th Congress, when James Delaney was chairman, the head Rules staffer would bring the letters requesting rules to the majority leader's office, where he and a majority leader's senior aide would make up the Rules Committee agenda. Although this no longer takes place, the chief Rules staffer described the frequency of his contact with the majority leader's staff in charge of scheduling as "hourly. We've even got a hot line." His interaction with the Speaker's staff is also extensive. Staff members discuss specific scheduling questions and share information gleaned from each one's own sources of information and own area of political expertise. Armed with the information gained from these sessions, staffers can often alert their bosses to potential problem areas at an early stage.

The relationship between 'Tip' O'Neill and Richard Bolling, chairman during the 96th and 97th congresses, is a close one. They served on the Rules Committee together for many years. Bolling firmly believes in strong party leadership and was the leader of the proleadership forces on the committee for years before he became chairman. He is clearly part of the leadership team, as one participant observed:

> The Speaker and [Bolling] work very well together. [They] understand each other. The initiation of the consultation may come from either side. It's an interaction based on a good basic relationship. It runs the gamut from someone in the Speaker's office calling [the chief Rules staffer] to say "We want such and such" (usually they'll get "such and such") to [Bolling] calling "Tip" and raising a whole series of concerns, saying, "These are things we have to anticipate." It's very much an interaction. . . . [Consultation is] about the granting of rules, about the type of rules, and also about the negative aspect—the delay of rules.

Because all House members and especially those in leadership positions are extremely busy, consultation is often highly informal. A staffer illustrated the informality with the following story: "I know of one case where a change in the Rules Committee agenda was announced to the world because the technician neglected to turn off the Speaker's microphone when Bolling was taking over the chair as chairman of the Committee of the Whole. It was on a Thursday and O'Neill was handing over the gavel and said, 'Oh, yeah, for Tuesday we need such and such.' And Bolling said, 'Yea, we'll put it on.' "

Bolling's relationship with the leadership has made it possible for some things to be handled in a more systematic and less informal fashion. Toward the end of a Congress, the bills reported from committee always exceed the available floor time, and priorities must be established. In 1980, after the 4 July recess, senior staffers from Rules and from the leadership made up a list of legislation for which Rules had requests and legislation still in the pipeline. The Speaker, the majority leader, the majority whip, the chairman of the caucus, and the chairman of Rules met to review the list and to decide on a shorter list of priorities. According to a staffer, "It's the first time in my experience that any of them were willing to sit still—never mind sit still together—long enough to go over a list of some sixty items. And that basically has become the so-called priority list." Clearly decisions on priorities must be made toward the end of a Congress, and decisions made collectively avoid confusion and misunderstandings. Yet before Bolling became chairman, reaching a consensus in a formal fashion was impossible. As one participant said, "Bolling could hardly go to Delaney and say, 'Here's a list of priorities for the rest of the session.' "

The way in which the committee performs its "traffic cop" function, then, has changed. The committee grants rules on the legislation the leadership wants to consider and grants them when the leadership wants them. Disagreements, which are rare and usually based on tactical and not ideological grounds, are negotiated between the committee chairman and the leadership. When the leadership is being pressured to schedule a measure it does not want to consider, the Rules Committee often shares the heat. An aide explained: "As long as we can spread the blame out, as long as we can tell a guy, 'You haven't got a rule yet,' that spreads it out a little bit. We don't want to put it on any more than the Rules Committee does, or anybody else, but as long as we can keep [the Rules Committee] working in tandem with us, they can fuzz theirs up for several weeks; if they want to, they can fuzz it up for a long time. And then when it gets down here we can fuzz it up for quite a long time."

The "Field Commander" Role

Besides the change in how the "traffic cop" function is performed, its closer relationship with the party leadership has also allowed the Rules Committee to assume some new functions. Bruce Oppenheimer, a student of the committee, reports that some members play a "field commander" role for the leadership. He quotes a senior Rules Democrat:

It's sort of like people on the Rules Committee treating themselves as if they were responsible field commanders reporting to the chief in Paris. Intelligence comes from us to the leadership. Our responsibility is to inform, advise, and execute. We're in charge of the field operation, and sometimes you have to act on your own best judgement. You can't always confer. Sometimes you need reserves like Biemiller calling up Madden. At times you make leadership decisions for the leadership. Even in a military operation it works the same way. (1977, p. 104)

Bolling has instituted changes as chairman, which enhance his own ability and that of committee Democrats collectively to perform this function. The staff has been reorganized and all important bills are carefully tracked. On the most major and controversial measures, a Rules staffer attends the mark-up. In 1980 and again in 1981, for example, an aide was assigned to follow the budget process: "She had the dreadful job of becoming what we refer to as a 'budgeteer.' She spent many long evenings at Budget Committee mark-ups, conference committees, reconciliation." Staff members are expected to develop an understanding of the politics of the legislation that comes before Rules so they can inform Rules Democrats of the regional and ideological interests and conflicts at issue.

Bolling has instituted a meeting of Rules Democrats prior to each committee meeting. Opposition to these caucus meetings by some senior committee Democrats who feared they would lead to infighting among the Democrats was met by Bolling's reply that he prefers to be alerted to problems in advance. The meetings give Bolling an opportunity to explain both political and substantive issues and to tell members "whether it's a party vote or not. The members often ask." Both participants and close observers agree that the meetings have proven useful. One of them commented:

Bolling, unlike either the lax or the authoritative chairmen [of the past], has brought the committee into a much more consultative process within itself. A half hour before the [committee] meeting, the Democrats meet in the chairman's office. There's a specific discussion of the items on the agenda. Just a last shakedown before going in to make sure there are no big problems that are going to surface. And occasionally you'll have a case where the chairman comes back in the room at the beginning of the meeting and the agenda changes. Not very often, because when there's not a huge demand on the part of the leadership (which there sometimes is not) they try to find out, this vacuum being there, if anyone on the committee has something he's particularly interested in. And there is a real effort to accommodate the members of the Rules Committee.

Structuring Floor Debate

Bolling believes that the Rules Committee can use rules to structure debate for the benefits of the leadership and the membership collectively. A variety of changes during the last decade have made the floor a more important decision-making arena and have complicated the parliamentary situation. Because a number of the issues at the center of controversy—energy and health, for example—fall into the jurisdiction of more than one committee and because it was unwilling to realign committee jurisdictions, the House instituted a multiple referral procedure by which a bill may be sent to several committees. How such bills are to be handled on the floor presents a complicated and delicate problem (see Bach 1980, pp. 27–28). The recorded teller vote and the decline of intercommittee reciprocity have led to a large increase in the number of amendments offered on the floor. As a result of these changes, bills now take much longer to complete, and the acceptance of amendments that are poorly understood by most members has become more common. The new permissiveness has also encouraged members to use House rules for delay and obstruction.

In response to these developments the Rules Committee has made increasing use of complex rules. A rule—simple or complex—always specifies the amount of debate time allowed and who is to control that time. A rule may waive points of order and may restrict amendments in some way. Through the late 1960s the great majority of rules were simple open rules that allowed all germane amendments and divided debate time equally between the chairman and ranking minority member of the reporting committee. The exceptions were revenue bills from Ways and Means, which were considered under closed rules prohibiting all but committee-offered amendments. In sharp contrast, by the 95th Congress, slightly over 20 percent of the rules granted were complex (Oppenheimer 1981, pp. 219–20). Complex rules may divide general debate time among several committees, they make a particular amendment or substitute specifically in order, they may prohibit all but certain specified amendments; they may contain several of these features (see Bach 1980; Oppenheimer 1981). By naming specific amendments or substitutes, even though they may be in order anyway, the committee seeks to focus attention and debate on major alternatives to the committee bill and in this way to structure debate so it concentrates on the critical choices and not on "bogus, time-consuming nonsense." If there are several major substitutes, a complex rule specifies the order in which they will be considered, a specification many members believe can have a significant impact. If the House spends hours amending the substitute considered first, members will be unwilling to vote down that substitute and, thus, have to go through the amending process again. Many observers believed that the rule for the Alaska lands bill in the 96th Congress advantaged Morris Udall's substitute in just this way.

Rules that restrict amendments may simply require that amendments be "noticed," that is, printed in the *Congressional Record*, by a certain date. This requirement allows the committee staff to analyze the amendments and the bill's defenders to plan strategy. Consequently, it reduces uncertainty and the possibility that a disastrous amendment will be passed due to lack of information. Some rules allow only specified amendments to be considered on the floor. These rules usually shorten debate time, focus attention on major alternatives, and protect the legislation from attempts to unravel it on the floor. In 1980, for example, the first budget resolution, which in previous years had been open to all germane amendments, was considered under a rule allowing only eight specified amendments. Without such a rule, consideration would probably have dragged on for weeks (see chapter 6). A participant commented:

> Publicly there was the normal "arbitrary rule, chairman of the Rules Committee not allowing certain amendments to be made in order, tight-grip of the Speaker on the committee" talk. Privately, however, the reaction was entirely different. Privately, the members knew perfectly well that if the rule had not been tight they would have been here for three weeks doing the budget. There are about ten or twenty members that are just philosophically opposed to a closed rule on the grounds that every member should have the right to offer anything. And that's a legitimate argument, to some degree, if you can count on the responsibility of the member offering it, to offer an amendment that actually has substance. Unfortunately, you can't always count on that. Some see open rules as strictly a way to tie the House up in knots.

The reconciliation bill in the fall of 1980 was also considered under a highly restrictive rule. Since the bill included cuts in numerous popular programs, an open rule would almost certainly have resulted in the bill's emasculation on the floor—a series of amendments restoring most of the cuts would have passed. The restrictive rule protected members from having to go on record on such amendments. Complex rules in instances such as these can be used to protect members and to affect outcomes.

"The construction of special rules," as a student of the committee says, "has become much more an act of political and paliamentary craftsmanship" (Bach 1980, p. 22). Complex rules are powerful tools, but since a majority of the House must approve them, their construction calls for political astuteness. "You have to get the balance just right," a participant explained. "You have to protect the rights of the minority, protect the rights of a variety of different coalitions within the House in order to pass the rule. And sometimes it's a delicate balance." Bolling's method of running the committee maximizes his chances of striking that balance. Systematic information gathering by staff, the regular caucus meetings of the committee Democrats, and the almost continuous consultation between the committee and the leadership at both staff and member levels provide the committee with valuable information, often at an early stage. On important or highly controversial bills the leadership and the chairman of Rules discuss the type of rule that is to be granted. According to a senior leadership aide, "On major bills there's very close consultation. On the major issues, there are important tactical questions which are reflected in what kind of rule they bring. We talk about that."

The three instances of major conflict between the committee and the leadership during O'Neill's tenure as Speaker involved the type of rule to be granted. These were cases in which a minority of Rules Democrats (not including the committee chairman) opposed granting the type of rule the Speaker wanted. Early in his tenure as Speaker, O'Neill had committed himself to passage of a strong ethics bill. If the bill was considered under an open rule, the Speaker was convinced, it would be emasculated on the floor. A number of Rules Committee Democrats, opposed to the stringent outside earnings limit the bill contained, wanted to report a rule that allowed that provision to be modified. On 24 February, 1977 O'Neill invited the Rules Committee Democrats to breakfast and, as he later described it, told them, "Lookit. I've committed myself as the leader of the party to the strongest ethics bill in the history of the country. And I'm asking you, the Rules Committee, as the one hand-picked committee that's appointed by the Speaker. You're my handpicked people. Now, I've been able to get this through the Obey Commission without any difficulty and I would expect that I would be able to get it through here" (Malbin 1977, p. 943). A participant said that O'Neill then "went around the room and got them to pledge support. There was a lot of screaming and moaning, but they did." All eleven committee Democrats voted for the rule O'Neill wanted. The rule for consideration of the energy program at the end of the 95th Congress also occasioned some conflict. Carter's energy program had been broken down in the Senate into a number of separate bills. A rule providing for consideration of the package as a whole to prevent a separate vote on the unpopular gas-pricing section was desired by the leadership, which obtained the rule by applying great pressure on committee members. The third case, the rule for the 1980 reconciliation bill, is discussed in detail in chapter 6.

Serious conflict between the committee and the leadership is unusual. To a large extent the committee serves as an arm of the leadership in the design of as well as the granting of rules. Through its increased use of complex rules the committee majority is acting on behalf of the leadership, though frequently without detailed consultation. To the extent that complex rules focus attention on the more important alternatives and shorten total debate time, they aid the leadership. Those placing restrictions on the amendments that may be offered are even more helpful because they reduce uncertainty. The length of current floor sessions is beginning to erode opposition among many Democrats to restricting the amending process. As members become more willing to accept some restrictions in return for more orderly and efficient floor consideration, the leaderhip's control over the floor stage will grow and its close working relationship with Rules will gain even greater significance.

When Bolling became chairman of the Rules Committee in 1979 he established two subcommittees, one on the legislative process and the other on the rules of the House, matters of original jurisdiction that had received little committee attention in the past. These subcommittees' activities have benefited the leadership considerably. The budget-balancing, anti-big-government mood of the 1970s and early 1980s made proposals such as sunset legislation and the legislative veto attractive to many members. Enthusiastic members have advocated them and offered such proposals as floor amendments without serious scrutiny. Yet these are complex proposals with a host of nonobvious implications for the governmental process and the functioning of the House. The Rules subcommittees have provided a forum for thorough examination of the proposals, have publicized some of the problems inherent in them, and have reduced the pressure on the leadership to take immediate action on them.

The Rules Committee is no longer obstructionist; rather, it now performs a number of positive functions for the leadership. Committee Democrats have lost their independence of the Speaker, but in return interested members have become part of the leadership. The transformation was underway before O'Neill became Speaker, but O'Neill's belief in the strategy of inclusion has undoubtedly accelerated it.

Conclusion

███████████████ Changes in the House of Representatives have demanded new modes of leadership. The increase in member activity requires that leaders engage in more extensive information gathering. Members now expect to participate significantly at all stages of the legislative process and leaders ignore or attempt to thwart these expectations at their own peril. The legislative process is much less predictable in the postreform House than it was in the days of Sam Rayburn.

The current leaders' use of the whip system, the Steering and Policy Committee, and the Rules Committee are elements of a strategy designed to cope with these changes. These arms of the leadership serve as information conduits; each provides assistance in the coalition-building process. In addition, by involving them in leadership efforts, the leadership gives the many members of these arms an opportunity for meaningful participation—but on the leadership's behalf.

4

CONSTITUENTS, ALLIES, AND ADVERSARIES: RELATIONSHIPS IN THE LEGISLATIVE ARENA

House Democrats

For the leadership, the Democratic membership is by far the most important element of the human environment. The House Democrats comprise the leaders' constituents; to keep their jobs, the leaders must meet at least their minimum expectations. Successful coalition building depends on the Democratic membership.

In choosing their leaders, members of the House of Representatives have probably always asked, "What can he do for me?" (Fenno 1981). In more specific terms, however, member expectation of their leaders seem to have changed in the last several decades. Current members expect from their leadership access and services; they expect that the leadership, in doing its job, will not restrict members' opportunities to participate fully in the legislative process. Members also expect the leadership to be at least reasonably successful at building winning coalitions on legislation of interest to them, but they differ among themselves on both priorities and policy positions.

As the preceding chapters have discussed, the leaders both make themselves available to rank-and-file members and provide services to the membership collectively (the informational activities of the whip system, for example) and individually, by bestowing a variety of favors. By thus meeting member expectations, the leaders contribute not only to their own job security but also to party maintenance; they accumulate "chits" that can be used in coalition building; and they gain information that is vital to the effective performance of both of their primary functions.

The increased number and activity of freshmen have led the leadership to pay special attention to new members. Senior congressmen tell of a time not so long ago when freshmen were in the main ignored and had to learn the ropes on their own. One established member recalled that a frequent activity of his during his early months in the House had been wandering up and down the halls introducing himself to people. Now freshmen are vigorously courted: they are given temporary office space for the period between the election and the swearing in, orientation sessions are arranged for them, and they are wined and dined. Thus, coincident with the December Democratic Caucus meetings, the leadership presented a daylong orientation program for 96th Congress freshmen Democrats. Among the topics covered were history and structure of the House; "House Democrats: Organization, Leadership Procedures, Traditions, Expectations"; committee assignments; House rules and allowances; staffing; and use of the frank. During the December caucus period the Speaker, the majority leader, and the Democratic Congressional Campaign Committee each hosted a reception and dinner for all new Democratic members and their spouses. The Speaker's was held in Statuary Hall; previously only Lafayette and Queen Elizabeth had been so honored.

The leadership's attentiveness to the freshmen is expected to produce a generally favorable climate. The orientation sessions provide the leadership with an opportunity to affect, at least marginally, new Democrats' perceptions of the job of the congressman. (Thus in his presentation, Majority Leader Wright spoke about the tough votes in the future and about the need to be a statesman on such occasions. "Being a statesman," it was clearly implied, meant following the party leadership.) The social functions allow the leaders and the new members to begin to get to know each other personally. Because, ultimately, persuasion is personal, the better they know party members, the more likely the leaders are to be successful. And a member who knows and likes a leader is more inclined to go along when he can.

The extensive use the leadership makes of the whip system and the Steering and Policy Committee provides a considerable number of members with an opportunity for meaningful participation—participation that aids the leadership. Again, special provisions are made for new members. One of the at-large whips is always a freshman who is chosen by his class. The Speaker always appoints a freshman to the Steering and Policy Committee.

By meeting member expectations of access, services, and participation opportunities, the leadership establishes a generally favorable climate for coalition building. Such a climate, however, is far from sufficient to assure success. Given the heterogeneity of the Democratic membership, members, in pursuing their individual goals, are often at odds with the leadership. Building winning coalitions often requires that leaders persuade members to act differently from the way they would act if uninfluenced.

The Carrot versus the Stick

The Speaker strongly prefers reward over punishment as a persuasion tactic. "O'Neill is not a strong-armer," a senior aide stated. "His knack is being able to put people in a position where they don't want to disappoint him. Basically he has a reserve of goodwill built up over many years, from doing little things for people over a long period of time. Most of the people around here know that if you receive favors, eventually you are expected to return the favor. Persuasion around here is very soft. At its best, it involves evoking a sense of responsibility." Some members complain about the Speaker's sparing use of negative sanctions. One of the more impassioned of them said:

> I am trying to get the leadership to exert more leadership, to have some requirement of members of the Democratic party, to have discipline, in other words. If we have no discipline and if everybody goes off in all directions, then there is no direction, no direction from the party. And because there is so little direction from the party, when direction is exerted, and leadership is exerted, it's ignored. There is no punishment; there is no reward. In a place with as many members as this, we have to have punishment and reward.

"Several members have taken the Speaker on in Steering and Policy meetings on [the lack of use of negative sanctions]," a senior staffer reported. "_____ said to the Speaker, 'Jesus Christ, I'm telling _____ that you are really pissed off with him, really upset about how he voted and you come up and put your arm around him.' "

The members who advocate a greater use of negative sanctions, not surprisingly, are mainstream Democrats. Their more conservative colleagues do not share this view, and some believe they have been shortchanged in the committee assignment process. Asked if the leadership had sufficient tools and resources to lead, one conservative Democrat responded, "If the leadership doesn't become too narrow. And I think this is where many of the members in the Congress have felt the Congress encompasses a much broader umbrella within the Democratic party than what the leadership is willing to allow the umbrella to spread. There's got to be the understanding that in conservative states like Oklahoma and Texas and Arizona and Alabama, if you do not have a conservative Democrat, you're probably going to have a conservative Republican." Sentiments such as this preclude, in the leadership's view, frequent use of negative sanctions. Negative sanctions available to the leadership are limited, and coalition building is a continuing process. A participant explained:

> The theory behind that is not only peace and tranquility and "the polite thing to do" but also "there's always tomorrow"; there's going to be another vote on another issue and you can't stay mad at anybody. If something happens and it doesn't work out, you may get mad momentarily but there's no percentage in staying mad. You need the guy tomorrow. It's a very practical aspect. There's

always tomorrow. And some people say "Tip" ought to be tougher on these guys, he ought to do this and he ought to do that. That's easy to say, but you've got to look at the long run. When you need them tomorrow. And you can say, "You went against me yesterday, so you owe me one today."

The leadership, thus, believes that extensive use of negative sanctions would be detrimental in terms of party maintenance and, furthermore, that it would hinder rather than help coalition building over the long run.

Although it is reluctant to "crack the whip," the leadership has on occasion done so. In the summer of 1980 John Ashbrook, one of the Republican gadflies, offered an amendment that the presiding officer ruled out of order. Ashbrook appealed the ruling and forced a recorded vote on the appeal. Although the ruling of the chair was upheld, forty-four Democrats voted against the Speaker. Greater party loyalty is expected on procedural than on substantive votes; in the House, appeals from rulings of the chair are rare, and crossing party lines on such a vote is considered a real challenge to a Speaker of one's party. O'Neill reacted quickly, sending the following letter to each of the forty-four defecting Democrats:

> Dear _____: I was extremely disappointed to note that you voted against a motion to uphold the ruling of the Chair last week.
>
> It is elementary to our procedural control of the House that the Chair be supported by members of our party. That is basic to a parliamentary body. In other countries if such a vote were lost, the government would fall.
>
> You should know that from 1937 to 1968 there are no recorded votes on the Chair's rulings. From 1968 until 1979, there were four votes. Now we have seen three roll call votes in seven weeks!
>
> Members of the Steering and Policy Committee and the Whip's Organization have discussed these developments, some of them calling for disciplinary measures and meetings. I believe, however, that our best course is to call the above facts to the Members' attention.
>
> I fully understand the pressures that are brought to bear by single-issue groups on such occasions, but I believe members have to be ready to support the orderly process when a member seeks to confuse procedure with issue.
>
> I trust you will take all these facts into consideration in the future. We must work together to enact a legislative program.
>
> Sincerely,
> Thomas P. O'Neill, Jr., The Speaker
>
> (*Congressional Record,* 96th Cong., 2nd sess.,
> 28 August 1980, vol. 126, p. 8120)

Among the forty-four were two committee chairmen. The Speaker reportedly spoke to one of them in strong language, essentially threatening him with loss of his chairmanship if he ever repeated his actions. This conversation took place in a relatively public arena and, as an observer remarked, "those things get around."

Because the forty-four Democrats' behavior directly threatened the Speaker's and the majority party's control of the House, a strong leadership reaction was essential. That Democrats generally supported the Speaker's response and that most of the forty-four apologized to the Speaker for their action shows that crossing party lines on procedural votes is a violation of still widely-held party norms. A lack of response by O'Neill would have contributed to the weakening of those norms. In the aftermath of this incident party voting on a variety of important measures did, in fact, increase, and observers attributed the increase to the Speaker's actions.

In 1981 the question of discipline arose again, and with considerably greater intensity. House Democrats lost three big legislative battles because of defections from their own ranks. Phil Gramm and Kent Hance, who had received seats on the Budget and Ways and Means committees respectively in response to pleas from conservatives for fairer representation, took lead roles in the Republican efforts. The leadership was not pleased. Asked about the large number of Texas Democrats defecting on key votes, Majority Leader Wright said, "I feel like the wife who was asked whether she ever considered divorce. She answered, 'Divorce, no, murder, yes!' That's how I feel about those guys" (Ehrenhalt 1981, p. 1177). Democrats who supported the party on the votes were furious and liberals were especially bitter. "Liberals supported the Jones budget, which they ordinarily wouldn't have, because they figured it was the best they could get," a staffer said. "Then the conservatives did them in."

The leadership was under considerable pressure to discipline at least the most flagrant defectors. The leaders, however, are more aware than their members of just how limited their negative sanctions are, and they wanted to avoid any actions that would backfire and endanger the Democrats' formal control of the House. The strongest intraparty consensus existed for disciplining Phil Gramm because many Democrats believed he had acted as a "spy" within party councils. Stripping Gramm of his Budget Committee seat, however, would require a vote of the whole House, which the leadership was not certain it could win. Disciplining members whose conduct was less flagrant, especially when nothing was done to Gramm, would only be counterproductive, the leadership believed, and drive those members farther from the party. Given Republican successes legislatively and in the polls in the summer of 1981, it might lead some members to switch parties.

The leadership postponed action until after the August recess. The decision proved to be a wise one. When Congress returned in September, the improved political situation for Democrats made it easier for liberals to take a cooler, longer-range view. At that point Majority Leader Wright announced four guidelines at a caucus meeting held to consider disciplinary measures for defecting Democrats:

1. Amnesty. We have opened the door. Democrats who have defected may come back.

2. Distinction between punishments and rewards. We do not seek to punish anybody for voting his or her convictions, but there are rewards—leadership committees and leadership positions. . . . We expect some sense of responsibility to the party and our colleagues. In the future, anybody who aspires to receive a gift must be concerned with that responsibility.

3. Distinction between votes. In no circumstances will we seek 100 percent conformity. . . . We look to the Steering and Policy Committee to choose carefully those relatively few votes and issues throughout the year which are key policy issues. When these have been chosen, we expect the Speaker to notify all members of the action. If I, in the future, ask my colleagues to reward me with a leadership position, I must expect that they will look at that.

4. Making a distinction between an occasional aberration from those positions, but not demanding or requiring total compliance with those relatively few. There are some who may occasionally vote differently because of their convictions or constituencies, but we are talking about those who vote consistently against the Democratic position. A person who consistently connives with the opposition—we will refrain from rewarding that person with a leadership position.

I think this fundamentally represents what the leadership wants to do. No one will be punished. We open the door to anyone. We welcome the sinners to repent. We don't hold their sins against them any longer. (Speaker's press conference, 16 September 1981).

The announcement of the guidelines had the effect the leadership desired. Those who had been pressing for discipline were generally satisfied; but no action that would drive members away from the party had been taken. "Nobody will be Joan of Arc until he lights his own torch," Jim Wright said. Yet defectors had been warned: "Nothing will happen at the hands of the leadership," Wright had continued, "But something may happen at the hands of the membership." Most of those questioned believed the guidelines and the widespread sentiments that had led to their announcement would influence members' behavior. In regard to whether the statement would be taken seriously by the members at whom it was aimed, a moderate southerner replied, "I don't think there's any question about it. I've talked to too many of them. I think that they were surprised that we didn't go further."

The leadership, then, is willing to "crack the whip" when doing so is essential to majority party control. Yet even then the leaders' approach will be as conciliatory as is consistent with conveying their message. Both the Speaker's letter and the majority leader's four-point statement contained threats, but both also, in effect, offered amnesty for past transgressions. The leaders believe their limited resources should be used negatively only when not doing so would be more costly than doing so in terms of party maintenance and future coalition-building success.

The Democratic Caucus

The leadership deals with Democratic members not only as individuals, but also as a collectivity. The Democratic Caucus, as the organization of all House Democrats is called, elects the party leaders. In the days of Sam Rayburn this was the sole function of the group; after the organizing session at the beginning of a Congress, it never met. Liberal Democrats in the late 1960s seized on the caucus as the primary device through which to reform the House. In 1969 they persuaded Speaker McCormack to accept a rule requiring monthly caucus meetings. Most of the far-reaching rules changes adopted during the 1970s were proposed by a committee of the caucus.

At its organizational meetings at the beginning of each Congress the caucus elects party leaders and debates and votes on proposed changes in caucus and House rules. By secret ballot the caucus votes on members nominated as chairmen by the Steering and Policy Committee and on prospective Appropriations subcommittee chairmen. The 1975 deposal of three sitting chairmen established this procedure as a meaningful one. Since that time, one Appropriations subcommittee chairman has been defeated and two others have decided not to run for fear of defeat. The caucus must also approve the Steering and Policy Committee-nominated membership of all committees. This, too, is more than a mere formality. Caucus members may nominate additional candidates for Budget Committee positions and for vacancies on Appropriations and Ways and Means. In 1979 one Steering and Policy Committee nominee for Budget and one for Ways and Means were defeated by caucus-nominated candidates.

The caucus's role in committee personnel decisions works, on balance, to the advantage of the leadership. Leadership-supported Steering and Policy nominees have occasionally been defeated. However, that chairmen must be approved by caucus vote has made chairmen much more responsive to the sentiments of a majority of the party and to leadership appeals based on such sentiments. Chairmen cannot defy with impunity the leadership when the leadership is backed by a Democratic majority. "The leadership has really been strengthened by the caucus vote on committee chairmen," a long-time observer said. "The chairs have been cut down to size. It used to be a much bigger deal to be a committee chairman than Speaker. Bolling is always saying, 'The committee chairmen were constantly handing Sam Rayburn his head.' "

In the early and mid-1970s the caucus also actively took legislative positions. Frustrated by the tight grip often conservative chairmen still held on their committees, liberals used the caucus to instruct committees. Anti-war legislation or legislation from the Ways and Means Committee was most often at issue. In recent years the caucus has less frequently taken legislative positions. The current leadership and many members believe that persistent use of the caucus to influence legislation could undermine the committee system. One leader said of the Caucus, "It's a problem and an opportunity. We can use it to stimulate interest and support for major legislation. But it can really be a problem." A senior leadership aide said, "The caucus is too unpredictable. For making policy, there's Steering and Policy. Most members don't want any more meetings anyway. They've elected members to Steering and Policy." Asked about leadership use of the caucus, a staffer replied, "You've got other tools so much more effective. You get into caucus and you get some sort of a resolution—then you've got a problem of how to get around the resolution, when maybe the resolution wasn't a very good idea in the first place. The leadership almost never uses the caucus to get something done."

Some participants in the late 1970s believed the leadership could make greater use of the caucus. "The caucus itself is a power for the leadership that it never uses," one said. "I don't know why it doesn't—to get a party position hammered out, for ventilating the issues." Some members who believed the caucus should be used more blamed the decision to open the caucus to the press and public for its demise. One said, "You can't wash your dirty linen in public; you can't have a tough discussion and look up and see six Republicans sitting in the gallery." There also were members who wanted to see the caucus assume new functions. One expressed his view this way:

> I believe the caucus can be expanded as an information and communication mechanism for the House so that we don't feel threatened about going there. Too many members now don't show up at the caucus because they are afraid that if they go there and there's a quorum, some fool thing will occur. Well, you know, we need to break out of that. Democrats need to communicate with each other better around here, and express our differences. We need a better mechanism within the caucus for sharing our diversity of opinions rather than running away from our diversities out of fear that if we were to get together and have a quorum that some horrible resolution would come out that we wouldn't like.

Thus during the Carter administration the leaders preferred not to use the caucus because they believed it to be unpredictable, because they feared it might limit their flexibility on important matters, and because they believed superior instruments were available to them. Some members believed the caucus should play a greater role and some suggested alternative roles; but there existed no groundswell for a more active role. The 1980 election changed both membership and leadership views of the role of the caucus. The Democratic House membership that returned to Washington in January 1981 was demoralized by the election results, worried about the future, and badly split on both policy and strategy. Leaders and members alike perceived the need for an inclusive forum to discuss such matters. Although

Steering and Policy Committee and whip meetings offered a number of members the opportunity to discuss with the leadership party strategy, this was a debate in which all members wanted to participate. A senior staffer explained:

> We now have obviously a different party in the White House. And there's a greater need for Democrats to meet on a regular basis—one, to plan responses to announced administration programs, and two, and probably more important to most of these guys, to plot survival tactics. With the margin being reduced so greatly and with the possibilities existent that we may not have a margin at all a year from November, there's a much larger concern coming from the individual members to be thinking like Democrats as opposed to be thinking of themselves; in other words, they know there's no way that they can stay chairman of such and such a subcommittee by themselves. So there's a greater need to sort of work out things collectively to preserve the majority and I think obviously a much greater awareness of this.

Gillis Long, the newly elected caucus chairman, had run on a platform of revitalizing the caucus. "One of his themes at the time was the need for greater communication, to bring things out into an open forum much more than they were in the past, and he's been very effective at doing that," a leadership staffer said. Thus the caucus was more active in 1981 than it had been in the previous four years. After the organizational meetings at the beginning of the Congress, eleven meetings were held in the first half of the 1981 session; during the period from 1977 to 1980 nonorganizational caucus meetings had averaged slightly fewer than ten per session. More indicative of the increased activity is the number of meetings that attracted a quorum. Of the thirty-nine meetings called during the 95th and 96th congresses, only five had a quorum, while seven of the first eleven meetings in 1981 attracted a quorum (Malbin 1981, p. 1642).

Caucuses are called sometimes to discuss general party policy and sometimes to discuss specific legislation. Thus in 1981 meetings were held to discuss the budget resolution, the reconciliation bill, and the tax bill. Such meetings begin with a progress report by the committee chairman; then he answers questions from the floor. A general discussion in which members bring up other matters follows. The caucus has not taken official positions on legislation. Long's intention was to use the caucus as a forum for airing views, and the caucus has carried out his intention. "It's a way for the membership to communicate with the leadership and the leadership to communicate with the membership," a leadership aide said. "You can always say, 'Well, you can just talk to one of the leaders on the floor'; and a lot of people do that, but sometimes it's easier to say it in the caucus."

At the beginning of the 97th Congress caucus rules were changed so as to close meetings to the public. Everyone questioned agreed that this had made the caucus much more useful. A comment like this one is typical of those made: "The whole idea of an open caucus is something which makes no sense to me whatsoever. It's not a caucus, it's Democratic members of Congress on exhibition, if it's open. Very little is accomplished. If you're going to have a caucus, make it a caucus. So they can take off their ties and roll up their sleeves and call this guy an s.o.b and that guy an s.o.b. if you want to and get it out of your system. And I think the end result of something like that is very, very worthwhile."

Democratic defeats in the first three big legislative battles of 1981 produced a high level of frustration and a great deal of criticism of the leadership. The caucus has been useful as a safety valve. One participant commented, "There has been a lot of acrimony within the party. This is a forum for letting off steam." Because the top leadership attends all caucus meetings, members can voice their criticisms and, as another participant said, "know their message is received." Although conservatives have not participated as actively as liberals, many of them have attended caucus meetings. The leaders believe that keeping the conservative and the liberal elements talking to one another is an important function of the caucus. One leader said, "You get an umbrella as big as ours is—if we can keep everybody talking, everybody knowing one another and where they come from, it adds to the solution of problems."

The strategy debate that raged within the House Democratic party through much of 1981 surfaced repeatedly in the caucus. Many liberals argued that House Democrats should recognize their de facto minority status and present proposals that clearly differentiated the Democratic from the administration position. A number of conservatives argued for cooperation with Reagan. "If the president's way is successful, everybody's happy," one explained. "That's the best climate in which to have a political campaign. . . . If his effort fails, it is not our fault. We have the best of both worlds." A third group advocated a damage-control strategy whereby Democrats would do everything they could to protect key programs. After the first two legislative defeats, some members argued that a victory was essential for the party, regardless of how it was achieved; others contended that the defeats proved that the clear differentiation strategy had been the correct one. Although these debates often contained at least implicit criticisms of the leadership, they were in fact helpful to it. "The Speaker has mentioned to me that to give everybody an opportunity to get up and say, 'I think this is the strategy we ought to follow' broadens the leadership's ability to discern a consensus of which direction most of them are willing to go," a member explained. In addition, as other Democrats pointed out, when members believe they have had "input" into strategy decisions they are more likely to be willing to adhere to them. A senior nonleadership Democrat said:

> The caucus is the place where a great deal of freewheeling debate over an issue takes place and where sometimes a consensus develops as it has been in the last

couple of weeks with respect to how to handle reconciliation. Most of the discussions, although they have taken place at leadership meetings and at chairmen's meetings and in whips' meetings, have ended up in the broader forum of the caucus where every member of the Democratic party participates. You don't take a vote, but you try to develop a consensus and make concessions where they're necessary and develop the strongest possible position that can be supported by the maximum number of Democrats.

With the support of the Speaker and the majority leader, Long is also attempting to use the caucus to develop Democratic policy alternatives. Early in the 97th Congress a caucus task force was charged with working out a statement of Democratic economic principles. Long also appointed a committee on party effectiveness. With an ideologically and geographically diverse membership of thirty-three, the committee served as the first forum for the discussion of the task force's statement. The committee approved the draft of the statement, which was then endorsed by the Steering and Policy Committee and, on 8 April 1981, adopted by the caucus. The economic policy statement was "not very strong," a participant conceded, "but we did get everyone to agree, which was a major accomplishment." In September 1981 work began on six more policy statements in the areas of crime, housing, long-term economic policy, environment, women's issues, and small business.

Developing coherent policy alternatives has always been difficult for the party that does not control the White House. That party lacks both a single leader and a mechanism for making authoritative decisions collectively. The fate of past attempts to establish such a mechanism suggests the caucus is unlikely to succeed in its effort to have the policy positions it develops recognized as authoritative for the party as a whole. The effort, however, involves a large number of Democrats in a party-based attempt to develop policy and thus offers these members another opportunity to participate.

The change in political conditions thus led to an increased role for the Democratic caucus. During a period when the House Democratic party has been under considerable strain, it has served as a forum for communication and as a safety valve. It has made a significant contribution toward party maintenance at a time when party coherence was threatened more than it usually is. But even during its period of relative inactivity the caucus was, as Tom Foley has said, "a kind of gun behind the door" (*Congressional Quarterly Weekly Report,* 15 April 1978, p. 875). "The caucus hasn't been used a great deal in this last Congress," a senior staffer said in 1979, "but the memory lingers on. It's there. People know it." Both the party leadership and the committees are aware that if they were regularly to thwart the wishes of a majority of their party colleagues, the caucus would provide a mechanism through which they could be brought to heel. Since the party leadership is representative of the party mainstream, this role of the caucus is extremely helpful to the leadership, serving as a force for responsiveness on the part of committees.

Committees and
Subcommittees

████████████████   The legislative process in the House is committee centered. Despite the increase in amending activity at the floor stage, committees and subcommittees are preeminent in shaping legislation. In building winning coalitions on major legislation, consequently, the party leadership is highly dependent on the committees to report the legislation and to do so in a timely fashion and in a form basically acceptable to a party-based majority of the House. Because the floor has become a more important decision-making arena, Democratic committee leaders are in turn dependent on the party leadership for help in passing their legislation intact at the floor stage.

The relationship between the majority party leadership and the Democratic committee contingents is predominantly cooperative. The leadership sees itself as an active or passive (depending on the importance of the measure) supporter of the committees' legislation—so long as that legislation is backed by a majority of committee Democrats. The party leadership generally trusts the committee leaders and the latter's party loyalty during the tenure of the O'Neill-Wright team warranted that trust. As recently as the 92d Congress (1971–72), both committee and subcommittee chairmen scored considerably lower on the *Congressional Quarterly* party unity index than the average Democrat; during the 95th and 96th congresses, by contrast, committee chairmen averaged slightly higher than the mean Democrat, and subcommittee chairmen about the same (Deering and Smith 1980, table 3). Current committee leaders are quite representative of the party.

Frequency of Leadership
Involvement

Given the party leaders' inclination to trust the committees and the immense time pressure under which the leaders work, the bulk of legislation is routinely processed without leadership involvement at the committee stage and only minimal involvement at the floor stage. A senior aide described the process: "Many, many bills go through here which are not distinguished by having particular leadership support or leadership opposition. Most bills just work their way through the House, and there are problems here and there are problems there, and the leadership doesn't really take a hand at all except to say, 'We support our Democratic committees.' But that support is taken for granted; it's always there; it's residual and it's not particularly acted upon in most cases."

Although the committee leaders collectively are representative of the Democratic membership, the committees are not necessarily microcosms of the House. Because committee attractiveness is in part a function of members' districts, the membership of some committees is quite skewed. For example, members from farm districts are attracted to the Agriculture Committee; big city liberals find the Education and Labor Committee particularly attractive. As a result, agricultural interests are overrepresented on the Agriculture Committee and Education and Labor tends to be considerably more liberal than the House as a whole. A senior member commented, "I've served on committees where the committee does what *it* can do, but that has no relationship to what the House can do."

The form in which a bill emerges from committee affects both the probability of floor passage and the form in which it is likely to pass. Passing a bill on the floor, of course, is much easier if the version reported from committee is acceptable to a broad majority of Democrats. "You hope that the leadership of the committee figures out all the political pitfalls and cleans up its act before it gets out of committee, so that the leadership in the House doesn't have to come in here and do this technical, political job on a bill on the floor of the House," a leadership aide explained. If a bill emerges from committee in a form unacceptable to a large segment of the Democratic membership, the leadership is in a dilemma. Either support of or opposition to the committee position by the party leadership at the floor stage is likely to exacerbate intraparty conflicts.

On major legislation, then, the party leadership does have an incentive to get involved at the committee stage. Both time constraints and norms concerning committee autonomy prohibit indiscriminate leadership intervention, but new resources and, most importantly, the decline in the power of committee chairmen have made selective intervention possible. A senior aide commented:

> Carl Albert and John McCormack, they didn't get involved at the committee level because the committee chairmen were then very powerful. Now, they've been weakened; they all have to answer to the caucus, so they're weakened and because they're weakened there's more chance for "Tip" to be involved. Would Albert have gotten involved in the same circumstances? He probably would have. And "Tip"—would he have been more involved if we wouldn't have had the reforms? He probably wouldn't have. Because he would have gotten rebuffed. They would have told him to "butt out." But now with them weakened considerably and the power shifted from the committee chairmen to the subcommittee chairmen and they're only subcommittee chairmen, he's got a shot at them, at influencing them, because they're not all that powerful. The leadership gets involved because of the demise of the committee chairmen. Now they have that opening and they didn't have it before.

A senior Democrat who is not a part of the leadership agreed that the current leadership is much more heavily involved than previous leaderships were. "The leadership has become much more involved in the substance of legislation and the status, the progress, of legislation over the last several years. Albert didn't have the slightest idea what legislation had been introduced, what important matters were before what committees. Unless there came to be something in the nature of a crisis, it was never brought to his attention and he didn't know anything about it. He wasn't well staffed and he was relying all but exclusively on the operation of the committee system. With O'Neill, that changed rather quickly." This Democrat, too, attributed the change to the reforms of the 1970s: "With reform, the capacity of the leadership has improved as far as being involved in the legislative process is concerned."

Interaction between the party leadership and committee leaders is frequent. Early each year the Speaker hosts a luncheon for all committee chairmen. A party leader said, "We go around and ask 'What are you going to have this year?' and we get target dates." Additional meetings are held when the need arises. The loss of the presidency and the Democrats' lack of agreement on how to respond to the Reagan program dictated unusually frequent meetings during 1981. Priorities, specific legislation, and strategy required discussion. The reconciliation process, which involved fifteen committees, by itself occasioned a series of meetings. At these meetings, a participant revealed, "we debated the issue of reconciliation, debated what the committees had to do, talked about an approach on the floor, and tried to develop a scenario." Committee and party leaders see each other and often confer informally on the floor. Experienced committee leaders, a leadership aide said, "are in contact with the leadership throughout the bill process" (Deering and Smith 1980, p. 29). On top-priority legislation, committee leaders may brief the Speaker on a daily basis. When the 1981 tax bill was being written Chairman Rostenkowski met with the Speaker at the end of each drafting session. When the 1981 reconciliation bill was in conference the Budget Committee member overseeing the process reported developments to the Speaker nightly.

A 1980 survey found that subcommittee chairmen who were questioned had, on the average, twenty-five conversations with the leadership about matters falling within the policy jurisdiction of their subcommittees during the first three-quarters of the 96th Congress (Deering and Smith 1980, p. 10). The number of conversations reported varied widely, though, indicating that some chairmen are almost constantly in contact with the leadership while others seldom confer. Much of this interaction concerns scheduling, often of a bill that the subcommittee leader cares about much more than the party leaders do. Subcommittee chairmen, who now most typically act as floor managers, frequently approach the leaders with scheduling requests, and the leaders' ability to grant them through their power over scheduling provides one basis for persuasion on bills that are important to them. Leadership help in passing legislation provides another basis. An Appropriations subcommittee chairman said, "I've called on the

Speaker, I've called on the floor leader when I felt I had a real problem with my legislation, to give their assistance. And I'm sure other chairmen do the same thing."

Typically on major legislation the party leadership and the Democratic committee leaders work together in a close, cooperative fashion. "[Conferring with the party leadership is] a fairly constant thing, if you're handling something as complex as the _____ bill," one committee leader said. "When we moved with [our program's] reauthorization we had sixty-two organizations endorsing that legislation. That takes a couple of years to put together. But you're constantly working with the leadership and others in developing this, and as you report back to them that this kind of support is being generated for the legislation, it reassures them that this is something important enough that the party ought to take a position on and move on it." Leadership involvement of this nature is clearly welcomed and is not perceived as interference.

Leadership intervention in the committee process is restricted to major legislation. "Rarely do we try to influence legislation at the committee stage," one leader explained. "It would be only on occasions when the legislation is considered a big, essential part of the whole leadership initiative." He gave as an example the economic stimulus program that newly elected President Jimmy Carter and the leadership had agreed to make the centerpiece of the Democratic program:

> In 1977 we intruded once or twice into committee deliberations—once after an appropriations subcommittee had reported out a bill, because we felt it did not adequately accommodate the economic stimulus package. That, of course, was a major initiative. It was the single most important thing at that time from the standpoint of the Democratic leadership and the president. We called in the subcommittee chairman and some subcommittee members, Democrats all, pointed out to them that what they reported out of the subcommittee was not adequate to carry out the president's program and the programs to which we were committed as the Democratic leadership and asked them to go back and beef it up. They did, without complaining, and that was the first example of a situation of that kind.

Asking a subcommittee to change a decision that has already been made is a particularly intrusive form of leadership intervention. The leader emphasized the exceptionality of such leadership action and again justified it in terms of the importance of the legislation: "Speaker O'Neill has been generally loath to do this sort of thing, however. He hasn't wanted to intrude into the private sanctuary of the committee, because he is keenly conscious of the extent to which committee chairmen regard that as their privileged domain. There are exceptions, exceptions so rare, however, as to make the point I think that we do this only when it's a major initiative, and one on which the Democratic leadership in the Congress and the White House are deeply involved."

When the bill at issue is top priority and has been referred to several committees, the conditions for leadership involvement are maximized. "Obviously the more issues you generate the more the Speaker has got to be involved," a senior committee staffer remarked. "Because he is the leader of the House. It stands to reason when you increase the scope of something, you're going to increase the responsibility of anybody in the leadership position." The aide gave the 1981 reconciliation bill as an example:

> There were a number of clumsy issues that we had and still have in reconciliation. Like we had no report from the Energy and Commerce Committee. OK, well, what do you do about that? You have the black lung issue and the fact of jurisdictional differences between Ways and Means and Education and Labor on the issue, which is a half-billion-dollar issue. You know how touchy black lung is. That, of course, involves all the Connecticut insurance companies, so you get all the articulate Connecticut members involved and they go to the Speaker. Here you got Education and Labor putting a fee on coal mines which is really an amendment to the revenue code. They are calling it a fee but it's really a tax and it's passed out of Education and Labor. That's in the jurisdiction of Ways and Means, and if we allow, through reconciliation, the internal revenue code to be changed, you've absolutely wiped out the jurisdiction of Ways and Means. So you don't think that won't go to the leadership and the Speaker—of course it does. . . . The scope is broader, fifteen House committees involved, obviously the Speaker is going to be more involved.

Modes of Leadership Involvement

The aim of leadership intervention may be either the expediting or the shaping of legislation. A variety of means are used. Generally the first step will be simply to talk with the committee or subcommittee chairman. The Speaker may make a public statement and persuade the chairman to make one also. O'Neill, for example, had a long talk with Al Ullman, the chairman of the Ways and Means Committee, before the committee began consideration of the windfall profits tax. Ullman, who had expressed some reservations about the bill, subsequently held a press conference at which he said he believed the bill would pass.

Talking with the chairman and bringing some pressure to bear on the committee by expressing his interest during a press conference or by discussing the legislation in the Steering and Policy Committee is often sufficient action by the Speaker to expedite legislation. Committees seldom hold up legislation on which a strong majority of their party colleagues wants to vote—the threat of caucus instruction always lurks in the background. In addition, the Speaker frequently can set a deadline for reporting a bill: when a bill is referred to more than one committee, he may and often does so. "The Speaker's power to set time limits is a profound change," said a man intimately involved with the legislative process in the House since the

1950s. "Used with the Speaker's authority in the Steering Committee and with the authority of the majority party, it is certainly the most valuable tool in the book to help the leadership."

Leadership staff carefully monitor all major legislation. According to a senior Democrat who is not a part of the leadership, O'Neill, early in his tenure as Speaker, was embarrassed several times because he lacked information about committee decisions. He "resolved that was never going to be the situation again and he began to put together legislative review teams, an adjunct of course of the leadership's staff operation which now has become very sophisticated indeed," this Democrat explained. "And there is somebody who has access to the Speaker and/or Jim Wright at any time and these people have knowledge of all important legislation and its status." Such monitoring can provide the leadership with an early warning of trouble which makes timely leadership intervention possible. Furthermore, the presence of senior leadership staff signals the interest of the leadership to committee Democrats.

In addition to monitoring, aides get involved in trying to work out compromises among the interested parties. As a staff member explained, "You talk to members and try to find out if there is a position that can be put together with leadership backing that will move the bill." During the 95th Congress one staffer was instrumental in working out a compromise on the hospital cost containment bill, which as a result of his efforts picked up four votes in committee. (The bill nevertheless lost in committee because one member switched his vote at the last moment.) The aide explained his role this way: "I went in as [the Speaker's] agent to try to work something out on the labor pass through. [It] took about ten or fourteen days, maybe a little longer, of going back and forth and talking to people and just trying to work something out, and that did make it possible for the bill to proceed to the next step." In 1979 a Steering and Policy staffer acted as liaison between the administration and the committee on the Panama Canal Treaty implementation legislation. Another was heavily involved in the windfall profits tax. In 1981 an aide helped work out a dispute between the Budget and Appropriations committees on the Labor-Health and Human Services-Education appropriations bill. In these and similar cases the staffer acts as a facilitator, helping to put together a compromise acceptable to key interested parties—the administration during the Carter years, Democratic constituencies such as labor, a Democratic majority of the committee—and, always, to a party-based majority of the House.

The leaders frequently work through their friends on the committee. They will sometimes request that such a member undertake persuasion efforts on their behalf. "The other day the Speaker asked me to get a couple of the members to turn around on their votes in the _____ committee," a member reported. "They will sometimes get into it, saying, 'I wish you would work on so and so,' but no pressures."

The leaders also often work through friendly outside lobbyists in attempting to influence legislation at the subcommittee and committee stage. On the Humphrey-Hawkins bill, one in which the Speaker was very interested, labor and black groups helped the leaders by working to shape the legislation in committee.

On major legislation, the leadership may become personally involved, sometimes meeting with all the Democrats on a committee. During the 95th Congress the Speaker met with the Rules Committee Democrats and extracted a pledge for support of the outside earnings limit from each one. In 1979, when the Budget Committee began consideration of the first resolution, O'Neill invited the Democratic members to lunch and entreated them to save social programs. More frequently persuasion is on a one-to-one basis. A senior aide explained, "You can lean on the chairman, the ranking majority members, the key subcommittee chairmen, strong persons on the committee. . . . I think [the committees] do a pretty good job. If they don't, you can manipulate them to where they do by going to the second echelons, getting things voted out." Asked what the Speaker was doing about hospital cost containment, which was stuck in committee in the summer of 1979, another staffer said, "Well, the Speaker's been talking to the people who are against it over and over and over again. He uses the argument about the poor, the halt, the lame, and the blind and just stays on it. . . . So he brings the weight of his office and works very hard. . . . Ways and Means, he talked to them. He's doing it with Commerce now; he hasn't succeeded yet, but he's keeping it up." On the 1981 tax bill, the Speaker made it clear to Ways and Means Democrats from the beginning that he would not accept a three-year bill. "That's something he never would have budged on," an aide to a senior committee Democrat recalled. "So we knew through a series of conversations that Rostenkowski had with him, that he had with other members of the committee, that that's where our negotiations broke off with everybody on it."

Often the committee chairman will ask one of the leaders to lobby his own members. "The chairmen of committees will sometimes ask me to say a word to this one or that one on a committee that he has not been able to reach or influence," a leader said. Asked about a controversial bill still in committee, a senior staffer said, "[The committee chairman] will probably come to 'Tip' and ask for help. He will say 'We need "X" ' or 'We need two more votes and only you can get them.' " The leadership makes every effort to work in cooperation with the committee or subcommittee chairman. If the leaders believe the chairman's substantive or strategic judgments are seriously flawed, they will attempt to change his mind. For example, the leadership and most Democrats were convinced that 1981 was not the right time to make major alterations in the social security system. President Reagan had imperiled himself politically by proposing benefit cuts, and Democrats saw no reason to rescue him by making it a bipartisan effort. The leadership dissuaded the chairman of the Social Security subcommittee from joining such an effort.

In its dealings with chairmen, the leadership relies heavily on personal persuasion, but if that fails other methods may be employed. An aide explained that the leadership "may have a meeting with that chairman and bring in the people who disagree with the chairman and sort of hack it out and in the end sort of force the chairman to come to the conclusion he doesn't want to come to. That happens. You don't tell the chairman, 'Now, look, you've got to do it my way.' You call a meeting—get everybody in there and get everybody else working on the chairman—to tell him, 'This is what we've got to do to get the bill passed,' and sort of persuade him to come to your side." If such efforts fail and the party leaders believe the matter at issue to be vital, they can bypass the chairman and work on and through others on the committee. They will do so as subtly as possible to avoid embarrassing the chairman "if he doesn't want to be embarrassed." The changes in rules and norms have made such activities on the part of the leadership possible. If the chairman of the committee is supported by a majority of committee Democrats, however, there is little the leadership can do. Asked about an important bill that came out of committee in a form that O'Neill disliked, an aide said, "Once it came out, they weren't running around trying to torpedo it. That's not their type of operation. It's a rare thing, in my judgement, for the leadership to try to supplant its judgement for those on committees. Once in a while you can't do anything else. But for the most part they want to cooperate with the committee and they'll do their best in committee and accept the results."

The conflict between the leadership and the committee may not be over policy per se but over what will pass on the floor. A participant recalled that several years ago the leadership had constant trouble with one chairman and his committee:

> Every time a _____ bill came to the floor, it was hacked to pieces, totally rewritten because [the chairman] would not compromise—very stubborn old farmer. He would not compromise. He'd say, "We're going to take it to the floor and we're going to win," and he'd get his head beat in every time. They'd rewrite the whole goddamn bill. And it took weeks at a time [when] a _____ Committee bill was on the floor, taking up the time of the House, creating great animosity, dividing the party. This is the kind of stuff that committees are supposed to resolve before it comes to the floor. Most of the time they do.

The leadership will do what it can to avoid situations of this sort because they are detrimental to both party maintenance and coalition-building success. But opposing the Democratic committee majority on the floor is considered extremely detrimental to party maintenance, and the leaders seldom do so.

Leadership support at the floor stage can, however, vary in intensity. A member said that when Democrats attempt to pass a bill on the floor, "[the leadership's] attitudes become part of it, whether it's pro forma support or whether it's enthusiastic support or whether it's dramatic personal involvement." Because the floor stage has become a more active decision-making arena in which passing bills intact has become more difficult, committee Democrats increasingly have turned to the leadership for help. With their realization that the party leadership's aid is likely to be necessary comes a certain pressure on committees to report legislation that the leadership finds acceptable.

Nevertheless, even fervent leadership involvement does not guarantee success. Staff members report that O'Neill "worked really hard" to shape the 1979 tax bill in committee—yet he failed. During the 96th Congress O'Neill was unable to get legislation providing for public financing of congressional elections out of committee despite the fact that he was publicly committed on the matter. Occasionally, because of time pressures, the leadership does not get involved early enough. One participant said, "In my experience when the leadership seeks to involve itself with legislation at the committee level, it can be very effective as long as it does it early enough. People get locked in." In other cases, however, members' pursuit of their individual goals results in decisions that directly conflict with leadership wishes, and in these cases there is little the leadership can do.

Members' Views of Leadership Involvement

That leadership intervention at the committee stage per se is not perceived as a threat to member goal achievement seems to indicate a significant move away from the extreme committee autonomy characteristic of the prereform House; consequently, it offers the leadership new strategic opportunities. The leaders, unsure of how much involvement their members will tolerate, intervene as subtly as possible and on an ad hoc rather than a systematic basis. The junior members questioned by and large did not believe leadership intervention to be illegitimate, as long as it remained highly selective. One junior conservative described occasions for legitimate involvement by leaders: "If they know that an amendment is pending in committee that will be very detrimental to a bill, then they have a right to kind of discuss that and say, 'Hey, we need to defeat that.' Or they may have an amendment pending that's needed, maybe an administrative amendment." A junior member of Ways and Means elaborated:

If there's a big tax bill or social security bill or what have you, the leadership will sometimes get involved at the committee level in seeing that a bill comes out a certain way, but it only happens with very big pieces of legislation and it happens rarely. The leadership is not deeply involved in the matters that come before the committee on a day-by-day basis. I'd say maybe three times since I've been here they've really sent someone from the leadership over to follow the committee's daily activities, to work on a mark-up—the energy bills, the social security bill, the tax bill in '78 come to mind.

The windfall profits tax bill is another example of a bill that received leadership input. Significant bills are followed by the leaders, who "try to be helpful in bringing [them] out." There apparently is no feeling among junior members that this is not a legitimate thing for the leadership to do. As the junior Ways and Means member said, "I think the members want the leaders to lead; they want direction, they want to know what's going on. They want to know what the leadership wants." Senior members seem less convinced of the legitimacy of leadership involvement at the committee stage except under extraordinary circumstances, and both senior members' acceptance and junior members' endorsement of such involvement seems to be predicated upon the condition that it occur rarely. The major bills that the leadership cares about are, of course, a small proportion of any committee's work load. The current leaders thus can simultaneously intervene on important legislation and maintain the perception among the membership that their intervention is an unusual event.

Involvement in the
Budget Committee

Leadership involvement at the committee stage is most consistent on the Budget Committee. The leaders strongly feel that the budget resolution must be one that the leadership and the party "can live with." As an aide said, "It's a special relationship. [The Budget Committee has] become a sort of leadership vehicle. As [the Budget Committee] sets overall ceilings, the leadership has to be involved." And as the budget has moved to the center of controversy, leadership involvement has increased (see chapter 6).

Party loyalty seems to be given more weight in making appointments to Budget than to any other committee. At the beginning of the 95th Congress, the Democratic leadership responded to the Republicans' highly partisan approach to the budget process by prevailing upon the Steering and Policy Committee to replace conservative Democrats with more reliable members (see LeLoup 1979; Schick 1980; Ellwood and Thurber 1981). A newly appointed member in 1979 was told that his support for budget resolutions in the preceding Congress had been influential in his assignment. The House rules recognize the leadership's stake in the work of the Budget Committee by providing for a leadership appointee to it. That the leadership representative has always been the majority leader demonstrates the importance the party leadership places upon the budget resolution. Considering the time pressure under which he works, the majority leader participates actively in the works of the committee, especially at the mark-up stage.

Leadership staff monitor all of the committee's activities and sometimes become involved in working out compromises. "The committee cut out money for the administration's new countercyclical revenue-sharing gismo," a leadership's aide reported during the Carter administration. "I was sent off to try to convert two people and managed to keep in about half of it, because they recognized the Speaker has a view that they don't have and . . . they were really cooperative." In the case of the Budget Committee, the party leaders become personally involved on a regular basis. A committee leader said:

> Oh, we confer constantly. The Budget Committee and the Rules Committee, in my opinion, are both and have to be very closely allied with the leadership; in fact, [we] have to be sort of arms of the leadership, because when you put together a budget document, you're putting together a position paper. The committee leadership has to have leadership support or it won't go anyplace, so, therefore, we consult frequently and witness the fact that the majority leader is a member of the committee. . . . The conferring is with Mr. Wright on a constant basis, his being a member of the committee, but also then with Mr. Wright and the Speaker and the other members of the leadership who the Speaker and Mr. Wright decide to call in at specific times.

The legitimacy of leadership involvement in the writing of budget resolutions does not seem to be questioned by committee members. The committee is unique: it is relatively new; assignment to it is temporary, although highly desired; and the majority leader sits on the committee as a representative of the leadership. Other House committees regard Budget with suspicion and, often, hostility, and from the committee's inception the budget process in the House has been intensely partisan. Committee Democrats know that to pass the budget resolution, they must have wholehearted, active leadership support. "A budget document is obviously an economic document, but it's also a political document. And if you're going to ask for the party's help, certainly you're going to have to have the majority leadership there," a Budget Committee leader said. "Now if we had more bipartisanship, this might not be so, but in the House there's absolutely no intention of the Republicans to really buy into this process." The goal most committee Democrats pursue on the committee is, according to a student of the committee, "a process goal, that of implementing and protecting the stringent requirements of the budget process" (LeLoup 1979, p. 234). Attainment of that goal requires passing the budget resolution, and floor passage requires intense leadership effort. Budget Committee Democrats, consequently, not only tolerate but actually tend to welcome leadership involvement at the committee stage.

House Republicans

███████████████ The relationship between the Democratic and Republican leaderships in the House is largely adversarial. The minority party leadership also attempts to build winning coalitions, usually in direct opposition to coalitions built by the majority party leadership. Failures at party maintenance on the part of the majority party leadership tend to benefit the minority party. By and large, majority party leadership success means minority party leadership failure and vice versa.

During the Carter administration the Democratic leadership had limited contact with the Republican leadership or the Republican rank and file. The Republicans were not consulted about scheduling decisions, but the Democratic leaders would accede, if they could, to the occasional scheduling request made by Republican leaders. However, scheduling pressures on the Democratic leaders from their own members were intense; there remained scant leeway for accommodating Republicans. "We give them a copy of the whip notice after the whip meeting and shortly before we announce it, and we notify them of what's going on but don't include them in the decision-making process," a participant said. "They're the minority."

Most of the contact with Republicans came through leadership staff aides. This interaction was usually informal and took place on the floor. One aide said of his relationship with the Republican leadership: "I tell them what I can and [Whip] Michel does likewise, though Republicans always try to get more information than they give." Because the majority leader is responsible for a smooth flow of business on the floor, his staff was especially active in trying to discover Republican plans and stop Republicans from interfering with the flow of legislation. A staffer gave this example: "They'll be filibustering some innocuous bill, calling all kinds of quorum calls . . . and you go over and sit down with them and you find out that they're really not after that. They're after the one that's going on down the pike. Sometimes you can discern it without going and talking to them and you change it and let the word out and the filibuster will die out." During the 95th and 96th congresses much of this informal contact was not with the Republican leadership but with a group of very conservative Republicans who were extremely active at the floor stage.

Regardless of the administration, much of the information that flows between the two leaderships goes through committee leaders. Information about the minority's plans is often obtained from committee sources: "The chairman and the ranking minority member, they have to live together in committee every day, so they've got to have a good relationship. And that's where it exists; we find out what their strategy is and what's going to happen. It'll flow from the ranking minority member to the committee chairman, who will tell us. That's 99 percent of the time, that's the way it goes."

Information about the plans of the Republican "gadflies" also often came from committee leaders:

It will flow from the ranking minority member who will get wind on his side about the revolutionaries over there and what they're doing. And will tell us. Because he's not so hot for their ideas either, these ranking minority members. They aren't. They try for an orderly process too and it roils them too because they've developed a position of accommodation, of compromising in the committee and here these guys come on the floor and try, in effect, to roll them, so the camaraderie then is between the committee people rather than party. So we know ahead of time.

Of course, information also flows to the Republican leadership from committee leaders. If the Democratic leadership and a committee chairman, for example, decide to pull a scheduled bill, the Republican leadership is not kept in the dark for long. One participant observed: "The chairman tells his staff director, and if his staff director is worth a damn, he tells his minority staff counterpart because he's got to get along with him. And that feeds back to the minority leadership awfully quick."

Republican capture of the White House led to more contact between the Democratic and Republican House leaderships during the 97th Congress. Divided control always requires cross-party consultation and coordination. The longstanding friendship between Speaker O'Neill and Bob Michel, the new Republican leader, also contributed to closer contact. Interacting directly with the president was very difficult for the leadership and the Speaker believed he was upholding the prerogatives of the House by dealing with Michel rather than Stockman. Most importantly, Republican control of both the presidency and the Senate and their larger share of the House membership added weight to Republican decisions. Thus information regarding the Republicans' intentions obtained through contact between the parties became vitally important for Democratic leadership decision-making.

In March 1981, after extensive consultation, the Democratic and Republican leaderships made a formal agreement with regard to the scheduling of the components of the president's economic program. Announcing the detailed timetable on the floor on 11 March, the majority leader said, "Never before, to my recollection, have the majority and minority leaders of the House, the chairmen and ranking minority members of the committees on Budget, Appropriations, Rules, and Ways and Means, sat down together and established definite target dates for each step in the process—the budget resolution, the reconciliation bill, and such tax reductions as the Congress in its wisdom may approve" (*Congressional Record,* 97th Cong., 1st sess., 11 March 1981, vol. 127, pp. 867–68). As this comment indicates, consultation between the minority and majority parties on scheduling is rare in the House. The Democratic leaders initiated the agreement because they wanted to forestall charges that the Democratic House was obstructing the president's program—and because the Republican Senate could force their hand in any case.

This agreement aside, the consultation that takes place is primarily for informational purposes. "We talk about when things are going to come up, and in what order, under what kind of a rule," a leadership aide explained. "We may ask [Michel] what he would like, but that doesn't mean that's what he's going to get. But at least we have taken the time to sit down and talk to him and vice versa." "We try to keep them informed about what we're doing and they try to keep us informed about what they're doing," another leadership aide said. "We try to keep it civil. If you don't communicate, people may get the wrong impression about what you're doing." Like their staffs, leaders consult informally and on the floor. A participant said, "I've heard Bob Michel say, ' "Tip," I've got some of my members that are going to insist on a vote on this and are going to insist on a vote on that, so we're going to have to vote on that,' and those kinds of things are discussed. But let's be honest about it, the Speaker doesn't have enough time to meet his own appointments without meeting with those guys."

During the Carter administration the leadership made no attempt to build cross-party coalitions or to negotiate compromises with the Republican leadership. In the 95th and 96th congresses the Democratic majority was very large and the formal Republican leadership was perceived as being unable to control its membership and, consequently, to deliver. A participant explained: "On several occasions in the last Congress, John Rhodes for one reason or another agreed to support something only to find that he brought only two or three of his co-faithful with him, and at that point it became clear that he wasn't the one to deal with because he couldn't rally the troops necessarily on those occasions when we needed them or wanted to cooperate." Occasionally a committee Republican who supports the Democratic leadership's position becomes involved in a Democratic-leadership-directed effort to pass a particular bill. The involvement may include attending strategy meetings, and is most likely to occur on foreign policy matters. The passage of the Panama Canal Treaty implementation legislation and the fight for aid money for Nicaragua are recent examples. A Republican who engages in such an effort does so on his own initiative and over the intense opposition of his party's majority.

Commenting on the relationship between the Democratic leadership and the Republicans during the Carter years, an aide to the Speaker said, "Sometimes it might be easier if we could do what the Senate does, namely rely on the more moderate among the Republicans, even if it meant compromising a little bit more. Theoretically, I'd prefer that approach. Reality doesn't lend itself to that practice. I think we'd probably have to compromise more sometimes, but it might be worth it in the large. It might have the effect of diminishing the Republicans' appetite for blood."

The decreased size of the Democratic majority in the 97th Congress increased the theoretical attractiveness of constructing bipartisan coalitions because, without some support from moderate Republicans, the leadership's chances of winning floor votes were slim. Early in the Reagan administration, however, Republican unity was very high and Democratic leaders had no realistic chance of attracting moderate Republican votes. By the fall of 1981 some Republicans were beginning to have doubts about the Reagan economic program, and the Democratic leadership, mostly through agents, began to make contact with the "Gypsy Moths," a loose group of moderate northeastern and midwestern Republicans.

Contact between the majority and minority leaderships in the House, then, depends largely on the resources available to the minority for thwarting majority party goals; and minority party resources are a function of the size of the party's House membership and its control—or lack of control—of other branches of government. House rules make it unnecessary for the majority party leaders to accommodate a weak majority party as majority party leaders must do in the Senate. When the minority is strengthened, the incentives for consultation increase. Even when, as in the 97th Congress, the minority is in a strong political position, the majority leadership will consult with and share information with the minority but will seldom give it a say in the making of decisions. The relationship is predominantly adversarial and, especially when the minority is strong, the primary resources the majority leadership commands stem from its discretion over scheduling, rules for floor debate, and the like.

The Senate Leadership

████████████████ House passage, of course, is only one step in the process by which a bill becomes a law. It is to the House party leaders' advantage to expend their limited resources on measures that will complete the process, and the same is true for the Senate party leaders. Incentives for close coordination between the majority party leaderships in the two chambers would seem to exist; yet, even during the 95th and 96th congresses, when Democrats controlled both chambers, coordination was sporadic and limited.

During the 95th Congress the House and Senate leaderships met biweekly. House participants included the Speaker, the majority leader, the majority whip, the chairman of the caucus, and sometimes, the chief deputy whip. Majority Leader Robert Byrd, Majority Whip Alan Cranston, and Secretary of the Democratic Conference Daniel Inouye attended for the Senate. Despite the participation of all of the top leaders, House participants said that the meetings were not useful until near the end of the Congress. One called the meetings "worthless." Another commented, "They tend to be recitations of laundry lists and not especially productive. There are no real attempts to coordinate legislative agendas in any but the most mechanical terms with the Senate." Because of the unfavorable evaluations, no regular meetings were held during the first session of the 96th Congress, although the joint leaderships' biweekly meetings with the president provided some coordination.

Coordination becomes most critical toward the end of a congress, when difficult choices about priorities must be made. Fairly early in the second session of the 96th Congress the joint leadership meetings resumed on a monthly basis, and by late summer the two leaderships were meeting at least every two weeks. A list of priorities was hammered out, and to a large extent both chambers implemented the agreement reached. A senior staffer described the process:

> They got together with the Senate and decided what they were going to do. There's no point in the House doing it if the Senate isn't going to. All too often the House has walked the plank only to find out the Senate had no plans of taking it up. So this year things changed a little bit. In our meetings, the House was a little tougher than in past years. We put it to the Senate, "When you pass it, then we'll do it," rather than it being the other way around. That was true in a number of cases and the Senate turned around on a few. So we came up with a priority list.

According to a House participant, the meetings were fruitful because "the Senate was much more interested in getting things done efficiently than usual because of the election. Byrd very much wants to get things done so the Democrats up for election have time to campaign."

Participants offered a variety of explanations for the fact that successful coordination seems to be the exception rather than the rule. One said, "The leaderships of the two houses are very different, especially at the top level. Each institution is very jealous of its own prerogatives, and neither leader can truly speak for his body." Time constraints play a role; both the House and the Senate leaders find leading their own chamber time consuming. In addition, so long as neither the House nor the Senate leader can promise his chamber will pass a bill, each has an incentive to try to force the other chamber to act first. Neither leadership wants to ask its members "to walk the plank" on a controversial bill that the other chamber may defeat. Given the weakness of party discipline and the resultant inability by party leaders to make meaningful agreements about what their chambers will pass, the arguments for the benefits of coordination do not hold on highly controversial issues. The incentive not to make an agreement about the scheduling of such bills and to wait out the other house is especially strong for the Senate, since the Senate usually prevails in the standoff. Those who have a stake in the passage of the legislation usually direct their pressure to the House first, because no filibuster is possible there.

In view of the difficulties of leadership coordination when both chambers were controlled by the same party, it is not surprising that interaction between the two majority leadership teams fell to an even lower level when Republicans won control of the Senate. During the first nine months of the 1981 session, for example, only one meeting between the Senate Republican and House Democratic leaderships was held. "They do what they want to do and we do what we want to do and we try to agree on an adjournment date," a participant said.

The House and Senate Democratic leaderships met about once a month in the 1981 session. Participants reported that the meetings were actually more productive than those of the previous Congress. "It tends to be less of a laundry-list discussion of legislation," a leadership aide said, "and more, though certainly not entirely, a strategy session." The meetings provided an opportunity for an exchange of information. A participant revealed, "The other side asks, 'What are you guys doing on this?' and 'What are you do- ing on this?' It's amazing the lack of communication between the chambers. It's just important to hear from the horse's mouth what people think about what's going on." Thus the adverse political situation facing Democrats in 1981 stimulated more productive interchanges between the Democratic leaderships in the two chambers. Exchange of information and consultation on strategy do not, however, constitute true coordination of the two chambers' legislative business; and the Senate Democrats, even were they willing, were limited in the agreements they could make by their minority status.

The relationship between the two chambers at the majority leadership level, thus, is a distant one. Even when both are controlled by the same par- ty, the incentives for coordination are often outweighed by contrary forces. As one senior leadership aide said of the relationship between the House and the Senate, "It's a funny marriage. You walk in together, you leave together, but the rest of the time you're separated."

The President and the Administration

The party leadership's relationship with the White House and the executive branch is, of course, conditioned by the party of the president. At least since Franklin Roosevelt's presidency, whenever one party has controlled both Congress and the presidency, congressional ma- jority party leaders have considered passing the president's program to be among their central responsibilities. The president's program includes measures desired by interest groups that are traditionally aligned with the party; these must be passed in order to satisfy the expectations of both the groups and their congressional allies. Because the media focus on the presi- dent's program, the leaders and the congressional party are evaluated in terms of their success in passing the president's program. The party leaders are strong party men; they want to see the president succeed because they believe his success is important for the party. "I'm a partisan Democrat," O'Neill said during his first year as Speaker. "The President of the United States is the leader of my party" (Malbin 1977, p. 942).

In return for their support, the House leaders expect the president to consult them and to keep them informed. Congress, after all, is an independent branch of government—however close his relationship with the president, the Speaker must protect the prerogatives of the House. The prerogatives are, as O'Neill has said, "to make sure that we have input in the legislation that the President is interested in, because he is the leader of our party. And it's for us to give him our views and our voice, whether it's favorable or unfavorable. . . . The difference of opinion will never be so great that I hope that we can't get together" (Malbin 1977, p. 952).

The Carter Administration

Relations between the House and President Carter got off to a rocky start because of Carter's failure to consult. Five days after the inauguration O'Neill told Carter "You, Mr. President, should keep us posted on what the White House is doing on legislation, so that if we have responsibility for moving it, we know what is going on" (Johnson 1980, p. 155). Yet Carter decided to recommend cutting funds for nineteen water projects and to withdraw his fifty-dollar tax rebate without prior congressional consultation.

All recent presidents have met regularly with their congressional party leaders. During the Carter years breakfast meetings at the White House were held biweekly. The regular participants were the president and the vice-president; O'Neill, Wright, Brademas, Foley, and Shirley Chisholm, secretary of the Democratic Caucus, for the House; Byrd, Cranston, Inouye, and Warren Magnuson, president pro tempore of the Senate, for the Senate; and various of the White House's congressional liaison people. Various cabinet secretaries, White House staff, and selected other members of Congress were included when the subject matter warranted their input.

The meetings served primarily as a forum for exchanging information. Naturally the president can be more explicit privately than he can be in public. He made his priorities clear to the congressional leaders (the immense amount of media coverage of the president and the active Washington rumor will often obscure them) and told them what he considered unacceptable. He was also able to keep the congressional leadership up to date on his foreign policy through these meetings. The leaders, for their part, made progress reports on legislation, reported trouble spots on major administration bills, gave their assessment of the prospects of specific legislation, and sometimes requested presidential help in passing legislation. They reported to the president the strategy they were pursuing on his legislation, and he in turn told the leaders what he was doing—which members of Congress he had called, which prominent figures he had asked to send letters to members, whether he intended to give a speech. The congressional leaders also made recommendations to the president about various matters—when he should send his measures to the Hill, for example. A House leader summarized the value of the White House breakfasts:

> In a word, communication. These fortnightly meetings give the president an opportunity to communicate to the congressional leadership what's uppermost in his mind, what he sees as the big priority projects coming along in the next two weeks and to plead with us to do those things that he thinks are vital in the national interest. They give us the opportunity to familiarize him with the problems that exist in Congress, to tell him what we think the odds are on each of these matters of concern to him, to let him understand some of the problems that occur in Congress, some of the feelings of our colleagues, that he otherwise might not have thought about. So it's a two-way street and it's an opportunity on a regular basis for us to sit down and talk together, and communicate where we are and where we think we can go within these next couple of weeks. I think it's very useful.

The leaders also maintained close informal contact with Carter administration officials, most frequently by telephone, and the administration soon learned the importance of keeping the leadership informed. "[They call about an] almost endless variety of things," a leader said. "Sometimes they're calling to just advise me of something that's happening that they think I need to know about, so that I don't read it in the paper and suddenly get asked by a newsman what my reaction is and get caught flat-footed without having thought it through or having had information on which to base the comment." Administration-initiated contacts often involved a plea for assistance. The same leader went on:

> Sometimes the calls will be to ask my help in some special meeting that's coming up with the leadership in general. They'll maybe say, "See if you can put in an oar for so-and-so. We think his point of view is the right one." Sometimes it will involve a plea that I stand with them on a budget item or that I help them resist an amendment that may be offered by someone. During the budget processing time, twice annually, I'm likely to have a lot of calls from the White House. Then there are times when they'll call and want me to help them on the House floor and that's more frequent. They suddenly will be caught with a barrage of amendments. This happens annually on the foreign aid bill. So the White House comes to me. And they want me to help them beat certain amendments on the floor and I try to do that, when it makes sense.

Interaction between the leadership and the White House at the staff level was also frequent. "I meet periodically with some of the people down there to review the legislative agenda, to share notes, to look at the prospects of particular legislation," a Speaker's aide explained. "It gives me an opportunity to get a better sense of what's important to them. On a day-to-day basis there are a lot of communications among us, but it's very hard to get a sense of their priorities. I also get information on what's going on in the Senate with which I'm not as familiar as I should be." Carter's congressional liaison team spent most of its time on Capitol Hill. Bill Cable, who headed that operation on the House side, interacted with the leadership on a daily basis. A senior Speaker's aide, describing the relationship, said, "Bill Cable uses my desk and my phones and we work very, very closely. We rarely see Frank [Moore, chief of the liaison team]. But that's OK. We get our business done with Bill. And Bill Cable can walk into the Speaker's office if that door is open. So right now, the access is total, the interchange is total."

By a skillful use of its very considerable resources, the administration can contribute significantly to coalition-building success. Carter's initial reluctance to do for members of Congress the numerous small favors his office enabled him to do decreased the administration's effectiveness. House Democrats found the Carter administration recalcitrant on everything from schedule "C" jobs in the regional offices, which historically have been filled at the prerogative of congressmen, to sending birthday greetings to prominent constituents. Carter's congressional liaison office became notorious for not even answering members' phone calls. Carter seemed unaware that if he wanted members of Congress to help him, he had to help them in return, that his own success depended on his using the resources of the presidency to help members attain their individual goals. The president, as one House leader said, "was terribly naive about some very basic realities." Over time the Carter administration became somewhat more adept at dealing with Congress. The early troubles, however, had a lasting impact. Too many Democrats never developed any personal sense of loyalty to the president. This of course made the party leadership's job more difficult.

A skillful administration can use its resources to influence legislation at the committee stage. Administration officials testify before House subcommittees and committees; on bills of some importance, administration experts attend the mark-up in order to provide members with technical information as well as information on administration views. The Carter administration, many members complained, sometimes did not get involved early enough. The 1978 tax bill was frequently cited as an example. "If they're wise, they will [get involved early]," a leader said. "Unfortunately, we've seen situations in which the White House will wait until the bill is already reported by the full committee and then want to amend it. That occurred last year with regard to the tax deduction bill. After it was reported by the Ways and Means Committee, the White House decided it wasn't acceptable and came up with a proposed amendment which was offered on the House floor. It was the act of an inexperienced or thoughtless group of people. They should have been involved at the committee stage if they had wanted to influence that legislation in that direction."

A major and related complaint about the Carter White House was its failure to involve members of Congress in the formulation of its policy proposals. "Carter has been successful when he's consulted the congressmen involved beforehand—the leadership and concerned committee chairmen and others," a leader said. "This gives people a feeling they've had a part in developing the program. It's when he sends something over without talking to anyone on the Hill, where some important members may have already even come out against some of the provisions, that there's been trouble." A long-time participant in the House legislative process said, "It's the old idea, you've got to be in on the takeoff as well as on the landing." Simply informing members does not constitute true consultation, he pointed out: "I'm talking about a consistency where the White House staff, the departmental staff gets together with their counterparts up here; they really start to move through a problem. What are the problems? How do you get this through? Is this a politically viable thing to do at this time? What effect is it going to have? How do we package this? This kind of give and take, back and forth." Lyndon Johnson, according to this participant, was a master at drawing members of Congress into the program development process early, thus giving them a stake in his success. By the time Johnson publicly announced he was sending draft legislation to Congress, "everybody is cut into it from the youngest member on the Democratic side," the senior aide explained. "And the package is put together; this guy who has got a gripe has had it fixed; that guy who has got a gripe, he's had it fixed. It's fixed, in other words. This is what I mean when I'm talking about a cooperative effort between an executive and a legislature and it works."

Carter employed early consultation more frequently toward the end of his term. The formulation of his economic program in the summer of 1980 was influenced by the views of Democratic members of the House. Not only did Carter meet with party and committee leaders, he also sent his top economic policy advisors to a lengthy Steering and Policy Committee meeting. Member comments at that meeting resulted in some significant revisions in the economic program. "That wouldn't have happened in the first couple of years Jimmy Carter was here—that kind of dialogue," a senior leadership aide said. "They're making a conscious effort to do it."

White House involvement in coalition building at the postcommittee stage is discussed in the next chapter. Assessments of the effectiveness of the Carter White House operation varied; those familiar with Lyndon Johnson's operation were most critical. "You hear all kinds of views on that score,"·a thoughtful junior member said. "On specific issues, where they've really gone after things, they do a bang-up job. When they really put on a full-court press, they can do it as well as anybody can. I think they fail in not having a more consistent, long-term effort, where they deal with each member continuously—a long relationship. To give the member an idea of where they're going and why, to try to understand the member's problems, to try to communicate with him on a regular, continuous basis. I think that's where they fail."

Few participants questioned were satisfied with the White House operation. As a result, although the White House did get involved in persuasion efforts and, according to many, was sometimes helpful, the leadership bore the brunt of the effort. As a House participant said, "There's always something [the White House people] need help on. Sometimes it's the other way around. But they come to us for help much more than vice versa because the Speaker has a lot of credits, a lot of loyalty, and Carter doesn't."

Although the House leaders believe strongly in supporting a president of their own party, they also hold strong views on public policy matters, and their first responsibility is to their party colleagues in the House and to the House as an institution. Thus their support of a president is not unconditional, and it can vary in intensity. When Carter vetoed a public works bill because he disapproved of some of the water projects included, the leadership opposed him and attempted to override the veto. For Jim Wright, long a member of the Public Works Committee, the fight involved a matter of deeply held convictions. Others in the leadership believed that supporting Carter would be too expensive, as it would alienate those House Democrats hurt by the cuts. Several years after the water projects fight the memory still rankled members. "Carter wanted a fight with the Congress and with the leadership that had saved his hide on a lot of close votes," a participant said. "That was demagoging."

Carter's request that Congress lift the Turkish arms embargo split the leadership. John Brademas, the whip, who had long supported the embargo, vigorously opposed Carter; Jim Wright led the successful repeal fight; O'Neill "sat on his hands." In spring of 1980 the leadership supported Carter on his administratively imposed oil import fee, which would have translated into a ten-cent-per-gallon gas tax. The leaders attempted to keep the repeal resolution from reaching the floor, but they were unsuccessful because opposition to the tax was so intense. The leaders voted against repeal and against overriding the president's veto, but because there was no chance of victory, they did not expend their limited resources to attempt to persuade their colleagues. A senior staffer explained: "Carter hadn't sold it to anyone—to the members, to labor, to the conservationists. That's his job. The tax wasn't the leadership's program. They couldn't do Carter's job for him. There was no point in their working it. Say they'd gotten 20 votes, or even 100. You still needed 100-plus more and the people you'd have gotten would have picked up a chit and expected repayment." (The House votes on the matter were 376 to 30 and 335 to 34 against the tax.) Leadership nonsupport for Carter's legislative requests was the exception rather than the rule. Although the president sometimes had to persuade the leaders to stand behind him, he usually received active leadership support for his program. "By and large, we're on the same general wavelength and are trying to work together," a leader stated.

The probability of coalition-building success is greatly increased when the administration and the House leadership work in tandem. But because of the Carter administration's clumsy relationship with members of Congress, joint efforts were less fruitful during his tenure than they might have been. A president can enhance his chances of success by doing favors that contribute to members' reelection prospects and by involving members in the policy formulation process, which can further their policy and power goals. The broad distribution of influence in the post-reform House makes presidential sensitivity to individual members' needs even more important. Carter's problems with Congress stemmed in part from a lack of understanding of basic political realities.

The Reagan Administration

When Ronald Reagan was elected president the leadership knew, of course, that its relationship with the White House would change, that both partisan and ideological differences would introduce an element of antagonism into the relationship. Given the policies Reagan had espoused during the campaign, the Democratic leaders realized that they and the administration would often take opposite sides on domestic legislative issues. Yet the leaders still hoped for a relationship similar to that between President Eisenhower and Congressional leaders Rayburn and Johnson. In announcing the 11 March scheduling agreement, the majority leader said, "This agreement is a convincing demonstration of the capacity of responsible bipartisanship to help this institution to function at its best. It is reminiscent of the spirit of understanding and mutual trust which prevailed during the Eisenhower administration" (*Congressional Record,* 97th Cong., 1st sess., 11 March 1981, vol. 127, p. 867).

The relationship that soon developed, however, was the antithesis of a mutually trusting one. The Democratic leaders read the 1980 election returns as a mandate for a more conservative economic policy and they realized their majority was shaky; consequently, they were willing to make what they believed to be major concessions. The same factors seem to have convinced the administration that dealing with the House Democratic leadership was unnecessary. The leaders found the president unwilling to compromise with them. One of them said, "I set out with the expectation of trying to be a bridge between the Congress and the president. I wanted to make a demonstration of our ability to work with the president, to give him cooperation and to show that we could be constructive as members of his loyal opposition. That, unfortunately, has not been possible. Each time we have sought to meet him halfway, or in some cases more than halfway, he has publicly denounced our effort, claiming that it was obstructionism."

There are no regularly scheduled meetings between the House Democratic leadership and the president as there were during the Ford administration. Meetings are infrequent. "The Speaker gets invited down to the White House not more than once a month for anything serious," a Speaker's aide reported; the rest of the leadership team meets with the president even less frequently. Furthermore, on several occasions when the leaders accepted invitations to the White House they sensed, once they arrived, that they were being used. The House leaders went to a 1981 tax bill meeting that they expected to be a negotiation session, a participant explained, and found it was a press conference. "They don't consult with us *at all*," an aide concluded. A leader called that meeting a "charade" and said, "It became rather quickly apparent to those of us who were there that he had no intention of a compromise. He already had his mind set on the compromise he wanted and compromise to him meant surrender on our part."

The president's inability or unwillingness to discuss policy in any detail has further frustrated the leadership. "There have been three occasions on which we have attempted to discuss substantive policy with the president," a Democratic leader reported in June 1981. "On none of those three occasions have we discerned any real desire on his part to get into any depth. . . . He doesn't get into discussions as Carter and Johnson and other presidents whom I've known have wanted to do." An aide was blunt in his description of a meeting between the leadership and the president in September 1981: "It was more social than anything else. They did, however, have the opportunity to try to talk to the president about social security and other things. To sum up what many members, Jim Wright, Tip O'Neill, and Rostenkowski among them, have concluded in their meetings with the president, he is a nonsubstance man—he doesn't know that much."

Relations between the leadership and the Reagan administration at other levels are also minimal. "In the Carter days it was not at all unusual for cabinet officers to seek out the Speaker to discuss particular problems, and I would say that's also rare now. Of course they come with the courtesy calls, but little more," commented a Speaker's aide who also indicated that there is little contact at the staff level. One high-ranking leadership aide reported that early in 1981 the White House liaison people called him frequently but that by mid-year that contact had ceased. "It was more or less pumping each other, trying to figure out what the other's doing that day, and it turns out to be a social conversation because nobody's going to tell the other one anything," he explained. "Those phone calls have stopped and I'd say I haven't heard from them [for] at least three months." A Speaker's aide said, "There's less contact in terms of just White House liaison people walking through this office now than there was under the Ford administration."

The current low level of interaction and high level of hostility between the White House and the Democratic House leadership have not characterized all past cases of divided control. Presidents play the dominant role in determining the nature of the White House–congressional leadership relationship. Reagan's belief that a cooperative relationship with the House majority party leadership is unnecessary for the achievement of his goals accounts for the current relationship.

Interest Groups

█████████████████████ Interest groups are both allies and adversaries of the party leadership. A particular group may, in fact, be an ally on one issue and an adversary on another. Some groups have traditionally been allied with one of the parties, usually when coinciding interests over a long period have resulted in close relationships. For the Democrats, labor has a special place; as a House leader said, "Labor has for years functioned as a kind of informal adjunct of the Democratic leadership." The Washington lobbyists of the AFL-CIO are highly sophisticated politically and can be valuable allies.

The leadership is approached by a great variety of groups, not only by the traditional Democratic groups but also by business interests and others one might expect to have less frequent contact. "It ranges the full gamut," a Speaker's aide reported. Periodic meetings between some of the major groups and the Steering and Policy Committee provide a forum for a wide-ranging exchange of views. A call from an interest group to one of the leaders may indicate a need for information. The majority leader's office, for example, receives a multitude of calls requesting information about scheduling. Often the groups want some sort of assistance. "Generally speaking, they want some legislative advantage by way of scheduling, timing, maybe a word dropped," a leadership aide commented. "It's only rarely that they seek direct, substantial involvement with a committee's deliberations. A word spoken to a chairman can be effective. They want help with a bill when it comes to the floor, of course, but there are lots of stages before that." One leader revealed that labor lobbyists call him frequently: "They call about scheduling, they want help with amendments on the floor, they want me to talk with someone on a committee."

The traditionally Democratic groups can usually assume that the party leadership shares their policy views. Often when these groups call the leaders their purpose is not policy persuasion, but activation. A leadership aide indicated that the lobbyists for the AFL-CIO are highly influential: [The AFL-CIO] are kind of an ad hoc but nevertheless strong part of the whole Democratic party apparatus and have been for forty years, fifty years. They'll many times just assume that they don't have to ask Jim to support them on something. . . . But they don't mind asking for the extra things. They might stop short of asking him to make a speech for something that they knew he would be reluctant to do because they don't like to be turned down either, but they can generally depend on the Democrats' support. Mainstream Democrats vote labor most of the time." Because of the decline in intercommittee reciprocity and the consequent greater amending activity on the floor, unexpected amendments are frequently offered. When a friendly group's interests are threatened by a surprise amendment, the group will often call the leadership for help. "Sometimes we get a call from a lobbyist, the head of the AFL-CIO or something, and he'll say, 'Oh, oh, they've sprung a Davis-Bacon provision, strike Davis-Bacon,' " a majority leader's aide explained. "You have got to go down to the Speaker and be sure [he and his staff] know and, if you can, get Wright to work the well or work the door."

The relationship between the House leadership and interest groups is not one-sided. Interest groups lobby the leadership, but the leadership also lobbies interest group representatives. Leadership lobbying may simply involve attempts to persuade usually friendly groups not to oppose the leadership position on a matter in disagreement. During the spring of 1979, for example, labor was unhappy with the budget resolution the leadership supported. Labor believed the spending figures for social programs were too low, but the leadership believed the tight budget was a political necessity. A number of meetings were held at which the leadership attempted with mixed success to persuade AFL-CIO representatives not to oppose the resolution. The leadership also sometimes works to activate interest groups, to get them involved in a legislative battle. On the Panama Canal Treaty implementation legislation, the leadership and the administration tried to involve affected groups—shippers and maritime unions, for example: An organized and successful effort to activate interest groups was made on synthetic fuels legislation during the 96th Congress. As they came to the floor to vote on the legislation, Democrats found a mass of labor lobbyists at the door of the chamber urging support of the legislation; Republicans had to wade through a crowd of business supporters of the bill. Interest group resources can provide an important supplement to leadership resources in the coalition-building process. A group with strength in a member's district is often more persuasive than a leadership figure.

The relationship between the leadership and the traditional Democratic groups, especially labor, thus, is a symbiotic one. As one leader said about labor, "It's a two-way street. If you help them, they'll help you with lobbying members on things important to the leadership." Experienced groups lobby extensively at the subcommittee and committee level. Activity of this nature by friendly groups can be of considerable benefit to the leaders since it saves them from having to expend their own resources in attempting to influence legislation at this stage. On those occasions when there is a coincidence of interest, the leadership will also work with groups that are not usually friendly. Time constraints and the lack of established lines of communication, however, hinder close cooperation with such groups and restrict it to the most major efforts.

When the leadership and a given interest group work together to pass an important bill, the character of the cooperation depends on the level of trust between the leadership and the group and on the leadership's evaluation of the group's political sophistication. The extent to which a group's representatives are involved in the planning of strategy and the amount of credence placed in the group's information about members' voting intentions vary widely. Because of their long-term working relationship with the leadership and their reputation for political expertise, the AFL-CIO lobbyists are more likely than the representatives of other groups to be taken into the leadership's confidence.

Vote counts taken by interest groups, it is generally agreed, are not as good as member-to-member counts. A staffer intimately involved in the counting process explained:

> I pay attention to it, but I don't *rely* on it. Because the people aren't, for the most part, experienced vote counters and they tend to hear what they want to hear. Because members are practiced at not making commitments. The guy will get up from behind his desk and put his arm around a lobbyist and say, "Well, I think that this has been a fascinating presentation and I think your argument's persuasive and I'd really like to be with you on this." And they walk out and say, 'Well, he's all right," and the hell he is—he's not. Because if he was he would have said so. But he didn't. That's the dead giveaway—"I'd like to be with you."

Even the AFL-CIO lobbyists miscounted on the common situs picketing bill. They believed they had 225 votes, enough to pass the bill. The leadership told them its count showed only 205 pro votes. The leadership nevertheless acceded to labor's request to schedule the bill. A leader explained, "We told them they would lose, but they didn't believe us. We had to schedule it because if we didn't they would always think they could have won and we'd done them out of it." The bill was defeated on a 205 to 217 vote. A staffer attributed labor's miscount to a partial reliance on reports from the locals.

Although the information provided by even the best lobbyists is not considered as good as a member-to-member count, it is nevertheless useful. It allows the leadership to double-check its data on Democrats and to get some reading on Republican votes. "The groups talk to both sides all the time," a staffer said. "Their information isn't as good as the members' information because people lie to interest groups a lot more readily then they will to their fellow members. But you can still get an idea. You can't rely on it, and you sure wouldn't count on it to pass it, particularly when it's a political bill like CETA. But that doesn't mean you can't get any information at all—you can."

Interest groups friendly to the leadership's position can and do lobby Republicans—which the Democratic leadership cannot do. A leadership aide said that lobbying groups were sometimes "motivated" by the leadership to work on Republicans. During the 1960s, this aide said, "Clarence Mitchell of the NAACP would always take the Republicans with big black constituencies in cities and go to work on them. And that was the key to passing civil rights bills." The leadership relies on the large and diverse education lobby to produce Republican votes on aid-to-education bills.

Interest groups, then, are often useful allies of the leadership. They provide information and, to the extent that they can claim to speak for a significant segment of a member's constituency, their persuasion efforts have a force the leaders' efforts lack.

Recent trends, however, especially the proliferation of narrow interest groups, are of considerable concern to the leadership. The Democratic leadership has always had to contend with strong opposition groups that have competed with the leadership for the votes of Democratic members. But during the 1970s the number of groups increased enormously; many of the new groups are concerned with exceedingly narrow issues and many have become highly sophisticated. A senior staffer commented:

> I've been here a long time and I would say one thing has definitely changed. I don't care what you are for, the sunflower seed association, everybody has a lobbyist. They're proliferating at a level and at a speed that's almost beyond that of light and I think they make an enormous difference. They capture the media, and between the lobbyists and the media, they give poor congressmen hell. They do a lot of research; they try and find out who the key people are, find out how a congressman is vulnerable in his home district, and they go after him and they make it very, very difficult for him.

Persuading members, each of whom represents a small geographical area, to fashion legislation beneficial to the whole of society was difficult before the proliferation of interest groups, he continued, and the large number of groups has compounded the problem and has contributed to the decline of parties: "What these people do with the pressure groups, they take an already very difficult, paradoxical situation and they exacerbate it by their activities. That's why the situation has gotten worse. Now you get a guy who is good to his so-called lobby groupies and looks good on the tube, he's got it made. He doesn't need the Democratic affiliation, nor the Republican affiliation. I think that's the erosion of the party."

Some of the internal House reforms have interacted with the proliferation of interest groups to make the leadership's job more difficult. Open committee mark-ups seem to have increased the influence of interest groups at the committee stage. A member of Ways and Means said of the open mark-ups, "It was supposed to protect the public but has just opened it up to much more pressure. You've got a room full of interest group representatives and they are experts, specialists. We aren't, we're general practitioners. During mark-ups, you'll hear the buzzing as members confer with lobbyists, especially on the front row [where the junior members sit]." The leaders and their professional aides also are generalists and thus are at a disadvantage vis-a-vis expert lobbyists who can concentrate their effort on a single issue.

5

COALITION

BUILDING:

STRATEGIES

AND

TACTICS

Deciding to Get Involved

▬▬▬▬▬▬▬▬▬▬ Constraints on the leadership's time and resources prevent the leadership from becoming involved in every piece of legislation. The leadership uses the bill's importance and the expected closeness of the struggle to determine its level of involvement. In the highly unpredictable postreform House, judgments about the closeness of the vote are often hard to make, and the danger of expending precious resources inefficiently is a very real one. A senior leadership aide said, "The list (of options) comes together pretty naturally. The problem is to cut it down. This partly depends upon where victories are possible. We don't want to waste effort on a losing cause."

Some legislation is of sufficient importance that the leadership has little choice but to get involved. The leaders consider it their responsibility to pass a Democratic president's major legislation because they believe their reputation and that of the Democratic party rests on doing so. Expected closeness of the fight still affects the leadership's level of resource expenditure. If the leaders anticipate no trouble or if they think winning is completely impossible, they will not mount a massive effort. Even in such cases, however, the leadership will be involved. At the least, leadership staff will carefully monitor the legislation. Under a Republican president, the leadership has somewhat more discretion in "picking its shots." If the president's program represents a direct challenge to core Democratic party principles, however, as it did in 1981, the leadership must respond with an active countereffort. The leadership is consistently involved in legislation of central importance to major segments of the House Democratic membership and to traditional

Democratic groups. The leadership's reputation also rests on its ability to uphold the reputation of the House as a functioning legislature and, to this end, the passage of debt limit increases and budget resolutions is crucial. Although they were not highly visible outside of Washington until recently, these measures have been very difficult to pass and have required a massive leadership effort.

Other, less critical, legislation engages the leadership depending, in part, on the leaders' personal policy preferences. For example, because of his interest in the subject, Jim Wright has been involved in foreign affairs issues beyond the requirements of his leadership role. He has consistently sought to protect foreign aid bills from unwanted floor amendments, and he took the leading role on the politically perilous issue of aid for Nicaragua. With some legislation, the leaders will receive a call for help from the floor manager, to whom the leaders will lend their support if they believe it "makes sense." Because of limited resources, they cannot comply with all such requests, yet providing aid at the floor stage is a significant favor and contributes to party maintenance.

Shaping the Preconditions
for Floor Success

■■■■■■■■■■■■■■■■■■ Any effort at coalition building takes place within the context of the House's ongoing institutional life. The leaders' relationship with their members is a part of that context, and this relationship influences the leadership's probability of winning specific legislative battles. The leaders, by drawing members into close contact with themselves via the whip system, the Steering and Policy Committee, and more informal means, give members the sense that they have influence on leadership decisions (see chapter 3). Even the leaders' service activities (discussed previously) are aimed at shaping a favorable climate for future coalition building. By doing favors for members individually and providing services to them collectively, the leaders accumulate implied IOUs and develop a reservoir of good will. In addition, information crucial to effective coalition building is often gained as a by-product of these leadership activities.

Among more specific determinants of floor success, the condition of a bill when it emerges from committee is extremely important. As the discussion in chapter 4 indicated, the leadership gets involved at the committee stage on major legislation. The involvement is usually subtle, and the leaders try to work with the committee chairman. The postreform House's tendency to "mark-up" legislation on the floor has made such involvement more necessary, for if a bill is seriously flawed politically when it reaches the floor, anything can happen.

The reforms have made leadership intervention possible not only by weakening the authority of committee chairmen, but also by providing the leadership with some new tools. A 1974 rules change allows the Speaker to recommend the formation of ad hoc committees and, if the House approves, to appoint the membership; this prerogative is a potent tool for influencing legislation at the pre-floor stage (see Vogler 1978). For example, use of this device was instrumental to House passage of Carter's energy package in the 95th Congress. Components of the package were first referred to five standing committees under a reporting deadline. The ad hoc committee then reviewed the components and was given authority to recommend amendments for consideration on the floor. In selecting the membership of the ad hoc committee, O'Neill paid careful attention to regional and ideological balance, but he also made sure that the committee had a pro-leadership majority. Because the Speaker appointed the membership, leadership involvement in the committee's proceedings was perceived as legitimate. A senior member of the committee, commenting on the Speaker's intervention in the committee, noted the Speaker's special vantage point:

> If I was an adjunct as I suppose I was of the leadership, then I had to have recourse to the leadership and say, "Look, you can obviously vote any way you want, but this is the leadership position." . . . In order to get a resolution to it, it was necessary to get these enormously different sectional views in some kind of an arena that offered at least a hope of resolution, and that, in some instances, was in the Speaker's office. . . . It isn't that we were going after each other like alley cats, it's just that upon occasion we thought that there was no operating room, and in that kind of a situation we had to go back and put it in a somewhat broader context for the Speaker. He was no expert on energy, but he is a bit of an expert on the perspective of the overall House. . . . And we are looking at those trees and he was much better able to see the forest and get us away from the specific trees and change the orientation a little bit.

Despite its advantages, the ad hoc committee device has seldom been used. The standing committees oppose the encroachment on their jurisdiction which ad hoc committees represent; thus frequent use would be detrimental to party maintenance. Except under extraordinary circumstances, if the leadership wishes to influence legislation at the pre-floor stage, it must do so by intervening in the proceedings of the standing committees. Although such leadership intervention is much more feasible now than it was in the prereform era, the standing committees are generally less receptive to leadership intervention than are Speaker-appointed committees. The leadership, then, can sometimes influence, but it certainly cannot control, the form in which a bill emerges from committee.

Strategy and Logistics of the
Pre-Floor Persuasion Effort

■■■■■■■■■■■■■■ A series of strategic decisions must be made by a bill's supporters before the bill reaches the floor. Under what type of rule should the bill be considered? Should a whip count be taken? What sort of effort should be mounted? When should the bill be scheduled? On bills of lesser importance, the leadership may not be involved in making these decisions except in the most routine fashion. The leaders take an active role on major legislation, however, and the crucial decisions may be made well before the bill is reported from committee—or even before committee consideration begins.

Designing the Rule

The party leadership involves itself in the designing of rules only on particularly important and problematical legislation. Communication between the Rules Committee and the offices of the Speaker and majority leader is almost continuous, but its purpose is coordinating scheduling and exchanging information more frequently than designing rules (see chapter 3). If the chairman of the Rules Committee is experienced and skillful, direct leadership involvement in rules formulation is seldom necessary. The leaders are always informed of the intentions of Rules on legislation of consequence, and sometimes the committee clears its plans with them. In the 96th Congress, for example, the committee chairman "asked whether [the Speaker] had any objections if he went the way Udall wanted him to go" on the Alaska Lands Bill. He was given a negative response despite the fact that Udall was opposing the committee majority. A coalition of Republicans and conservative Democrats on the Interior Committee had defeated Udall, that committee's chairman. In such a case, the Speaker did not believe he had to support the committee majority. By acquiescing in a rule that favored Udall he in fact helped the committee minority, which included a majority of Interior Committee Democrats. A senior staffer indicated that leadership involvement in the design of rules occurs when necessary, which is "when it's a national Democratic program. When you have a difficult bill. When you have a bill that the Democrats are going to have a hard time holding because the Republicans plus a minority of their own party may take it out. Where you have particularly contentious issues among senior Democrats who are at each other's throats on something and you've got to structure it as best you can so that neither side feels slighted. Most bills don't need that attention, but the toughies do; I mean, that's the definition of a 'tough one.' "

From the leadership's point of view, rules that place restrictions on the amendments that may be offered can be extremely helpful because such rules reduce uncertainty at the floor stage. Rules can also sometimes be designed to give the leadership position a strategic edge. Every rule, however, must be approved by a majority vote on the floor, and one thrust of the 1970s reforms was against restrictive rules. Consequently, the leadership must be careful in its use of such rules. A leader said:

> So long as it is not an amendment which would be ruled out of order under the rules of the House, the member is inclined to feel, I think, that he or she ought to have the privilege of offering it on the House floor. Now a modified closed rule, for all intents and purposes, would limit that freedom. So you've got to weigh orderly, expeditious processing against the individual rights of the members. There are trade-offs; therefore, I think modified closed rules ought to be employed only on rare occasions where you have a piece of legislation of major national importance that needs to be considered expeditiously in an orderly way, and it shouldn't just be employed willy-nilly on every piece of legislation that comes to the floor.

Sometimes a highly restrictive rule offers the only real hope of leadership success. The rule for consideration of the energy program conference report in the 95th Congress was vital to its passage. The rule specified that a vote be taken on the package as a whole; separate votes on less popular components were barred. Passing this rule was difficult; the vote on the previous question* on the rule was 207 to 206. Once the rule was approved, however, members were faced with a straight up-or-down vote, and the conference report was adopted by a vote of 231 to 168.

In 1977 and again in 1979 carefully designed rules were used to structure floor choices on congressional pay raise bills. Most members, of course, want pay raises but hate to vote for them. Especially in difficult economic times, pro-votes on pay raises are hard to explain to constituents. But passage of the 1977 pay increase was crucial to O'Neill's prestige; he had promised members the pay raise if they would pass the tough ethics code. In 1977 the rule allowed for a vote on only one pay raise amendment. Consequently, to kill their own raise, members would have also had to deprive top-level executive branch officials of a raise. This packaging changed members' decision-making calculus, and the pay raise was approved. The national budget-balancing mood of 1979 dimmed the prospects of an across-the-board pay raise. The rule allowed only one amendment, which lowered the

---

*A vote for the previous question is a vote to end debate. A vote on the matter being debated (the rule in this case) is then the next order of business. If the motion to order the previous question on a rule is defeated, the successful opponents of the motion may then propose their own rule.

congressional pay raise from 7 to 5.5 percent. The amendment was approved but the legislative appropriations bill of which it was a component was then defeated.

The budget-balancing mood also threatened the debt limit increase sought by the president in the spring of 1979. Debt limit increases are always difficult to pass, but in this case an additional problem emerged. Phil Gramm and Jim Jones, conservative Democrats, proposed amending the bill so that, except on a vote of two-thirds of both chambers, the debt limit could not again be raised until the federal budget was balanced. The parliamentarian advised the amendment's sponsors that the amendment was not germane, so Gramm and Jones requested that Rules make the amendment in order. Rules refused their request on a straight party-line vote. Gramm and Jones then decided to attempt to defeat the previous question on the rule, which would allow them to amend the rule. The leaders, unsure of winning the previous question vote, still preferred that the test come on the previous question roll call than on the Gramm-Jones amendment. As Gramm said, "The leadership wants the confrontation to come on a procedural vote where they have a better chance. People can say, 'I'm for it, just against the procedure.' On a straight up-or-down vote [the amendment] would pass." The leadership won a narrow 201 to 199 victory on the previous question. It is in this way that the Rules Committee majority and the leadership working together can sometimes structure the floor situation so that the key vote occurs on a procedural rather than a substantive matter. Because procedural roll calls are less visible, members are more willing to follow party lines, and as a result the majority party leadership is more likely to prevail.

Complex rules on major legislation require careful political calculation. Although members are more likely to follow party lines on procedural than on substantive roll calls, they can and do vote down rules they consider unfair. In designing such rules, the Rules Committee has to bear in mind that the rights of all significant segments of the membership must be protected. The leadership is involved in the making of such decisions; and, since the use of complex rules is on the increase, so too is leadership involvement in the design of rules. The rule for consideration of the first budget resolution in 1980 and that for the 1981 reconciliation bill are particularly notable examples. In 1980 a budget resolution was for the first time considered under a restrictive rule. The decision on which amendments to allow was made at a meeting of the leadership and the chairman of the Rules Committee. The most important strategic decision in the battle over the 1981 reconciliation bill was that on the rule. The leadership eventually decided that its chances of victory would be best if members were forced to vote separately on the various budget cuts the president wanted. The Rules Committee reported out such a rule, but Reagan managed to focus sufficient public attention on what is usually a low visibility vote to defeat the previous question. (For a discussion of the 1980 and 1981 rules decisions see chapter 6.)

A variety of factors has led to a significant increase in the use of complex rather than simple open or closed rules (see chapter 3). As a result, when any given rule is being written, there are more and more complicated choices, and the decisions made can significantly affect floor success. The design of the rule for a major bill is now often a critical element of legislative strategy.

Taking a Whip Poll

The Speaker decides whether a whip poll will be taken. According to a staffer in the whip's office, "The committee chairman normally requests [a whip poll], and sometimes the decision is made solely by the Speaker and sometimes it's made collegially by the leadership. There are certain things that are just understood we [will] count, such as budget resolutions." Most major bills will be counted, as will less important ones if there is reason to suspect trouble. Sometimes, however, a strategic decision to avoid a whip count will be made. "Sometimes a whip count can hurt you; it alerts members that maybe there's some reason they should vote against [a bill]," a participant explained.

Timing the whip count correctly is important. Normally the count is taken after the bill has been reported from committee, when it is about to be scheduled for floor consideration. "We try to time it early enough so that you've got time to work after you've got your data base," an aide said. "If we come up with a poll on the morning that the bill is coming up and it says we're going to lose by twenty votes, that's interesting but it hasn't fulfilled the purpose of the thing, which is to be able to prevail with our position. And on a tough bill, you normally need more than a day, or more than three or four hours." The count, then, must be taken early enough for there to be time to work the bill but late enough for the right question or questions to be asked. The less predictable floor that currently exists has made early discernment of the key voters more difficult. Sometimes it is necessary to delay a poll until the political situation has clarified—until Republican strategy has become evident, for example. Furthermore, an early count may not be accurate because members have not yet focused on the issue. A zone whip explained:

> Members of Congress have so much to do, and they have their fingers in so many pies, that they don't really have time to play theoretical games like, If so and so were going to be brought up, how would you vote on it? You bring in some question as a bolt out of the blue, you get a whip advisory and attached to it is a little whip question that says, Ask the members in your zone how they would vote on this amendment. Well, I look at it, and I try to keep up with what's going on, and it's the first time I've ever seen it. Well, I can logically

assume that it's also the first time every other member in my zone has ever
seen it. He doesn't know how he's going to vote. And there's no point in my
asking him how he's going to vote if *I* don't even know how *I'm* going to vote.
I say, "How you going to vote?" and he says, "How are *you* going to vote?
What is it?"

Special circumstances sometimes compound the problems involved in
deciding when to take a poll and what to ask. In the summer of 1980 the
reconciliation bill was stuck in the Rules Committee. Until a rule was
granted, deciding what question to ask was impossible, but by the time the
rule was granted, a poll would no longer have been useful because persuasion efforts were so far advanced (see the case study in chapter 6). Counting
the vote on Carter's stand-by gas rationing plan in the spring of 1979 was
difficult because Carter kept changing the plan to accommodate the Senate.
"It was tough to say from one day to the next what the 'it' was that we were
going to vote on," a whip's aide remarked. The 1981 tax bill presented
much the same problem. Both the Democratic and the Republican alternatives were being revised almost until the day of floor consideration. Given
high uncertainty, a bill will sometimes be counted more than once. "You
may find that you've asked the wrong question," a participant stated.
"Things have changed. Or that you may have asked the right question, but
then there's another question that needs to be asked too that is equally
important."

The regional whips poll their zone members; "riding herd" on the whips
so that they will complete that task in a timely fashion is one of the jobs of
the whip's office. The count results in a division of Democrats into support
categories: right, leaning right, undecided, leaning wrong, wrong, absent,
and not contacted. The whip poll conducted by the zone whips provides an
initial "data base." The next step depends on the type of effort the leadership has decided to mount.

A Typology of Vote
Mobilization Efforts

The highly unpredictable environment in which the current leadership
operates requires more extensive vote-gathering efforts on its part. In order
to procure help in coalition building for the core leadership and in order to
satisfy members'—especially junior members'—expectations of meaningful
participation in the legislative process, O'Neill has developed the strategy of
inclusion, whereby he attempts to involve as many Democrats as possible in
the coalition-building process. A major effort in which many members are
brought in is, however, time consuming. An efficient allocation of the leadership's limited resources requires gauging just how much leadership
involvement is necessary to pass a bill intact, a difficult task in the postreform House.

One can, without being too arbitrary, isolate four types of vote mobilization efforts. In committee-centered efforts, Democratic committee leaders bear the primary responsibility for passing the legislation, but the party leadership is available to help in case of trouble. Joint committee-party leadership efforts are characterized by shared responsibility for the planning and implementation of floor strategy. Informal inclusionary efforts are those in which the party leadership and committee leaders involve other interested members. Task force efforts are characterized by the Speaker's appointment of an ad hoc group that he charges with passing a specific bill.

Committee-Centered Efforts

Committee-centered efforts are the most common. Even quite important bills are often handled in this fashion as long as they are not leadership top priorities and are not expected to present unusual trouble. Appropriation bills and foreign aid bills usually fall into this category. A whip count may have been conducted, after which the appointed whips receive names of those who need some persuasion. An aide to the majority whip explained, "I'll just cut up the list, we put the names on little cards and send them around. Or I'll take them in my pocket on the floor and give them to the deputy and at-large whips and say, 'Will you talk to these people?' and so forth." The top leaders may also take some names.

Significant bills handled in this fashion are usually ones on which passage is not in doubt; amendments are the problem. If asked to do so by the floor manager, the whips and sometimes the majority leader will work the doors on particularly troublesome amendments. In some cases no request is necessary; everyone knows where the trouble spots are and that some leadership help on the floor is needed. A leader commented on foreign aid bills: "You know, that's a demogogue's delight. It doesn't have any constituency. Nobody's for it; everybody's against it. Every time it comes up every year, there's a long hassle on the floor, while amendment after amendment is considered. If all of them were to be accepted, you'd wind up with the most utterly unworkable kind of bill. So I try to help."

Joint Committee—
Party Leadership Efforts

When the party leadership and committee leaders jointly plan floor strategy, a second level of leadership effort is reached. The consultation may be relatively informal, but it usually involves a meeting to discuss the results of the whip poll and plan floor strategy. "The Speaker may just call up four or five of his people and those he's got to have, and he and the majority leader and others will meet with them and they'll thrash it out," a senior aide explained. "It can be done very informally, in the hall or on the floor."

Time-consuming formal meetings are justifiable only if the bill is of some importance and nonroutine strategic decisions need to be made. For example, the 1979 Taiwan legislation necessitated by Carter's official recognition of China and his break of official relations with Taiwan presented some unusual problems. The bill had to be passed quickly and in a form that did not conflict with the United States' agreement with China. Yet the legislation was unpopular in the House, and the introduction of a great many amendments, some of them "killer" amendments, was anticipated. O'Neill responded to the administration's call for help by assigning a Steering and Policy Committee staffer to monitor the bill in committee and work with the administration to assure that the committee bill was acceptable. When the bill emerged from committee the leadership had at its disposal full information on the trouble spots and was able to play a meaningful role in making strategic decisions on amendments. It knew that the defeat of all amendments that gave the United States' presence in Taiwan any sort of official status was essential. Some senior Democrats on the Foreign Affairs Committee were less than enthusiastic about the administration's position, and as a consequence leadership involvement was extremely important.

A bill that requires leadership involvement in strategy planning almost always requires refinement of the initial whip count. "You don't go out and do a poll," a staffer said, "and then lock it up like George Gallup does. These are not Gallup polls." The count taken by the zone whips only provides a base line—its results require interpretation. "We look at the distribution of members who are causing the trouble," a whip's office staffer said. "Is it a regional group or spread all over the party? We try to figure out which interest groups are putting on the pressure and which are with us." The initial count is then refined by recontacting those Democrats who were recorded as not being committed to the leadership position as well as members whose proleadership response "looks funny." "If you get a tough whip count and the members don't want to say how they'll vote, you keep going back to them," a leadership aide revealed. "Or use somebody else on them. You follow-up, time and time again, with other members or with the leadership or constant phone calls." The deputy and at-large whips receive a list of names and are asked to report back to the whip's office with their findings. Their job is persuasion as well as information gathering. A whip's office staffer described the process: "You start rolling that list over, constantly. As people come back and say, 'I talked to so-and-so and he said this,' you check him off as OK or continue to work him, send somebody else to see him, and you keep rolling the list over and over and over until you get where you want to be."

If the appointed whips are to be effective at persuasion, they must understand both substantively and politically the legislation on which they are working. In a move to increase the appointed whips' information, the majority whip in 1980 instituted special meetings prior to the regular Thursday morning whip meetings. These meetings, which include only the appointed whips, do not occur every week, but are scheduled as needed. Their purpose is to provide a forum for conveying information on specific legislation to the appointed whips and for discussing strategy. The bill's floor manager usually attends and briefs the appointed whips on the substance of the legislation, on the areas he expects trouble in, and on the arguments he believes likely to be most persuasive.

Informal Inclusionary Efforts

When a higher level of effort is deemed necessary, the party leadership and committee leaders enlist the involvement of other interested members. Those brought in may be junior members of the committee of origin or members with a special interest in the legislation. This somewhat more formal process is likely to include several scheduled strategy meetings, and staff will serve as information conduits among the many members involved.

This type of coalition-building effort actually spans a broad range in terms of intensiveness and extensiveness. On one end of the spectrum is the annual effort on the foreign aid appropriations bill. A fairly standard floor scenario has emerged for this bill, and as a result no particularly complex strategic decisions need to be made. In addition, the leadership knows in advance which members are committed to the foreign aid program and are willing to work on the appropriations bill. Thus, in 1978, for example, the effort began only a few days before the bill was to be considered on the floor and involved members who had worked together on the matter in previous congresses. A leader said, "I did try to elicit all the help I could get—we organized a little committee and successfully warded off most of these really mischievous amendments last year."

The efforts on the 1979 Panama Canal Treaty implementation legislation and on the 1980 and 1981 reconciliation bills represent the other end of the spectrum. In these cases, the leadership involved itself at the committee stage. Strategy planning and persuasion efforts were begun weeks before the bills reached the floor (for full discussions, see chapters 6 and 7). An aide described the special effort required on the 1981 tax bill, another bill that demanded a high level of leadership involvement:

> We took a subcommittee room down the hallway and we stripped the walls, we collected staff from all over, the committee, personal staffs, and some Ways and Means members, Steering and Policy Committee staff, leadership staff, some of the lobby organizations, trade associations that were helping us pass the bill. And we had the walls filled with charts with all the Democrat members' names, where they were. You name it, we did it and we made it sort of like the control center. Now a lot of it was for PR purposes. We wanted to

show the administration that we were serious about this, and while we didn't have the resources at our command, in a comparable way with the administration, we were certainly giving it everything we had. . . . It was a very coordinated thing really. Steering and Policy, leadership, individual members, staffs, outside organizations, all working under the aegis of this boiler room thing. Every time you went in there, four people were on the phones and the charts were on the wall and we were there till midnight.

Task Force Efforts

The fourth type of effort is an O'Neill innovation. On certain bills that the leadership considers both centrally important and difficult, the Speaker appoints a special task force, an ad hoc group that is charged with passage of the bill. The leadership believes that task forces, the ultimate expression of the strategy of inclusion, provide both immediate and long-range payoffs. By increasing the number of people working in an organized way to pass the bill at issue, a task force increases the probability of success on the bill. If the membership of the task force is broadly representative and thus includes members with ties to all segments of the party, the chances of success are further increased. In the long run, giving a large number and a wide variety of Democrats "a piece of the action," but under the aegis of the leadership, and thus giving them a stake in the leadership's success will, the leaders believe, make those members more responsive to the leadership generally. Work on a task force is thought to be especially likely to influence junior members, to teach them the value of joint action under the aegis of the party.

The basic notion underlying the task force concept—that of joint organized effort to pass a specific bill—is not new. "People have been doing task forces of one kind or another for a hundred years or more," a senior aide stated. "Any time that there's an interested group of people, they're going to get together and work on it in some kind of common front." The informality of the more traditional arrangements distinguishes them from the current Speaker's task forces. A senior staffer closely involved in the process observed that early in the 95th Congress, O'Neill's first as Speaker, the leadership had narrowly lost an important bill. The formally designated task force was the Speaker's response to the loss, which the leaders were convinced resulted from a lack of organization.

The decision to appoint a task force is solely the Speaker's, although he may do so on the advice of other leadership figures or staff. He will, of course, confer with the prospective floor manager of the legislation. A Steering and Policy Committee staffer described how the decision is made: "You see, we all have our committee responsibilities. If we see a bill coming up out of committee and think, Oh, oh, we've got real trouble, if it's sufficiently major, then you go to the boss. Then a determination has to be made: Is it that important? Now if it is that important, do we want to play it this way [establish a task force]? Will it have a better chance if we don't call too much attention to it, or will it have a better chance if we work it hard? All those things are taken into consideration." Another senior staffer listed the types of bills for which task forces are formed:

> They are significant leadership issues where the Speaker has some prestige on the line, and, much more importantly than that, where the core of the party has to have the bill. Now, that's pretty easy to pick out. You look down the list of bills which came up in the Congress and you'll find the eight or ten bills that really had to pass. We had to have the budget, we had to have the debt ceiling; some elements of the party had to have Humphrey-Hawkins; CETA comes in the same bag; energy, the Democratic party had to have; a tax bill we had to have. And you look down the list of other bills, and I would guess that there aren't any that if they had not passed they would have done as much damage to the party or to the leadership or to the House, the Democratic members of the House, as those bills if they had not gone through, so that's how it's done.

A different staffer made the same point in the imperative mood: "They should be used only on significant legislation that is clearly part of the Democratic Party program." Table 5.1 lists all task forces appointed during the 95th and 96th congresses. The bills for which these task forces were established are ones on which trouble was expected and ones that the Democratic party as a whole or some significant segment thereof "had to have."

Table 5.1

SPEAKER'S TASK FORCES, 1977-80

Task Force	Chair	House Vote (yes, no)	Democratic Vote (yes, no)	Date
Energy Organization Act (HR8444)				
Natural Gas	Sharp, Inc.	199–227*	72–210	8/3/77
Plowback	Gibbons, Fla.	198–223*	74–208	8/4/77
User fees	Mikva, Ill.	221*–198	212–68	8/5/77
Passage	Sharp, Ind.	244*–177	231–50	8/5/77
Social Security (HR9346)				
Fisher amendment	Fisher, Va.	386*–38	257–24	10/26/77
Pickle amendment	Tucker, Ark.	196–221*	74–206	10/26/77
Passage	Gephardt, Mo.–Tucker	275*–146	235–46	10/27/77
Conference report	Gephardt–Tucker	189*–163	174–54	12/15/77
Humphrey-Hawkins (HR50)	Rose, N.C.	252*–152	233–41	3/16/78
First budget (S. Con. Res. 80)	Derrick, S.C.	201*–197	198–61	5/10/78
Debt ceiling (HR13385)	Gephardt, Mo.	205*–202	196–74	7/19/78
Second budget (H. Con. Res. 683)	Derrick, S.C.	217*–178	215–42	9/16/78

Table 5.1—*Continued*

Task Force	Chair	House Vote (yes, no)	Democratic Vote (yes, no)	Date
CETA (HR12452)	Miller, Ca.-Oberstar, Minn.-Mineta, Ca.			
Obey amendment		230–175*	114–152	8/9/78
Jeffords amendment		221–181*	101–162	8/9/78
Passage		284*–50	206–18	9/22/78
Tax (HR13511)	Gephardt, Mo.			
Kemp amendment		177–240*	37–237	8/10/78
Passage		362*–49	224–47	8/10/78
Energy (HR5289, HR5037, HR5263, HR5146, HR4018)	Sharp, Inc.			
Previous question on rule		207*–206	199–79	10/13/78
Adoption of conference report		231*–168	185–81	10/15/78
Debt Limit (HR1894, HR2534)	Gephardt, Mo.			
Previous question on rule		222*–197	221–44	2/28/79
Passage		194*–222	191–73	2/28/79
Previous question on rule		201*–199	200–54	3/15/79
Passage		212*–195	209–53	3/15/79
First budget (H. Con. Res. 107)	Mineta, Ca.			
Passage		220*–184	211–50	5/14/79
Conference report		144*–260	108–152	5/23/79
Conference report		202*–196	174–80	5/24/79
Second budget (H. Con. Res. 186, S. Con. Res. 36)	Mineta, Ca.			
Passage		192*–213	188–67	9/19/79
Passage		212*–206	212–52	9/27/79
Chrysler aid (HR5860)	Blanchard, Mich.	271*–136	209–48	12/18/79
Second budget (H. Con. Res. 307)	Gephardt, Mo.	205*–195	195–55	6/12/80

Source: Task force membership lists.
*Indicates leadership position.

President Carter's top domestic priority during the 95th Congress was passage of a comprehensive energy program. His prestige and that of the party and the leadership hinged on success in the energy area, but the leadership knew passage would be difficult because energy policy deeply splits congressional Democrats along consumer versus producer lines. As a consequence, a full-fledged task force was appointed on the Energy Organization Act. The task force for this bill, the first bill to receive the treatment, consisted of three subgroupings, each charged with defeating or passing a key amendment. The Senate drastically changed the energy legislation so as to make final House approval more difficult. Liberals were extremely upset by the gas-pricing section, and House approval of the conference report rested on passage of a rule that prevented a separate vote on that section. The anticipated closeness of that vote made an organized task force effort necessary.

Both the president and the party leadership considered legislation to place the social security system on a sound financial footing among the priority domestic items of the 95th Congress. The steep increase in social security taxes that this entailed resulted in a far from popular bill. The social security task force consisted of subgroups charged with responsibility for specific amendments. The Fisher task force was charged with passing an amendment deleting mandatory coverage of federal workers. The passage of the amendment by an overwhelming majority makes that task force something of an anomaly. A staffer who worked with the task force explained that the preliminary counts had not shown such a large margin and, further, that the drastic consequences of failure had made a major effort necessary. "The crucial thing is, what if it hadn't [passed]? We had no social security bill, plain and simple," he said. "It had to pass and, while most people would say the chances are 9 out of 10, it was not a situation where one was willing to take that 10 percent risk."

The steep increase in social security taxes which the social security bill mandated made it politically advisable to pass a tax reduction bill before the 1978 elections. The form, not the passage, of tax legislation was at issue. Representative Jack Kemp (R-N.Y.) and Senator William Roth (R-Del.) had received extensive publicity for their proposal to cut income taxes by 30 percent, and the leadership knew Kemp would offer the proposal as an amendment to the tax bill. Its obvious appeal combined with what the leadership saw as drastic consequences if it should pass led to the establishment of a task force charged specifically with defeating the Kemp amendment.

The reputation of the House Democratic leadership rests, in part, on the success of leaders in gaining passage of a Democratic president's priority legislation. It also depends on the leaders' ability to uphold the reputation of the House as a functioning legislature on less highly visible matters. Two areas that have been especially problematic for the leadership are the biannual conflicts over the budget resolution and the recurrent fight to raise the federal debt ceiling. In a time of high inflation, successful coalition building in these areas has become increasingly difficult. Both budget resolutions and debt limit votes offer congressmen nearly irresistible opportunities for grandstanding. An intensive and well-organized vote mobilization effort has become a prerequisite to success on this legislation.

The remaining bills on which task forces were established between 1977 and 1980 were bills of central importance to a major segment of the Democratic membership. Big city liberals needed the Humphrey-Hawkins bill and the CETA bill, and both of them seemed to be in deep trouble. Michigan Democrats and other members with Chrysler plants in their districts considered the Chrysler bail-out bill a "matter of life or death." Because of its relatively narrow range this bill fits the criteria for the establishment of a task force least well. The Michigan Democratic delegation, it was reported, "begged" the Speaker to establish a task force. The task force technique, then, has generally been restricted to significant legislation on which the prestige of the leadership and the party as a collectivity were on the line as well as bills badly needed by a major segment of the party.

Once the decision to establish a task force has been made, the Speaker appoints the chair. Staff may suggest one or several names, or the Speaker may ask the chairman of the relevant committee for the name of a "bright young guy who would do a good job on this." All but the first task force were chaired by junior members, members first elected in 1972 or later. Dick Gephardt of Missouri chaired several task forces during his first term. Junior members are chosen in part because they have more time to devote to the task than senior members, who have heavier committee responsibilities. In addition, giving junior members an important job to do and drawing them into the leadership's orbit are aspects of the strategy of inclusion. One of the leaders said that an effort was made "to pick members who will stay around, who intend to make a career of the House." The chair is usually though not invariably a member of the originating committee.

The Speaker frequently suggests names for part of the membership of the task force, but he also gives the chair considerable discretion to include anyone else he would like to work with. In selecting the membership, the task force chair works closely with the Steering and Policy Committee staff, who provide staff work for the task forces. Over time the selection process has become rather elaborate. Prior to a meeting between the chair and Steering and Policy staffers, the latter prepare a list of potential members, including their record of support on similar legislation. Commitment to the legislation in question, of course, is a prerequisite to membership. Within that constraint, attention is paid to getting "regional, seniority, and ideological balance." An effective task force must include members with ties to all sections of the party and, especially, ties to those elements that will require the most persuasion. As a task force chairman explained: "It just depends, you know, in the roller-coaster politics of the Hill whether at that given point in time your task force is composed of people who can logically expect to be listened to by the people you need to reach. And you may reach the conclusion that this is a great task force but 'you guys ain't the ones we need' to pick up the votes that we don't have. So then you go out and get the Speaker to help you solicit more bodies to serve on the special task force."

Although inclusion is an objective of the task force concept, passing the bill at issue is paramount. Task forces must be a manageable size. The fourteen task forces under discussion averaged twenty-eight members, ranging from the sixteen-member CETA task force to the social security task force and the energy conference task force, each of which had forty-one members.

An analysis of all 95th and 96th Congress task force memberships reveals the extent to which the aim of involving in the legislative process a large number and variety of Democrats, especially junior members, is actually met. During the 95th Congress 40.3 percent of the Democrats (116 members) served on at least one task force (see table 5.2). There was considerable membership overlap among task forces. One in five Democrats served on two or more task forces during the Congress. Although fewer task forces were established in the 96th, approximately 30 percent of the membership (81 Democrats) served on a task force during that Congress; one in eight Democrats served on two or more.

Table 5.2

REGIONAL REPRESENTATION ON TASK FORCES

Number of Task Forces Served on	95th Congress		
	Percentage of All Democrats	Percentage of Northern Democrats	Percentage of Southern Democrats
0	59.7	58.7	62.7
1	19.4	22.1	12.0
2	8.7	6.6	14.7
3 or more	12.2	12.7	10.1
Number of Task Forces Served on	96th Congress		
	Percentage of All Democrats	Percentage of Northern Democrats	Percentage of Southern Democrats
0	70.7	67.6	79.2
1	17.0	19.6	9.7
2	5.8	4.9	8.3
3 or more	6.3	7.8	2.8

Source: Task force membership lists.

Note: The total number of Democrats in the 95th Congress was 288; there were 213 northern Democrats and 75 southern Democrats. The figures for the Democratic membership of the 96th Congress are 276, 204, and 72, respectively. Border Democrats are included in the northern category.

The strategy of inclusion refers not only to involving a large number of members but also to including members from all sections of the party. Overall, the task forces have been fairly representative in terms of region. In both the 95th Congress and the 96th Congress, 74 percent of the Democratic membership was from northern and border states and 26 percent from the South (see the first note in chapter 1 for the regional categorization). The average northern and border membership across the fourteen task forces was 77.5 percent; the average southern membership, 22.5 percent. The regional balance on each task force varied but only one task force was highly unrepresentative: no southerners served on the CETA task force. It seems the unpopularity of the program made southerners unwilling to work for the leadership position on the bill.

Table 5.2 presents data on the proportion of northerners and southerners who served on task forces during the 95th and 96th congresses. Southerners were less likely to have served on a task force than northern and border Democrats, but the differences are not substantial. The leadership has succeeded reasonably well at including southern Democrats in the coalition-building process via task force membership. In fact, a larger proportion of southern than northern and border Democrats served on two or more task forces during the 95th Congress. Clearly those southerners willing to participate are given opportunities to do so.

The requirement that task force members be committed to passage of the bill in question prohibits strict ideological balance, just as it makes absolute regional balance somewhat difficult. As one would expect, task force members as a group are more loyal to party than non–task force members. Considering each of the fourteen task forces separately, and using *Congressional Quarterly* party unity scores, one finds that members of a task force have a higher average party unity score than nonmembers and that this pattern holds for both of the regional groupings. The differences between task force members and nonmembers are especially great among southern Democrats.

Table 5.3 displays party unity scores broken down by frequency of task force membership and region. Democrats who served on one task force are, as a group, appreciably more loyal (with a unity score of 78.4) than those who served on none (68.4), and those who served on two or more, slightly more loyal (79.6) than those who served on only one. The difference in party unity between those who served and those who did not is especially marked for southern Democrats. Nevertheless, task force members are relatively heterogeneous ideologically. Southern Democrats who served on task forces are significantly less loyal as a group than northern Democrats who did not. The leadership finds it possible on specific bills to involve members who otherwise frequently defect—a few Democrats who are generally highly disloyal have served on task forces.

An interesting outgrowth of the strategy of inclusion and an indicator of the decline in committee insulation in the House is the committee make-up of the task force membership. Although the chair usually is a member of the originating committee, a majority of the task force membership is not. Excluding the two energy task forces (for which the figures would not be meaningful), on the average 31.5 percent of task force members are also members of the committee reporting the bill.*

*The energy bill was referred to five standing committees and to the Ad Hoc Committee. Of the members of the first energy task force, 64.3 percent were from Ways and Means or Com-

Table 5.3

PARTY UNITY

(By Frequency of Task Force Membership and Region)

	95th Congress					
	Number of Task Forces Served On					
	None		One		Two or More	
Group	Unity Score	Number	Unity Score	Number	Unity Score	Number
All Democrats	68.4	171	78.4	56	79.6	60
Northern	77.0	124	81.2	47	84.9	41
Southern	45.6	47	63.8	9	68.2	19

	96th Congress					
	Number of Task Forces Served On					
	None		One		Two or More	
Group	Unity Score	Number	Unity Score	Number	Unity Score	Number
All Democrats	72.5	194	84.5	47	85.3	34
Northern	79.0	137	86.1	40	88.7	26
Southern	57.0	57	75.2	7	74.3	8

Sources: Task force membership lists and the *Congressional Quarterly*'s party unity scores. Scores have been adjusted so that absences do not affect them.

Note: Border Democrats are included in the northern category.

The subgroup of members of the social security task force charged with passing the Fisher amendment included a number drawn from the Post Office and Civil Service Committee. Since the Fisher amendment concerned federal workers and thus was related to the Post Office and Civil Service Committee's jurisdiction, the inclusion of members from that committee on the task force was a recognition of their legitimate interest in that aspect of the bill. That case, however, is the exception and not the rule. On other task forces, members who were not from the originating committee held positions on a wide variety of committees. They were congressmen with an interest in and a willingness to work for the bill in question.

A primary aim of the task force concept is involving junior members in the coalition-building process on the leadership's side. That objective has clearly been accomplished. During the 95th Congress 51.7 percent of the Democratic membership had begun their service in 1973 or later, and on the average 69.4 percent of the members of that Congress's nine task forces

merce, the two committees with major jurisdiction, and 44.4 percent were from the Ad Hoc Committee. On the second energy task force, 22 percent were from Ways and Means or Commerce and 26.8 percent from the Ad Hoc Committee.

were drawn from this junior group. Democrats first elected in 1972, 1974, or 1976 accounted for 45.8 percent of the party's members and for 60.1 percent of the membership of the first two task forces in the 96th Congress. Freshmen constituted 15.2 percent of the Democratic membership and 18.5 percent of those serving on the two earliest task forces in that Congress. The first task force of the 96th Congress was set up only one month after Congress convened, yet freshmen were included in it: 12.1 percent of the debt limit task force membership consisted of freshmen. Of the budget task force established in late spring, freshmen constituted 25 percent of the membership.

The relationship between task force membership and seniority can be seen in table 5.4. During the 95th Congress slightly more than one-half of the Democrats first elected in 1972 or later served on at least one task force. Junior members also were more likely than their senior colleagues to be frequent task force participants. The same holds true in the 96th Congress: junior members were more likely both to have served on a task force and to have served on multiple task forces than senior members. The leadership has been successful in involving a large proportion of Democrats generally, and of junior members specifically, in task force efforts. Membership has been drawn fairly proportionately from northern and southern members and, to some extent, from conservatives as well as liberals.

Table 5.4

SENIORITY REPRESENTATION ON TASK FORCES

| | 95th Congress | |
Number of Task Forces Served on	Percentage of Senior Democrats	Percentage of Junior[a] Democrats
0	70.5	49.7
1	16.5	22.1
2	5.8	11.4
3 or more	7.2	16.8

| | 96th Congress | | |
Number of Task Forces Served on	Percentage of Senior Democrats	Percentage of Junior[a] Democrats	Percentage of Freshmen Democrats
0	75.0	67.5	69.0
1	21.3	16.7	7.1
2	1.9	7.1	11.9
3 or more	1.9	8.8	11.9

Source: Task force membership lists.

Note: There were 139 senior Democrats and 149 junior Democrats in the 95th Congress. In the 96th Congress there were 108 senior, 126 junior, and 42 freshman Democrats.

[a] First elected in 1972, 1974, or 1976.

Strategy Planning

According to one experienced Democrat, most committees try to report out their bills in a form they believe acceptable to a majority of the House: "During the debates on a piece of legislation, at mark-up in committee, that is the constant theme: Can we get it passed on the floor? So a great deal of accommodation is done within committees external to, or free from, any pressure by the leadership. The bill that comes out of subcommittee is almost inevitably modified by the full committee. And the major modifications are in terms of how much we can accept to assure passage without doing violence to the intent of the bill." Nevertheless, a bill sufficiently controversial and important to require extensive leadership involvement is ipso facto not assured of easy floor passage. Its fate may well depend on the strategic decisions made before it reaches the floor, among the most important of which are decisions on how to handle various expected amendments: Does the whip count or other information indicate that an amendment can be defeated? Is an amendment so disastrous to the integrity of the bill that an intense effort to defeat it must be mounted? If an opposition amendment has sufficient surface appeal to make it difficult to defeat on an up-or-down vote, can it be amended so as to make it innocuous?

The "amending to harmlessness" tactic has become standard operating procedure on foreign aid bills. An amendment to prohibit aid to some unpopular country will be offered; a member of the Foreign Affairs Committee will then offer an amendment to the amendment which adds a clause to the effect that the original amendment is binding "unless the president decides it is against the national interest." If it is adopted, the amendment to the amendment "pulls the teeth" of the original amendment. The tactic makes it unnecessary for a congressman to cast a vote that would be difficult to explain back home; a vote that could be interpreted as favoring foreign aid for Syria, for example, would pose a problem in almost any district. The same tactic was used on the Panama Canal implementation legislation: the floor manager offered what he called "a Zablocki–Foreign Affairs type amendment" to a major killer amendment and thus defanged it (see chapter 7). Another version of the same tactic involves offering a mild and not very specific substitute for an amendment considered unacceptable. This tactic allows members to go on record as being in favor of some popular objective without doing damage to the bill. In 1978 the leadership knew Republicans planned to offer an amendment to the Humphrey-Hawkins bill setting an inflation goal of 3 percent. The proposal seemed to be picking up support in the days before the vote, so the leadership countered with a substitute. Offered by Majority Leader Jim Wright, the successful substitute required that the president annually set inflation goals. Wright's offering the amendment was itself the result of an important strategic decision, and it placed the full imprimatur of the leadership on the substitute.

Parliamentary tactics occasionally can be used to block opposition amendments. Nongermane amendments can be ruled out of order, but members usually have sufficient information to craft germane amendments. The leadership's control of the Rules Committee means, however, that waivers for nongermane amendments opposed by the leadership will not be granted. House rules specify that only four forms or degrees of amendments can be pending on the floor: an amendment, an amendment to the amendment, a substitute amendment, and an amendment to the substitute (Oleszek 1978, p. 119). Sometimes this restriction can be used to block an amendment. A participant explained: "In order to prevent an amendment that you know is expected, you'll come along and recognize either a leadership figure who gets recognized first or a member of the committee who is senior to whoever is going to offer this bad amendment. You'll come along quickly and offer your amendment first as a strategic move to fix it so his amendment can't be amended further. And so you take up the slack that way." If the leaders are confident that an amendment will be dropped in conference, an all-out fight to defeat it on the House floor may not be necessary and may, in fact, be counterproductive. If the strategy is to drop an unwanted amendment in conference, a recorded vote will be avoided if possible because the conference agreement is easier to justify if the House has not gone on record in favor of the deleted amendment.

Decisions about how to handle various amendments must be made in light of overall strategy on the bill, which must be consonant with the political situation in the House. On Humphrey-Hawkins, for example, it was decided that intense effort should go into defeating amendments because, as a participant reported, "All you had to do was have one big bad amendment and the bill was finished. . . . Too many didn't want to vote for it anyway [so] that, if you gave them a chance to say, 'Well, it's got this bad amendment on it now'—no bill. You had to win everyone." In contrast, strategy on the 1978 CETA bill involved simply preventing amendments that totally gutted the program. Passage of the committee bill without change was the preferred outcome, but in the case of CETA, "the continued existence of the program was very much in doubt." A compromise, discussed later in this chapter, was required in order to get any bill at all.

Sometimes it becomes evident that, because the committee misjudged what would pass the House, or because the political situation changed after the bill was reported, a postcommittee compromise on substance is necessary to obtain passage of the bill. Usually committee leaders fashion the compromise under the general oversight of the leadership. After the Chrysler bail-out bill was reported out of committee, the need to toughen the bill became manifest. It appeared that the Senate would pass legislation requiring much more stringent sacrifice from Chrysler workers and that in the House too many members regarded the committee bill as a "cream puff." Consequently, the decision was made to draft a "toughening" amendment for the committee to offer on the floor. The administration, the

United Auto Workers, and the Michigan Democrats, with the task force chair in the lead role, negotiated a compromise that proved to be instrumental to passage of the bill. Another occasion for compromise arose when the 1977 social security bill reported out of Ways and Means made participation by government workers mandatory, a provision the leadership considered politically untenable. "Why that came out of the House committee the way it was I'll never understand," a participant said. "There was never a hope to pass that and, whatever you thought about it, it was just poor politics." Consequently, the leadership decided that an amendment deleting the provision would be offered on the floor.

Vote Mobilization

Once the initial strategic decisions have been made, the organized persuasion effort can begin. Strategy is subject to revision as information is gathered or as a response to new events. The type of effort being mounted determines the next step. If a task force has been appointed, an initial meeting will be called which typically will begin with a "pep talk" by the Speaker. "The Speaker launches them; he meets with them; he urges them on," a participant reported. "He's in a better position than anybody else in the House to have the most information, so he can help to steer in the right direction on what needs to be done and what doesn't need to be done." The top leaders are ex officio members of every task force. Their frequency of attendance at meetings depends on personal interest, conflicting commitments, and just how much trouble they believe the bill to be in. When the leaders cannot themselves attend, they send senior aides in their stead.

At the first meeting, strategy will be discussed and the task force members will be assigned a list of Democrats "they will be responsible for working throughout" consideration of the bill. Usually, though not always, the whip system conducts an initial count for the task force. In the absence of a whip poll the task force will take a count, so a decision on which votes to count is sometimes made at the initial meeting. The counting process has been complicated by the large number of amendments offered in the postreform House. The large number of bills for which the whip system conducts polls demands that the questions asked by the whips on a given bill be restricted in number and fairly simple. Task force members concentrating on a single bill can collect and convey more information. "Task forces are especially helpful if the issues involved are very complicated substantively and you really need to run an information campaign to inform members," a leadership aide reflected. "And where there are lots of possible permutations and you need to really get a 'feel' for the members—that is, what they'll do under a variety of circumstances."

When the zone whips conduct a whip poll, they only count. For task force members, counting and persuasion are always combined. Consequently, the process differs only slightly if the task force begins with a whip poll.

According to a leadership figure: "We'll kick around arguments—discuss which ones will be good with which members. Then we'll go through the whip poll and assign names. The list of names will be read, and a member will say, 'I'll take that one.' Or maybe no one will volunteer and someone will say, '_____, why don't you take him?' and _____ will say, 'I don't want to.' But finally all the names will be assigned." Or, as a senior staffer expressed it, "There will be candid discussion until they pin down where the 'trigger' is."

Region and seniority are the primary bases for assigning names because, according to the participants questioned, they are the primary bases on which friendships form. "Let's say _____ from Washington is a member of the task force," a task force chairman said. "You want to give _____ the Washington and Oregon types. If you give him South Carolina and Mississippi, there's no camaraderie there, so to speak." "It helps to have a contemporary doing the lobbying," another task force chair said. "I'm going to feel a greater sense of kinship with people who came here when I did" (Davidson and Oleszek 1981, p. 196). The belief that members will be more successful at persuading their contemporaries provides an additional reason for the large junior component of task force memberships.

Sometimes more ephemeral relations among members provide the basis for the assignment of names. A member explained: "I might say I'll take him because he's a young fellow who is on my subcommittee and he's got a bill that he wants me to hear in my committee and, you know, he'll listen to me real carefully right now. He'll pay attention if I call him. Or you don't want me to call that guy because I opposed his amendment last week on the floor and, you know, he wouldn't listen to me very carefully at all." As in other vote mobilization efforts, finding the "trigger" may mean going outside the House. According to a staffer, one of the ways of "motivating" members is via outside groups: "To get ____'s vote, you get Kenny Young [of the AFL-CIO] to call him."

If the leadership effort does not include the appointment of a task force, a meeting to assign names may be called, or the assignments may be made more informally. If the effort consists mainly of people who have been involved on similar bills in the past, a meeting may not be necessary. A whip's aide explained:

> The bigger, the more consequential, the issue the more likely there will be a meeting. It will be the Speaker, Jim Wright, Brademas, Rostenkowski, Foley, and other key people, certainly the floor manager. The best function of these meetings is to discuss substance and the political aspects—the arguments to be used, strategy. It's really a waste of time to assign names at these meetings because the same people always take the same names—so I can do it. If there's no meeting I assign names, mostly to the [appointed] whips, but also to other key people who are interested in the legislation.

The criteria for assigning names are the same as those used by task forces. A whip's office staffer said, "Sometimes [it's done] geographically, sometimes by who knows whom, a mixture of things. Ideology, region, all those things." Members who are recorded as being firmly opposed to the leadership position are usually contacted. A task force chairman described how the issue also determines who is approached:

> On the debt limit, there are a certain group of people that we know are going to vote against it, no matter what. They have always voted against it; they have proclaimed their intent to always vote against it for whatever reason. And so you pretty well leave them alone. And you deal with the people who have at least shown the willingness to vote for it at least one time. On the budget, everybody's fair game because the budget has so many elements in it that attract or don't attract people that you can't write anybody off. And everybody has voted for a budget at least once somewhere along the line.

Once the initial assignment of names has been made, whether through a task force or not, the one-on-one persuasion begins. A wide variety of arguments is used. "You can argue the substance, you can argue the politics of it; you can argue party loyalty, you can argue personal friendship, you can argue any variety of things all mixed up together sometimes," a participant said. Because substantive arguments play an important role in persuasion efforts, task forces are especially useful on complex bills. "Normally the reason a task force is set up is the thing is substantively complicated in a way that's going to take a lot of explanation, a lot of argument, and you try to get people working it who have more than ordinary knowledge of what's involved," an aide explained.

In their persuasion effort, members emphasize the "consequences, political and to the country, of a wrong vote" and add an appeal to party loyalty. A member described the typical arguments: "You say, 'We're asking you to vote for this, not only because it's a good idea, not only because it's a bill that came out of the committee, but because it's a Democratic party position and the Democratic Steering and Policy Committee has unanimously endorsed it and we would ask your loyal support of the Democratic party position.' These are the kinds of things that you say. How you say it depends on the individual you're talking to, but that's the message you try to get across."

Arguments vary with the bill at issue. On budget resolutions and on the major energy bill, for example, the carefully balanced nature of the committee product is emphasized. About persuasion on debt limit votes, a participant remarked, "You ridicule the opposition arguments, minimize the (electoral) impact, and appeal to their sense of responsibility." When a constitutional amendment banning busing was discharged from committee, persuasion efforts placed emphasis on the irresponsibility of amending the Constitution in such a casual fashion. When the Reagan administration came up with a last-minute substitute to the reconciliation bill written by the committees, Democrats argued that approval of the substitute would represent a threat to the power of the House and to the integrity of the legislative process. Sometimes a fortuitous circumstance provides an effective argument. In 1979 a number of members were pushing an amendment to the foreign aid bill which would have sent United States observers to Rhodesia for its election and would have authorized $20 million in aid to that country. Some of the amendment's proponents justified the $20-million expenditure on the grounds that Rhodesia needed the money to help fund its election. Supporters of the Carter administration, which opposed the amendment, were provided with an obvious and effective counterargument through one of the amendment's major Democratic supporters, who was a prominent opponent of public financing of congressional elections. This member, they said, seemed to believe in publicly financed elections in Rhodesia but not in the United States. This line soon made the rounds, and the member's subsequent—and quickly abandoned—attempts to lobby Democrats were greeted with laughter.

The most persuasive argument also varies from member to member. A participant remarked: "It's very individualistic, you go by instinct. Members have different motivations. Some you have to puff up. _____, you tell him he'll get credit, that he's a leader. _____, you persuade him he's being patriotic. Others, you persuade them it's the devious thing to do politically. Some you have to convince it's the liberal thing to do; others, that it's conservative." Southern Democrats asked to persuade their generally conservative regional colleagues have the most difficult assignment. A southerner with a reputation as an effective persuader talked about his technique and its limitations:

> You can go to the well just so many times, and if I really go all out, I can get a substantial majority of the members in my zone to vote for almost anything once or twice a year, but you can't do it on everything that comes down the pike. You can say to the other members in your zone, "Look, this is _really_ important, I know that it's not going to be the most politically popular thing with us, but I'm going to do it," and I usually know who the other people in my zone are who will go along on most things, but I get at least three or four of us who I know are going to go, and then I say, "Well, I'm going to do it and this one's going to do it. If we can all do it together it will minimize any impact that it has." And we are able to do that several times a year.

As work on the persuasion effort continues, members contact the Democrats assigned to them and then report back their results. A progress meeting may be held, during which the names of congressmen now committed to voting with the leadership are marked off and the remaining names, if necessary, are reshuffled. On a difficult bill, this process continues until floor action is completed.

The top leaders always participate in the persuasion effort by taking some names. One of the purposes of a task force, however, is to minimize the number of members the top leaders must persuade. They are busy, and their personal appeals for votes are most likely to be effective if they are not made too frequently. Consequently, an attempt is made to save the top leadership, especially the Speaker, for "the tough ones." A member described task force procedure and the role of the leadership within it:

> You just physically go to your weak spots and see if you can change them and, if you can't, you then present all this to the Speaker and let him make the decision as to whether or not this is somebody he wants to call on the telephone. As a practical matter, the Speaker could pass an awful lot of legislation around here if he did nothing but stay on the phone, calling members asking them to vote for something, but he ain't got time to do that, so that's why the leadership functions have to logically spread out under him. And work like this task force work is basically a delegation of authority from the Speaker, and the majority leader of the party, to the workers to make the contacts.

The leaders, of course, bring the prestige of their offices and the backlog of favors they have done to their persuasion efforts. They also make it their business to know as much as possible about individual members' political situations. The "key" to effective persuasion, according to a leadership aide, "is knowing how far you can ask an individual member to go. For that, you must know his district. That's why [the leaders] travel." In addition, there are some arguments only the leaders can use. A leader said, "Often you can get a chairman by saying, 'It's a party issue and since you got your chairmanship from the caucus, you should vote with us. If you vote against the party too often, you might have trouble in the caucus.' "

Whatever the type of effort mounted, the floor manager is involved. If a task force has been appointed, the floor manager is always invited to the meetings. A top leadership figure envisions the relationship among the party leadership, the floor manager, and the task force this way: "The leadership is the general staff, the floor manager the battlefield general, and the task force the company commanders." Generally floor managers appreciate the help the task force provides, and the floor manager and the task force chairman seem to work together well. The prospect of a smooth working relationship between the task force chair and the floor manager is no doubt an important consideration in the Speaker's choice of the task force chair. A task force chairman described his relationship with the floor manager, who was also the committee chairman: "Well, of course, Chairman _____ sat in on every one of these sessions. So he saw whatever strategy we were developing within the task force and could say, 'Hey, I don't think you ought to be doing that.' Whenever I had a chance before going into the meetings, I'd try to check with him on certain things. I'd say, '_____, this is what we're thinking about doing; what do you think?' He'd say yes or no." Another said, "My experience has been that the chairman of the committee is an integral part of the task force effort, but his focus is on actually shepherding the bill through, dealing with the procedure, managing it on the floor, et cetera."

Occasionally the relationship is not so smooth. In one case the chairman of the committee and the chairman of the task force disagreed about major aspects of the bill at issue. Inconsistent signals from the Carter administration had led to a generally confused legislative situation. On the matter at issue between the two chairs, the task force membership itself was split. The primary charge to the task force, however, was to defeat a particular Republican amendment, and on that the task force and the committee chairman did manage to work together. "Even people who are getting divorced will get together to stamp out a rattlesnake in their tent," a participant remarked. "But that doesn't mean that the marriage is going to go real well from then on."

When time and circumstances allow, an effort is made to work with friendly interest groups. When a task force has been appointed, its chairman may meet with interest group representatives to coordinate strategy. The chairman of the task force on the Humphrey-Hawkins bill, for example, met with about forty interest groups. During the budget battles of 1981 members of the leadership and Budget Committee leaders met with numerous interest group representatives. One open gathering, just before the vote on the reconciliation bill, turned into a mass meeting because it attracted so many lobbyists. Interest groups are a useful supplemental source of information on members' voting intentions.

The leadership generally does not share the results of its whip polls with interest group representatives, as an accurate count depends on keeping members' responses confidential. Nevertheless, on really tough issues the leadership may need interest group help and wants interest group efforts to be targeted efficiently. In such cases the necessary information is usually conveyed to the appropriate group via the floor manager. As one participant explained, "That's kind of a sensitive thing because we don't want the members to think we're giving away their names to other people. Most of that's done on a committee level anyhow. We tell [the committee chairman] this guy won't give us an answer and he says, 'I'll take that one.' And he gives it to the educational lobbyists—he deals with the educational lobby everyday and he knows them; he's working with them to get a bill through."

If the bill is of central concern to powerful interest groups, their lobbying effort can be of immense help. Both the Chrysler Corporation and the United Auto Workers were deeply involved in the effort to pass the Chrysler aid bill (*Congressional Quarterly Weekly Report,* 17 November, 1979, pp. 2582-83). Chrysler sent top executives to Washington to meet with congressmen and hired Thomas Boggs, a prominent Washington lawyer and the son of Congresswoman Lindy Boggs and the late Majority Leader Hale

Boggs, to lobby Democrats; William Timmons, a former Nixon and Ford aide, was hired to lobby Republicans. In addition, Chrysler attempted to activate its 19,000 suppliers and its local dealers to lobby. United Auto Workers President Douglas Fraser joined the UAW's Washington lobbyist in his efforts. "Fact books" outlining the impact of a Chrysler bankruptcy on individual districts were sent to all congressmen.

In this instance the task force chairman coordinated the interest group effort with the very intense task force effort. The task force met repeatedly and pored over the voting lists at each meeting. Most of the task force members had a direct constituency interest in the bill, and they worked it extremely hard. They were "very intent upon getting absolute commitments," and those congressmen not yet committed were often visited by a number of task force members as well as by interest group representatives. "They may be overdoing it," an aide said. "At the last task force meeting, there were some reports that members were complaining about the intensity. But this is life or death to the Michigan people."

With Chrysler, the UAW, and such groups as the NAACP, the Urban League, and the U.S. Conference of Mayors supporting the bill, the arguments could be carefully tailored to fit each congressman's vulnerability. The impact on large cities and especially on blacks was emphasized to liberals; government's responsibility through regulation for Chrysler's problems and government's resultant responsibility to help the company was the argument presented to conservatives. The impact on jobs was stressed with Democrats; the impact on the business climate with Republicans. New Yorkers were reminded that Michigan Democrats had supported aid to New York City. An opponent of the legislation described the effect: "You have a situation where all of the [lobbying] elements push different legislators in the same direction. . . . Each group [of legislators] one would expect to oppose the bill is neutralized by one of these interests or another" (*Congressional Quarterly Weekly Report,* 17 November 1979, p. 2583).

The Carter White House's involvement in vote mobilization efforts varied with the legislation at issue. Because Bill Cable spent a great deal of time in the Speaker's rooms, he was aware of leadership strategy on a day-to-day basis. The Carter liaison team, however, was never an integral part of the strategy planning group as the Kennedy and Johnson liaison teams had been. "[The White House liaison people] will not usually attend the strategy meetings," said a leadership aide. "They will talk to the Speaker separately. They are usually content to leave the details to the House leadership. They will lobby individual members themselves."

When the leadership believed itself in need of help, the Carter administration sent prominent figures to the Hill to speak to Democrats en masse. In the spring of 1979 the House had defeated a debt ceiling increase, and the count on the second attempt indicated a close vote. Secretary of the Treasury Michael Blumenthal sent every House member a letter explaining what would happen if the increase was not approved quickly and on the morning

of the vote appeared at a special whip meeting and "really laid it on thick."
To bolster a budget resolution that was in serious trouble, Vice President
Walter Mondale came to the Hill and spoke to a group of about one hundred Democrats.

The Carter administration engaged in considerable one-on-one lobbying
of House members, of course, but in those efforts directed by the House
leadership its involvement tended to be peripheral rather than central. A
member frequently engaged in leadership efforts said, "On the debt ceiling,
they've always been involved; they give us some of their lobby help. We
often assign them some names. When you have one of these elaborate operations, when you want three people to hit everybody, one of them might be
an administration lobbyist from Treasury or from the White House." A
leader elaborated: "Toward the end, if we still don't have the votes, we may
give them a list of names—people we think they might have some influence
with who we haven't been able to bring around. They don't seem to be able
to change many votes. They can maybe once or twice a year, but it costs
them. They have to make commitments."

The Reagan liaison team and Reagan himself proved to be considerably
more adept at lobbying members. Since the Democratic leadership and the
Reagan administration seldom agree on policy, the greater skill with which
White House resources are used in this administration makes the leadership's job a great deal more difficult. An aide who was deeply involved in
the tax bill fight spoke of the administration effort:

> They do things which we wouldn't think of doing, to tell you the truth. I come
> from an organizational background—the Daley organization. When you think
> about that, you think about all sorts of terrible things. But the things that the
> Daley organization would do are nothing compared to some of the things that
> the White House would do, and they do it in a very, very nice, pleasant
> upfront PR kind of way. I think a lot of what the president does at the White
> House—the cuff links and all—that's all very, very, very important, but I think
> it's been overdone in the press. It's important because Carter did such a bad
> job and so by comparison it's important. But the other things that they did—
> the peanut price supports and the sugar price supports and a deal on this and a
> deal on that. These are things that . . . . we couldn't do and I'm not so sure
> we would do. But they're good.

Although one-on-one persuasion is central, there are other actions the
leadership can take to influence floor success before a bill reaches the floor.
The leadership can ask the Steering and Policy Committee to endorse the
legislation, which signals to Democrats that the leaders see the bill as important and as a party matter. On policy matters the Speaker largely dominates
the committee; there may be heated discussion, but so far the Speaker has
received every endorsement he has requested. An aide said, "I've seen many
times they'll have discussion and it will be controversial and they'll argue

back and forth with the Speaker and one another. And then somebody will finally say vote, and they'll vote. And [opponents] will wind up saying, 'Let it be reported that I'm not here.' So that just adds a little bit of extra sex to the bill by saying the Steering and Policy Committee voted unanimously to support this legislation.''

Participants, nevertheless, do believe that an endorsement has some effect. "It's sort of the last word in whether the leadership supports the bill," a staffer said. "When the Steering Committee does take a position, it does seem to get around that, OK, this is one that if you're going to go wrong on, you'd better think twice because somebody's going to get you in the back of the chamber over here and ask you why you did it and make clear that it was not helpful." Two members described the effect of a Steering and Policy endorsement this way:

> There is a pressure on members who otherwise might not want to go along with the position, that if it's important to the Democratic party leadership, they'll appreciate that factor and will often go along because of that factor.

> I think it's all part of a process. Singly out there by itself, no, it doesn't make a great deal of difference. But as part of the Speaker's opinion, as part of the majority leader's opinion, as part of what the newspapers may be saying, it's all part of the process that helps steer opinion in the House of Representatives. As that it is very important.

A whip explained that a Steering and Policy endorsement helps him to persuade: "It's easier for me as a whip to say it's Policy and Steering and the Speaker that want it than it is for me to use my personality or lack of it to persuade a person as to what's good for him or her in their own district."

The leaders use the Thursday morning whip meetings to let the whips know which bills they consider critically important and to try to persuade the whips to vote with the leadership. Although the leaders do not count on the zone whips for persuasion, their exhortations at the meetings give the impression that they do. The exhortations themselves exert some pressure on the whips, and if they can activate a few whips, the effort is worthwhile. A conservative zone whip indicated that the leaders' entreaties do have an impact: "They've said, 'Hey, we need you.' They say how important this bill is. And I think there's a degree of persuasion when you say, hey, the Speaker wants this bill, the majority leader wants this bill, and the majority whip wants this bill, and you can read between the lines. I think this is an important factor."

Another leadership device is the "Dear Colleague" letter sent to the membership. Although the arguments used vary with the bill at issue, the substance of the bill, its importance, and party loyalty are usually emphasized. Substantive arguments are phrased as explanations that members can employ at home in explaining their vote. Jim Wright's "Dear Colleague" on aid to New York City in 1978, for example, was clearly aimed at providing members with such an explanation. It read, in part,

Please bear the following thoughts in mind when the *New York City Financial Assistance Act* (H.R. 12426) comes before us for a vote this Thursday:

New York has faithfully repaid every penny of the loan extended in 1975, on or ahead of schedule, and with interest. That loan has not cost the nation's taxpayers one red cent. . . .

The City has *tightened its belt* and accomplished every internal reform it pledged to accomplish in 1975. . . .

Think of the *alternative:* If the rest of us should refuse, after all of this, to extend the needed guarantees, the bankruptcy of America's largest city would send shock waves throughout the entire economy. . . .

Members of Congress from New York City have *consistently supported* progressive measures to help the *rest of the country.* A substantial majority of them, over the years, have supported flood control for our own smitten communities, water projects for the American West, the Great Plains conservation program, drought relief for the Southwest, the Appalachian Development program, and the entire range of other programs when the rest of our country has come to them in our time of need. . . .

Now it is our turn to reciprocate. To turn our backs on America's largest city in its hour of need would be not only ungrateful and undemocratic; it would be downright stupid!

If the parliamentary situation or the strategy being pursued is complex, the "Dear Colleague" can provide a concise explanation of the importance of a procedural vote, the vote on the previous question on the rule, for example, or the substance and politics of a leadership-supported amendment.

Scheduling the Legislation

■■■■■■■■■■■■   Control over floor scheduling is probably the majority party leadership's single most important power, and on major legislation it is used strategically. An initial scheduling decision may have been made soon after the bill was reported from committee, or even earlier, but the leadership is always free to make a change, even after a bill has appeared on the printed schedule. "You don't have to tell anybody a damned thing if you pull a bill," an aide explained. If the minority asks why a bill is not taken up as scheduled, the leadership can simply reply, "The chairman of that committee decided that he wasn't quite ready to bring it to the floor yet."

Certain rules of thumb on strategic scheduling have developed. Liberals are still more likely than conservatives to spend long weekends in their districts, so the day of the week on which a bill is scheduled is important. "You can clearly put DOD [Department of Defense] and the hawkish bills on

Mondays and Fridays,'' a participant explained. ''But if you got on something with liberal connotations, you really want to position it either Tuesday to be completed on Wednesday or Wednesday first thing up to be completed by the close of business or to be completed no later than Thursday.'' It is generally believed that putting a ''mean'' bill on the floor the day before a recess will at least shorten debate, as everyone wants to leave.

Sometimes a bill is scheduled quickly so as to prevent a full-scale campaign by unfriendly interest groups. As a staffer explained: ''The Chamber of Commerce says they can trigger 50,000 people and they in turn trigger 25 apiece. They can inundate you but it takes about six weeks to get the flow started. If you give them six weeks, they can kill almost any bill if its controversial. So, clearly, if you've got one like that, the thing to do is to move before they move—before they've got time to gin up.'' Conversely, if opposition interest groups have brought masses of constituents to Washington to lobby, the vote may be postponed until these grass-roots lobbyists have gone home.

The order in which legislation is considered may affect the outcome substantially. In the summer of 1979 sentiment in favor of lifting sanctions on Rhodesia was growing in the House, despite the Carter administration's opposition. Two appropriations bills to which a rider lifting sanctions could have been added were on the schedule. Because the leadership feared a rider might pass, the appropriations bills were delayed until the Foreign Affairs Committee could come up with separate legislation that was much less embarrassing to the president. This bill was ''slid in'' ahead of the appropriations bills, thus diffusing the sentiment in favor of adding the riders. In the summer of 1980 the conference reports on the synthetic fuels bill and on the bill creating the Energy Mobilization Board were ready for House action. ''I told the leadership that the synfuels conference report should be scheduled first, before the energy mobilization conference report,'' a leadership aide said. ''It's contentious, it might actually be defeated. Certainly there will be hot debate. I don't want it to sour the atmosphere, which might hurt the synfuels bill.'' The synfuels conference report was scheduled first and was easily approved, while the energy mobilization board, in fact, was defeated.

Whenever possible the leadership tries to space out the tough bills; scheduling such bills close together is likely to lead to disaster. In 1979 four major and difficult bills were scheduled for consideration in the first week or so after the August recess. All required quick action, but, as the defeat of all four indicated, the scheduling decision was a major mistake. When difficult bills are bunched together, there simply is not enough time to work each bill thoroughly, and each of these four—the second budget resolution, the Panama Canal bill conference report, a congressional pay raise bill, and a bill raising the debt limit—required an organized effort. Considering the bills so soon after a recess exacerbated the time problem. In addition, the bunching meant that members were asked to cast four difficult votes in one week. An aide explained the result: "People were saying, 'I'll give you [votes on] two of the four', so it was easier for them to get out of going with the party." When difficult bills are considered close together, one legislative battle may have a spillover effect on another. Speaking of the defeat of the budget resolution, one participant said, "There was not enough time and not enough work done, but also the pay raise came up first and created a lot of bad blood." That faulty scheduling was responsible for this particular debacle is indicated by the later reversal of all four votes.

Strategic scheduling involves putting a bill on the floor when its chances of passing are highest. This often requires delaying a bill. If a postcommittee compromise on substance proves to be necessary, the leadership will delay until the compromise has been worked out. More than a month elapsed between the report of the Chrysler aid bill and its consideration on the floor because the time was needed to put together an agreement to modify the bill. The leadership may also delay so as to give friendly interest groups an opportunity to mount a full-scale campaign. When the leadership finds that its persuasion efforts have not borne the fruit expected, it sometimes delays a bill for weeks while it attempts to build a winning coalition.

Reliable information on members' voting intentions is critical to strategic scheduling. The whip count, refined by the follow-up persuasion effort, provides that information. The decision to schedule is not based simply on being able to count 218 votes, however." One of the things that's important is . . . the movement and how it changes over a period of days and weeks," an aide to the majority whip explained: "Are the regional and/or ideological groups breaking in your direction or not?" How important the numbers are also depends on the kind of legislation at issue. Although a short delay in consideration is almost always possible, long delays often are not. Some legislation can be delayed indefinitely in the hope that the political situation will improve; many bills, however, must be considered expeditiously, and, for scheduling those, momentum is more important than the specific numbers. A leadership aide explained:

Look, you've got two different kinds of situations—one is when you have to make a judgment on whether the legislation should be called up or not—that was an issue in the consumer protection bill in the last Congress and on common situs picketing, and a few other things. In each case it was decided to throw it on the floor although, given the numbers, we knew it wasn't likely to pass. So you have that kind of judgment occasionally and sometimes the judgment goes the other way—we haven't the votes, don't bring it up now. And in the first instance the numbers are very important. And then you have the second kind of situation in which the legislation is going to come up. Now, on Panama we delayed it three or four times, but we were going to reach the point where it had to come up because we had to get this done in order to meet certain time constraints including those in the treaties themselves. In the second kind of situation, the numbers aren't so important. It's working it that's important. And the better indicators are movement and shifts and just your general "feel," but it's almost become irrelevant for action purposes what the precise numbers are. It's not irrelevant for strategy purposes in deciding how to handle it, but as far as taking action, it's irrelevant what the numbers are because the bill is going to come up.

On the Floor

The extent of leadership floor activity depends on the type of effort being mounted. If the bill is important but not top priority and no unusual trouble is expected, the party leadership relies on the committee leaders to direct the floor effort. The chief whip and several appointed whips may work the door on the most controversial amendments; the whip and the majority leader may vote early as a signal; during particularly touchy roll calls the majority leader may stay on the floor to signal the leadership's interest by his presence and to engage in some last-minute persuasion if necessary.

Many bills, however, require that the leadership become very involved on the floor. Sometimes winning one or two specific votes is the key to overall victory and effort can be concentrated on that. If the rule for the bill prohibits most or all amendments, the key votes are often on the previous question on the rule and on the rule itself. In these cases the leaders and members working with them will all be on the floor. The majority leader may speak for the rule; all the doors will be covered, often by more than one person; a system for calling in pocket votes—votes promised "if you really need me"—will have been developed; and the Speaker, if he is not in the chair, may stand at the monitor examining how members voted, and senior staff and members working the vote may bring to him Democrats they believe he might be able to persuade. Toward the end of the vote the leaders will cluster in the well to do some last-minute persuasion if it proves necessary.

Highly restrictive rules are still the exception. Most bills are considered under an open rule, and if the bill is controversial a large number of amendments can be expected. Counting every amendment in advance is not possible because of the numbers involved and because some amendments will be offered without warning. Amendments can be extremely complicated, and their actual effects can be obscure. Consequently, although vote mobilization efforts in the days before a bill reaches the floor are essential, holding the coalition together during floor consideration and warding off amendments that could seriously damage the bill are equally crucial.

The floor manager plays a central role during the amending process. As one senior staffer explained, a politically astute floor manager facilitates the other proponents' efforts:

A skillful floor manager knows the mood of the House; he can read the mood of the House and knows when to accept [an amendment] and he knows which ones he can accept and sweep out in conference; he knows which ones he can accept and live with. He's in communication with the administration. Let's say it's a foreign aid bill and they want to ban aid to Uganda—well, there isn't any damn aid to Uganda, so if the guy wants to do it, you stand up and you argue against [the amendment] and then you accept it without asking for a vote. You don't even ask for a roll call. Sometimes you have to fight it tooth and nail because you know you can't do anything with it. You don't want to screw up your bill. This certainly plays a major role.

Even the most skillful floor manager needs help on highly controversial bills. When a great many amendments are offered, a task force can be especially helpful because the members can talk to their colleagues during the amending process and get an informal up-to-date count—a "continuous count"—on amendments. A continuous count also provides information on how the amending process is affecting the bill's chances for final passage, information that may allow for a timely change in strategy. A participant explained:

When a bill is on the floor—a bill where there are lots of amendments and it's a tough philosophical issue—you can literally count as you go along and see people getting on and off. And a task force can do that; they can keep on it: "Hey, Joe, I know that that amendment wasn't exactly your favorite thing. You voted against it; I knew you were kind of tenuous on this bill to begin with; are you still with us?" That kind of thing. They can alert you early on to where your weak points are and keep you in touch with what's happening, whereas with the more traditional kinds of whipping, there's just no way you can stay on top of it that well. They won't get the right answers, and they certainly can't get them as fast, because you're talking about being there on the floor, able to sit down next to a member and ask him, as opposed to going through the telephone, which is much more distant, much less likely to get the actual, honest, eye-contact-to-eye-contact truth—harder to lie to your face, you know. Now, I mean like this budget conference report, that's irrelevant. People who were on, were on; people who were off, were off. You just had to beat them into shape. The previous year, though, with the budget resolution, it was quite possible to add and subtract votes as amendments were adopted, defeated. And that helps you to know which ones you've got to beat and which ones you've got to pass and it helps you to frame your amendment. If you get to the end and you don't have the votes, you can frame your amendment to create passage. That's not a new game, it's just being done a little differently, a little more formally.

Task force members stand at the chamber's doors and hand out information on the amendment pending to members as they file in for roll calls. One of the duties of task force members is to keep track of the people assigned to them and work on them during a roll call if necessary. The task force chairman, who stays on the floor the entire time a bill is being considered, and some of the members "cluster around the monitor and look at the vote state by state. If they find someone has voted wrong, they will chase him down and work on him. Even if he comes to the floor, votes, and then runs, he's got to be around somewhere and they will find him." When no task force is in operation but the bill is an important and difficult one, the appointed whips aid the leadership in carrying out these functions. On the Taiwan legislation, for example, whips worked the door on all major amendments; Jim Wright gave two floor speeches, remained on the floor during voting on most amendments, and worked the door on the most troublesome ones. On 8 March the House defeated an extremely damaging amendment on a very close vote. The leaders immediately divided the names of defecting Democrats among themselves and talked to all of them. When consideration resumed on 13 March, killer amendments were defeated with relative ease. One "rather silly" amendment did pass, but a House leader conferred with the Senate Democratic leadership, which thought the amendment could be deleted in conference, and as a consequence, the House leadership decided not to attempt to reverse the vote.

Disseminating Information

Because of the number of amendments offered and the ease with which a recorded vote can be obtained, the establishment of an effective method of providing information to members has become necessary. Members simply will not blindly follow the leadership over and over again, especially when their votes are to be made public. This need has been met by the development of the "bullet," a mimeographed, one-page summary of an amendment. Developed by the Steering and Policy Committee staffer working with the Humphrey-Hawkins task force, bullets have now become a regular part of the process. Bullets are prepared by the committee staff prior to floor consideration for amendments that are expected. For amendments offered without warning, bullets are written and duplicated on the spot. The originating committee staff and the Steering and Policy staff work together, often using an Appropriations Committee room located close to the House floor.

There is widespread belief that the bullets are effective. "On bad amendments, you need something to give the members," a staffer said. "You've got to give them a rationale for voting against. Otherwise, ... if they have nothing and they go in, they'll look at the vote totals and may be stampeded." He explained that many amendments are complex: "There may be only three or four or five people on our side of the House who understand what some of these amendments really do, and if they don't have a way to reach the whole Democratic Caucus, we're in trouble. On the _____ bill, every time we didn't have [a bullet] we lost.'' The use of bullets has extended beyond task force efforts. Democrats with task force experience have begun to use bullets to explain complex amendments in other floor efforts. ''They got some new tools, they saw that they worked, and now they're carrying them back into their work for their committee,'' a participant commented. ''You see members of the committee taking sheets of paper to the doors. It seems to be becoming more the way you handle things, a more routine kind of thing, and I think that's just great.''

The automatic telephone system also aids the leadership in disseminating information quickly. From the Democratic cloakroom the telephones in the offices of all Democrats can be rung and a taped message played automatically. Typically the message will say, ''The Democratic leadership asks you to come to the floor and vote against the X amendment,'' and then give a concise description of the amendment. Before the automatic system was installed, every telephone numer had to be dialed individually; this time-consuming calling was done infrequently, and when it was, no explanation for the request could be offered. ''It's magnificent,'' a senior leadership aide said of the automatic system. ''Now, putting out a whip call to get people to the floor, I'll many times do it myself. Just say, 'Such and such is happening; the majority leader wants the member on the floor.' ''

Floor Tactics: Old and New

The electronic voting system, which was installed at the same time as the automatic telephone system, has, most members believe, made the leadership's task more difficult by shortening the duration of the vote and thus the time the leadership has to work on members. A senior staffer explained the advantage of the old system: ''The old alphabetical voting system by the time it was abolished had been developed to a very high state, where if you saw Mr. Blumenthal in the B's go along, you had a pretty good chain of seven people who would go along following this, and you could go around and talk to those seven people and turn them around before they got around to Mr. Ranew in the R's or Mr. Stevens in the S's. It took nearly an hour to have one of those votes. That gave you time to work.'' Because there are multiple voting stations, locating a specific member on the floor is now more difficult. ''They come in all kinds of different doors, vote, scoot out,'' a participant commented. ''The key thing in the old system was that it was $A\ B\ C\ D\ E$, and when F answered his name you could spot where he was, and go get him if you had to. But now you can't.''

Strategies for working within and even taking advantage of the electronic voting system are evolving. On major efforts, appointed whips or task force members may be ''staked out'' at the voting stations. Successfully implementing this strategy, however, is difficult, a leadership staffer reported: the members assigned to the voting stations ''tend to wander away.'' The majority leader and the chief whip voting early and the same way as a signal to members is a positive use of the system.

The "fast vote" is another positive use of the voting system. A senior staffer said, "You know how, if the cargo on a ship gets off-balance, if it gets too much to one side, you'll get to the point where suddenly the ship keels over. It's that way on some votes. I call it 'the lurch effect.' " A "fast vote" takes advantage of the "lurch effect." "We've developed the fast vote," a participant explained. "We've gotten 120 votes on the board in the first minute and a half. Then when members who intended to oppose it came in, they'd see the overwhelming vote and decide to go along. It can be very effective." The "lurch effect," an aide said, was accidentally discovered:

> We learned on the consumer bill that it did make a difference because the Republicans did it to us there—inadvertently. They had David Rockefeller and a whole bunch of Republican fat cats down in the members' dining room. And the leadership on the Republican side was running around their half of the floor shouting and yelling, "Vote and get downstairs, vote and get downstairs; we can't leave them alone down there!" And they clobbered us; they put a great many votes on the board in the first thirty seconds and in the first minute and that established a psychological edge. They were on the high ground, and we never could catch up. The guys who said, We'll hold back and wait and see how it's going, all had a chance to make sure it went that way. Because we were behind, we were down, and how can you hold their votes when you're down? So, I can't say that we would have won it for sure, but in my bones I believe we would have won it if we had not been outmaneuvered—by the inadvertent tactical edge. So, that's one tactic which when we came to the B-1 we applied.

The fast vote is effective only on selected issues. If, because of intensely held personal views or direct constituency interest, members' "feet are set in concrete," the tactic is unlikely to sway their votes. But, as a member commented, "There's a lot of peer pressure around here. There's constituency pressure, there's philosophical pressure, there's ideological pressure, and then there's also peer pressure, and if you develop peer pressure, well, people don't like to be too isolated. They like to be part of the team, they like to get the benefits of the team operation."

The electronic voting system has made essential an efficient mechanism for calling in pocket votes. Members sometimes promise to vote with the leadership if their votes will be decisive. "Sometimes you'll be working a bill and you'll get a report back that so-and-so doesn't want to vote for this thing and just about has to vote against it, but if you *absolutely* have to have him, he'll vote with you," a leadership aide revealed. "So he goes on that list of potential last-minute votes in the well, and that's normally the way it occurs. Although there are some people who are party stalwarts, who will change their vote for you. We try not to ask them too often." Members occasionally convey their willingness via their zone whip during the initial count, but they more frequently do so later in the persuasion process, and often the promise is made personally to one of the top leaders. A senior staffer said, "Some of the Texans might tell that to Jim; some of the liberal guys might tell it to Brademas. More often than not, though, it's the guy telling the Speaker because he wants to get a credit with the Speaker."

The ability to convert pocket votes into actual votes when needed takes careful prior organization in light of the constraints of the electronic voting system. "We very often will have a list of names and you've got to create a mechanism for being able to call that in right quick, like sometimes within a space of thirty or forty seconds," a participant explained. "The main problem is logistical, keeping them on the floor. We have used a buddy system. You get someone to stand with them." A female task force member was reported to have kept a Democrat assigned to her from leaving the floor by "practically sitting in his lap. He would have to have been a real boor to have gotten up."

If the bill is on the floor for more than one day—an increasingly common occurrence—formal or informal strategy meetings may be held between sessions. If it is a task force effort, formal meetings are the rule. Committee staff brief the members on amendments expected, arguments to be used are discussed, and voting records to that point are analyzed. The task force may decide that on a given amendment "twenty members are targets and everyone will work on them."

Responding to "Nasty Surprises"

No amount of organization and prior work can guarantee smooth sailing on the floor. Because of the high rate of amending activity, "nasty surprises" can occur all too easily. Choosing to pull a bill off the floor after one or two amendments have been lost or to finish it regardless of the hour of adjournment can have a major effect on outcome. On important bills, the floor manager and the leadership make such decisions, but if a task force has been appointed its chairman can provide another judgment. A staffer told of an important bill that ran into serious trouble on the floor. The committee majority was inclined to continue consideration, but the task force chairman, "sensing the mood a little better," said, "Hey, look, I know you'd like to stay and finish the bill. Well, I happen to think that if we stay here another five minutes, we're not going to have a bill to manage anymore." The task force chairman, by insisting the bill be pulled, saved it, according to the aide; "We went back and we had a day and a half to regroup."

When things go wrong, the majority party leadership's power to pull the bill off the floor becomes critically important. Pulling the bill, of course, prevents immediate further damage to the bill and also gives proponents time to revise their strategy. Sometimes the trouble is due simply to generalized member irritation during a late session and all that is required is a cooling-off period. A senior aide explained: "Lots of times late at night the House will start deteriorating. It'll be nine or ten o'clock at night and the committee's had to eat two or three bad amendments for no reason at all except the House is in a bad mood; they're irritable and they're mad at something the president's done and you just sense the feel of the House. So [the leaders] will go out and persuade the committee chairman to just pull his bill and rise and let's adjourn. We'll come back to it later."

Sometimes a killer amendment that "sounds good" will pass because of a lack of information. In 1977, when a bill to revise the Hatch Act was on the floor, John Ashbrook offered such an amendment. Innocuous at first glance, the amendment would have placed severe restrictions on the political activities of labor unions. Neither the floor manager, who was a junior member, nor the other proponents were prepared for such a situation, and the amendment passed. "There was nobody on the doors when Ashbrook passed," a staffer said. "Nobody saying, 'This is good'; 'this is bad'— which is how something like Ashbrook could pass. It would have destroyed the bill." The increasingly large percentage of junior Democratic members has increased the likelihood of such occurrences, according to the aide. "You had a tremendous changeover in the House, a new voting system, members, almost a majority of whom no longer even know who Mr. Ashbrook was, except by distant reputation, and it would never occur to them that he would sandbag them as badly as he did." The bill was pulled and Democrats were informed of what the Ashbrook amendment actually did to it. It's a "legislative lemon," Stephen Solarz (D-N.Y.) said. "It looks sweet on the outside but tastes bitter on the inside" (*Congressional Quarterly Weekly Report,* 11 June 1977, p. 1145). When the bill was brought to the floor again, the bill's manager offered an amendment that negated the Ashbrook amendment and it was easily adopted.

Sometimes damaging amendments pass simply because they are politically popular; then often the best that can be done is to work out a compromise. When the CETA reauthorization first came to the floor in August 1978, the prospects of passing the bill ungutted looked dim; many legislators perceived CETA to be "the second most unpopular program in the country after welfare" (David Obey, quoted in *Congressional Quarterly Weekly Report,* 12 August 1978, p. 2107). Despite a task force effort, the House adopted two damaging amendments: the Obey amendment lowering the ceiling on CETA wages and the Jeffords amendment slashing authorized funding for public service employment. Fearing additional disasters, the leadership pulled the bill. During the recess that followed a compromise substitute bill was worked out and it passed easily in September.

When a bill of some importance runs into unexpected trouble on the floor, direct leadership involvement is often necessary to repair the damage. In mid-1979 a standby gas rationing bill was on the floor. Earlier in the year President Carter had submitted a standby gas rationing plan to Congress for approval as specified by a 1975 law. Much to the embarrassment of the leadership, the House had rejected the plan. The rejection was due, in part, to House members' annoyance with Carter, who kept changing the plan to accommodate the Senate. The more basic problem, the House leadership believed, was the extreme sensitivity of members to constituency interests on the matter. They concluded that, barring an emergency, no plan could win majority support. After the initial defeat, the Commerce Committee drafted a new bill that would not require prior congressional approval. Congress could still veto the plan, but only at the time when the president wanted to implement it.

When the new bill reached the floor Republicans made a concerted effort to weaken it through amendments. An amendment to reinstate the same review procedure as that in the 1975 bill, a proposal the leadership considered completely unacceptable, was offered by James Broyhill (R-N.C.) and was rejected, 235 to 182. A little later Benjamin Gilman (R-N.Y.) offered an amendment that did essentially the same thing, and it was unexpectably accepted by a 232 to 187 vote. "We were able to reject the first several weakening amendments," a participant said. "But then the Republicans offered an amendment through Ben Gilman. He's more popular with Democrats than most of them. He's not seen as a firebrand, he's not a highly partisan person. In this instance, it wasn't his amendment though. It was handed to him by staff who had prepared it as they were handling amendments to other Republican members to offer, for the express purpose of weakening the bill, and for the purpose of embarrassing the president." The leadership immediately pulled the bill. According to a participant, "The Speaker agreed that this was an amendment that we should not have to suffer; that, further, if we suffered it without rolling it back, it would set the stage for a succession of weakening amendments and it would make the bill relatively worthless."

An amendment approved in the Committee of the Whole may be voted on again in the House after the amending process is completed. Alternatively, one can negate the effect of an amendment by passing another carefully drafted amendment. The leaders decided to adopt the latter course because they did not want to wait until the amendment process was completed. A leader explained the decision:

> That decision was made on the basis that this obviously was not one isolated amendment but was part of a concerted effort to weaken the bill—to rend it, to tear it to shreds, and indeed there were some twenty-odd amendments offered, each with the effect of weakening the bill, making it unworkable. We felt it important to establish a pattern of victory out there instead of a pattern of defeat. If we turn this around, then it's going to be easier to ward others off. If we don't, it's going to encourage the Republicans to offer more and still more and make it easier for our Democratic colleagues to go ahead and vote for them. So we thought it had to be turned around psychologically at that time.

The committee staff quickly drafted the amendment, and at the same time the leaders began their persuasion effort. A strategy-planning lunch was held. "I had a kind of cross section of people interested in that bill," a leader said. "Liberals like Toby Moffett and Andy McGuire and a conservative or two like Phil Gramm, and we took the list of those Democrats who had voted right on the Broyhill amendment and wrong on the Gilman amendment and assigned them, knowing that if we turned those around, or a substantial majority of them, we would be able to prevail." The members involved in the effort talked to their assignees and reported the results to the leadership. "There were some they had not been able to persuade, and I then would go to them and talk with them," the leader said.

When the bill was again considered five days after the approval of Gilman, the majority leader offered the amendment. He did so because, as one member said, "Democrats tend to recognize that when the majority leader offers an amendment, this is one they're supposed to rally around on." The Wright amendment was approved 234 to 189. "We turned 45 votes around and that was more than enough to make the difference," a leader said. The next day, by a vote of 263 to 159, the House passed the bill.

The leaders' resources, though far from negligible, certainly are not unlimited, and it is important that they not expend any more resources than necessary in any particular effort. If it becomes clear that a particular vote will be lost, members who have promised to vote with the leadership are released: "You don't want to use your chits." In most cases the leadership wants to win, regardless of the margin; once a solid majority is assured no effort to add to that is made, and if members want to change their votes they are not discouraged so long as it does not change the outcome. There are occasions, however, where there is safety in numbers. On the 1977 pay raise, for example, the leaders believed a large margin would protect members. "When the vote ended and members were given the chance to change their votes, a solid line of Democratic House leaders . . . formed in the well to discourage members who had voted for the raise from changing their votes" (*Congressional Quarterly Weekly Report,* 2 June 1977, p. 1368). The same rationale held on the constitutional amendment to ban busing. The larger the margin against it, the less vulnerable any one opponent would be. In addition, as a leadership staffer said, "It was one of those situations where you didn't want to see it come out [of committee], but since it did, it was just as well to stomp it into the ground, because now it won't be coming out again for a long, long time."

The Conference Committee

■■■■■■■■■■■■■■■ The House and the Senate must pass a bill in identical form before it can become law. When an important bill passes the chambers in different forms, a conference committee is often appointed to work out a compromise version. If the two versions are very different, or if the issues in disagreement are highly charged, coming to an agreement that will win the approval of both chambers is a delicate political task and may require leadership involvement.

House conferees are officially appointed by the Speaker, but precedent has severely constrained his discretion. The chairman and the ranking minority member of the committee of origin recommend a list of conferees to the Speaker, and tradition requires him to defer to them. But the Speaker has always had some discretion in determining the ratio of Democrats to Republicans, and recent House rules changes have enlarged the Speaker's discretion in the appointment of Democratic conferees. House rules now require that the authors of major amendments be appointed as conferees, but because the determination of whether or not an amendment is major is not always clear-cut, the rules provide some leeway. For example, conservative Democrat Phil Gramm, who cosponsored the successful Republican substitute to the 1981 reconciliation bill, was not appointed a conferee. On a bill that has been referred to more than one committee, the Speaker has considerable discretion in determining the number of conferees allotted to each of the committees involved as well as in deciding whether the members will act as conferees for the entire bill or only for specific sections. At times this leeway has provided opportunities to advantage the leadership's position. On the Panama Canal implementation legislation, for example, O'Neill decided that all House conferees would be conferees for the entire bill and thus diluted the influence of Merchant Marine Committee members who were hostile to the administration's position.

Leadership involvement in the deliberations of the conference committee is restricted to the difficult cases, but very often the leader of the House conferees will request leadership help. "Like on a budget resolution, they're going to get involved," a Speaker's aide said. "The chairman of the conferees will come to 'Tip' and say, 'You have got to talk to this guy.' 'Tip' will talk to him instantly, use the power of persuasion. I won't say it's rare, to get involved at the conference level." Leadership staff also get involved in working out compromises at the conference stage. If an aide has been assigned to work on an important bill, he is expected to see it through the conference.

Carter's energy program, one of his and the leadership's top priorities, presented extraordinary problems at the conference stage and required unusual leadership involvement. The versions passed by the House and Senate differed fundamentally. The year-long conference frequently threatened to break down completely, in which case there would have been no bill. A senior conferee described the problem and the Speaker's role in managing it:

> It was a very delicate balance that we were working with at all times where important policy matters were involved. What I'd say to the Speaker is, "I think it would be a good idea on the resolution of the natural gas matter if we'd have a meeting. . . ." We were in there every day, all day—or most of it—and under enormous pressures, and we didn't fly to him at every turn. It was really quite rare when we did, but when we did we had to because we were about to be stalemated. Before we got ourselves into an absolutely rigid position where people were saying, "Goddammit, I'm not going to go one step beyond this"—just short of that—we would say, "Well, let's try something else because we're just about to take positions from which retreat will be all but impossible."

Leadership staff were involved in working out language and the like. The Speaker's role was a more general one. As another participant said, "The issue involved long histories of disagreements. There were past enmities that had to be overcome; there were new enmities that had to be overcome. The leadership was a constant pressure in the direction of agreement."

Leadership involvement in the synthetic fuels bill conference was even more extensive. An unusual set of circumstances led to the majority leader's central role. On 26 July 1979 the House passed a 14-page synthetic fuels bill. Jim Wright had been extensively involved in the legislation and had offered a successful floor amendment enlarging the program in the committee bill. (See chapter 7 for a case study of this legislation.) In mid-July President Carter announced a new energy plan of which synthetic fuels was a major part. In response the Senate passed a 300-page bill that consisted of ten sections; thus the conference was forced to deal with a bill that included nine sections that had not been in the original House bill. The Banking Committee had reported the House bill, but the Senate bill involved the jurisdictions of the Commerce and Science and Technology committees as well. Conferees were chosen from each of these committees; Tom Foley from Agriculture was appointed; and the majority leader was a conferee. Because most of the Senate bill had not been considered in the House, a great deal of staff work was required, and a de facto staff director was needed to coordinate the staff work because each of the conferees had a vote on each section of the bill. An aide of the majority leader assumed that role. During the long conference this aide directed the day-to-day work, which often involved delicate in-House political considerations. The Senate bill, for example, included a section dealing with an energy conservation bank. The House Commerce Committee had under consideration a somewhat similar bill, and the Banking Committee was considering a solar bank bill. Thus extended negotiations were required before the two committees were able to draft a combined proposal that constituted the House position in the conference. Given the scope of the synthetic fuels bill, numerous difficulties requiring the personal involvement of the majority leader arose. Jim Wright talked to the conferees individually and collectively over and over again. When most of the major disagreements had been worked out but numerous smaller difficulties remained, Wright decided to force the issue through the use of a high-risk tactic: he publicly set a deadline for agreement. The tactic proved to be successful; the conferees reached an agreement and the deadline was met.

Leadership involvement at the conference stage is most frequently aimed at facilitating an agreement so that a bill will emerge and at influencing the form of the compromise. It may also serve to protect the prerogative of the House vis-à-vis the Senate. In 1980, for example, Senate Majority Leader Robert Byrd tacked a relaxation of strip-mining standards onto an unrelated Merchant Marine Committee bill. Speaker Tip O'Neill foiled Byrd's attempt to maneuver around the House Interior Committee, which opposed the change, by appointing Interior Committee members as conferees for that section of the bill. Of the Speaker's action an aide said, "That was straightforward. That was really a question of protecting the Interior Committee's jurisdiction over the issue." Another commented, "Bobby Byrd was on the phone to 'Tip' frequently on that. But 'Tip' didn't do what Bobby Byrd asked him to do and he couldn't because he had to protect the prerogatives and power of the Speaker and also stick to germaneness and House rules and the House position."

The Strategy of Inclusion:
An Evaluation

██████████████████ In building coalitions, the majority party leadership employs a wide variety of techniques. Most of them are not new, although some of the rules changes of the 1970s did augment the techniques available. The multiple referral rules, for example, offer opportunities not previously available. The transformation of the Rules Committee into an arm of the leadership gives the party leaders true control over scheduling and makes possible structuring the floor situation via the design of complex rules. The strategy of inclusion—the current leadership's active attempt to involve as many Democrats as possible in the coalition-building process—much more than specific techniques differentiates the current leaders' approach to coalition building from that of their predecessors.

New leadership strategies became necessary as the House was transformed by changes that took place in the 1970s. The legislative process in the postreform House is fraught with uncertainty, and the majority party leadership needs help with coalition building. The Speaker's strategy of inclusion is in part a response to that need. An aide said, "He gets task forces involved; there's a Steering Committee involved in issues. He's a good listener so that everybody feels like he's a part of it. But all of a sudden on one bill he's got fifty guys involved in the bill. And that's a big jump-off. Makes everybody feel they're a piece of it. I think that's why he succeeds."

The strategy of inclusion has an immediate payoff: it increases the probability of floor success. The members thus involved can perform tasks the small core leadership group is not able to carry out alone. A task force, for example, can explain the provisions of a complicated bill on a member-to-member basis; obtain a detailed and precise count of Democrats' voting intentions; and engage in face-to-face persuasion efforts with a large proportion of the Democratic membership. It has the organization and the numbers to respond quickly to unexpected floor developments.

The leadership believes that the strategy of inclusion has longer-range payoffs as well. By involving members in leadership efforts via the expanded whip system, the Steering and Policy Committee, and task forces, the leadership satisfies members' expectations for meaningful participation in the legislative process and thereby contributes to "keeping peace in the family."

Task forces provide an especially useful way of channeling a junior member's desires for participation into activities beneficial to the leadership and the party. Participants believe that task forces have been useful in socializing junior members. Working on a task force gives them a piece of the action; it also provides them with an understanding of the problems of the leadership and, in some cases, results in an identification with the leadership. "It's helped the leadership to get to know the new members and the new members to get to know the leadership," one participant said. "And it's certainly helped the new members who I've spoken to—my personal friends—to understand the need for leadership and followship. I think the guys who have served on task forces know a lot more about the need for a party structure with some loyalty than those who haven't." According to another participant, "The task force members, particularly the chairmen, got an awareness of the problems of leadership and a feeling of meaningful participation that paid dividends on later legislation, as they felt some obligation to cooperate with other task forces. Many of the task force members . . . became emotionally involved with the leadership."

As the socializing effect of task force membership has become clearer, the membership selection process has changed. There is now a conscious effort to include Democrats specifically for the effect membership may have on their attitudes toward intraparty cooperation:

Initially—though not necessarily total consciously—we chose those people who might be most amenable to working in the same philosophical mold as the chairman and the Speaker and the leadership as a whole. Though not totally— I mean that's not the only reason you choose somebody. We have since then

changed the nature of the invitation process a little bit to try and broaden it
and bring in people who we're not that used to working with. And there's been
some discussion about that, and there is a conscious effort currently being
made to broaden it, to reach into places we haven't reached into before. You
can't always do it because the places you haven't reached into before may be
philosophically totally opposed to your bill. But we try, and we're trying pretty
hard.

Increased awareness of the socializing benefit of task force membership had
by the 96th Congress led to another form of reaching out in the composition
of task force membership lists. Every one of the five new Democratic members of the Ways and Means Committee was included in the debt limit task
force in early 1979, and of the eight new Budget Committee Democrats, six
served on the spring 1979 budget resolution task force (deep policy disagreements precluded the inclusion of the remaining two). This appears to represent a conscious attempt to draw new committee members into the leadership's orbit, to accustom them to working with the leadership on major bills
within their committee's jurisdiction. Thus, rather than attempting to
dampen the high rate of rank-and-file participation—an enterprise almost
certainly doomed to failure—the leadership seeks to direct it into productive
channels.

The strategy of inclusion thus provides a means of reconciling the leadership's two primary functions, coalition building and party maintenance,
within a context of limited resources and high uncertainty. The leadership's
resources certainly are not negligible, but the importance of "keeping peace
in the family" places constraints on the use of those resources that extend
beyond their inherent limitations. Because coalitions must be built repeatedly, tactics that exacerbate intraparty conflicts or create dissatisfaction are
counterproductive in the long run even if they work in the short run. As a
leadership aide said, "What you've got to remember is, when you're playing the game today, you can't figure it's the last game you'll ever play; you
must always think about how what you do today is going to affect your
chances tomorrow." The need to consider the effect of today's tactics on
future success dictates that a heavy emphasis be placed on positive rein-
forcement and that negative sanctions be avoided. The majority leader commented, "After a tough vote, I sit down and write a letter to some of these
guys and thank them and try to give them some material to defend their vote
to their constituents. It isn't worth it to demand someone's vote, even once.
It's a continuing process. If you get one vote under duress, it will be harder
in the future" (Malbin 1977, p. 944).

The strategy of inclusion does not, of course, guarantee leadership success. As the next chapter shows, leadership success is a function not only of
the skillful use of limited resources but also of a variety of factors outside
the leadership's control. The strategy of inclusion does maximize the leadership's probability of success in the highly unpredictable postreform House.

CHAPTER **6**

THE

LEADERSHIP

IN ACTION:

BUDGET

POLITICS

Budget Politics 1979

Because the budget resolution sets an overall framework for spending decisions, the House Democratic leadership considers passage of a resolution that is a majority party document crucial. Since the beginning of the congressional budget process in 1975, passing budget resolutions has been difficult in the House. Unlike their counterparts in the Senate, House Republicans have provided little support; there were nineteen recorded votes on passage and on adoption of the conference report taken from 1975 through 1978; on these roll calls, the mean number of Republican votes in favor of the budget resolution was 8.4 (LeLoup 1979, p. 238). Given the lack of Republican support, a majority must be built from the Democratic membership. Passing budget resolutions requires considerable leadership involvement. The House Budget Committee Democrats are highly dependent on the leadership for the floor success of their resolutions; thus the leadership has substantial influence over the committee.

Continued and rising inflation promised to make the process even more difficult than usual in 1979. In the wake of California's passage of Proposition 13, a budget-balancing mood seemed to be sweeping the country. Liberal interest groups, on the other hand, responded to President Carter's austere budget with dismay. As in the past, the House Budget Committee (HBC) staff, working under the direction of Chairman Robert Giaimo, developed a preliminary budget document that included estimates broken down into the nineteen broad functions (such as defense, energy, health) into which the budget is divided. The staff worked under two premises: the budget had to be austere, but not so austere that liberals would be unable to

175

vote for it. Thus countercyclical aid and mass transit funds were carefully protected. Unlike in previous years, the chairman decided to consider the document first in the Democratic caucus of the HBC. During a series of meetings over the course of a week, committee Democrats reviewed and revised the preliminary figures. Giaimo and the leadership hoped these meetings would "build some unity among the Democrats."

The chairman's mark (the document from which the committee works) came out of these meetings. With one major exception, it was not very different from the document brought to the caucus. David Obey, a leading liberal on the committee, provided the exception by persuading his fellow Democrats to transfer $1 billion from defense to social programs. The mark-up was long and rancorous. Yet, with the exception of the overturn of the Obey amendment and the deletion of Carter's real wage insurance, the changes made were marginal. According to one HBC staffer, "Everyone knew Obey would be changed back in full committee." Because of broad-based doubt about the wage insurance proposal both in the committee and in the full House, its defeat was not unexpected.

The party leadership was involved throughout this period. At the beginning of the mark-up Speaker O'Neill invited all the HBC Democrats to lunch and made an impassioned plea for saving social programs. Contact between the HBC staff and the Speaker's staff was "constant" throughout the mark-up period. The Speaker used his influence to preserve social programs where possible, but he too recognized that the political climate dictated a relatively austere budget.

Majority Leader Wright and Chairman Giaimo worked together closely during the mark-up, trying to find a balance between supporting decisions of the HBC Democratic caucus and producing a resolution that would pass on the floor. Because the original document had been carefully prepared to find acceptance with a wide range of Democrats, the two goals were not usually in conflict, although they were on the Obey transfer—against which Wright and Giaimo voted along with five other Democrats and all of the Republicans.

Although all of the Democrats except Obey voted to report the resolution out of committee, the leadership knew that floor passage would be difficult. The support of many committee liberals was far from enthusiastic. The HBC staff has held a number of meetings with the representatives of traditional Democratic constituencies, especially with AFL-CIO lobbyists, and these groups, although seemingly resigned, were not happy with the product. Conservatives were no more pleased: in order to win liberal support, support, however grudging, committee Democrats had cut Carter's defense request and restored some of his proposed cuts in jobs, education, health, and social service programs. At a leadership meeting with Chairman Giaimo shortly after the mark-up was completed, all participants agreed that a major floor effort was required.

This was a case in which "everyone knew" there would be a task force. The Steering and Policy Committee staff drew up a list of possible chairmen for the task force from which O'Neill chose Norman Mineta of California. First elected in 1974, Mineta had established a reputation for intelligence and legislative responsibility and had previously served on a number of task forces. On being named chairman, Mineta met with several Steering and Policy staffers to draw up a list of members for the task force. Prior to the meeting the staff had prepared a list of potential members which included information such as their record of support on previous budget resolutions.

The broad strategy that is to be pursued on a bill usually evolves out of what has happened during committee deliberations. In this case, related one participant, "We made up a careful package in committee. The strategy on the floor was to sell it as a carefully crafted package and beat back all [non-committee-sponsored] amendments." A package amendment adding funds for various social programs, as well as for two destroyers ordered and then cancelled by Iran, was to be offered on the floor by the committee. "Bringing the additions in the Simon amendment to the floor rather than adding them in committee was a conscious strategy," a HBC staffer said. "The purpose was to reinforce the notion of a package."

The first task force meeting began with a "pep talk" by the Speaker. After some discussion of strategy, task force members were assigned a list of Democrats they would be responsible for working throughout consideration of the resolution. No whip count had been taken, so the task force would have to conduct its own count; a decision as to what questions to ask had to be made. "So then we had to decide what was the critical issue," a participant explained. "We knew we were going to have a series of amendments, but I didn't want at the start to have to give seven or ten questions to a person to have to ask and so, in our discussion in the task force, we reduced it finally to two." The task force decided that the most critical votes would occur on the Republican substitutes to the resolution. Because it appeared that several Republican substitutes would be offered, in their first approach to the Democrats assigned to them task force members asked whether they would oppose any Republican substitute. Because this first poll indicated a very close vote, the key decision for the leadership and Chairman Giaimo was whether they should try to defeat all Republican substitutes or offer a compromise amendment to the substitutes. The HBC staff were instructed to draft a perfecting amendment in case it was decided that one of the Republican substitutes could not be defeated.

The task force continued to work in the days prior to floor consideration. As they attempted to persuade their colleagues, members emphasized the carefully balanced nature of the committee product as well as party pride. "Our strategy was that this was basically a majority party document," a member commented. "This was written by the Budget Committee majority, and we ought not let the minority party dictate what the majority party is going to pass." A "Dear Colleague" letter signed by the Speaker, the majority leader, the majority whip, the chairman of the Budget Committee, the chairman of the task force, and the chairman of the Democratic Caucus made the same arguments. It read, in part,

> The committee Resolution responds to the national mood on inflation and deficit spending, while still reflecting traditional Democratic concern for human needs. It deserves your support. . . .
> We also urge your support in defeating weakening amendments such as the Republicans' Holt-Regula substitute which would significantly reduce budget levels. It would emasculate traditional Democratic programs and injure the economy.
> We Democrats have the responsibility of passing this Resolution. Since the inception of the budget process, Republicans have refused to cooperate in passing a resolution. We are hopeful that we can count on your help.

Floor consideration of the budget resolution began on 30 April. On 1 May the proponents suffered a potentially crippling defeat when, by a vote of 212 to 198, an amendment cutting $250 million worth of targeted fiscal assistance passed. If the decision had been allowed to stand, it would have split the coalition supporting the resolution and made the adoption of other major amendments more likely. A participant explained the problem: "We were using the argument, 'Look, this is a very carefully written budget resolution to make sure we're satisfying the agriculturalists, the urban community, the East, the West, the whole thing, and don't monkey with this very tenuous balance we have.' As soon as that 250 million [dollars] was taken out, you could hear people saying, 'Well, the hell with it; I'm not going to vote for this damn thing.' "

The committee chairman immediately met with a group of his members and with Budget Committee staff to draft a substitute, the Solarz amendment, which would restore $200 million worth of fiscal assistance. At this point the existence of an organized working group was crucial. "Once we had [the Solarz amendment], we got to work," the task force chair explained. "We recalled everybody and said, 'All right, here's what's happening, we need the votes on this one. Make sure the people you have as your responsibility vote "yes" on the Solarz amendment.' So within two days we came right back and got that thing reversed and got the [$] 200 million added in."

Between House sessions, the task force met with HBC staff for briefings on amendments expected. The task force chairman remained on the floor during the entire period of floor consideration, and members were expected to be there during each roll call to work on their assigned congressmen. "There were some of these amendments that were very appealing considering the 'Prop.' 13 mentality," a task force member said. "So we had, really, to explain to them why we ought not to be succumbing to this kind of thing.'' Because of the complexity of many of the amendments offered, bullets played an important role. A participant described the use of a bullet during the pressure of voting on amendments: "You know these members are coming in through the door and they have essentially seven to two minutes—or even a minute—to vote on an amendment. They're running in and asking, 'What is it?' and you can't explain a four-page amendment, changing aggregates and everything else and subfunctions. So you say, 'This is the Grassley of Iowa amendment, vote "no,"' and hand them the sheet. It points out as succinctly as possible what's in it: that it adds $380 million to the deficit, that it cuts out all programs for babies.''

On 9 May the showdown came, as both the Latta and the Holt-Regula substitutes—both of which proposed major cuts in social programs—were voted on. Majority Leader Wright sought to rally the Democrats in a rousing floor speech:

> Now we have [an amendment] which is almost seductive in its allure. It combines the admittedly impelling attractions of a big tax cut and a lower deficit.
>
> There are only a couple of things wrong with that. The trouble is when we look below the superficial figures at the premises upon which they are founded, we see that they are about as insubstantial as a big wad of cotton candy. . . .
>
> I see people on the Republican side laughing. Maybe it is funny. Maybe it is great fun to cut these programs for those who can afford least to be cut. . . . Is this to become a veritable who's who of those who do not count with the Congress? Well, I think not.
>
> We have a responsible budget resolution which is the result of the careful deliberations of the Budget Committee for many weeks and of this House over some 7 days of debate. . . .
>
> Further, to take the heart and soul out of the programs which are the lifeblood of America, for which this country has stood, would be indefensible.
> (*Congressional Record,* 96th Cong., 1st sess., 9 May 1979, vol. 125, pp. 2931–32)

The Latta substitute was defeated by a 191 to 228 vote; Holt-Regula, by 198-218.

The Republicans' inability to agree on one substitute contributed to Democratic success. Because Republicans introduced and brought to a vote two alternative plans, the leadership and the task force were able to persuade those Democrats who believed they had to go on record as favoring budget cuts to vote for one or the other, but not both. As long as these members divided their votes between the two alternatives evenly—and the task force saw to it that they did—both of them would fail. In fact, thirty-three Democrats voted "yes" on one and "no" on the other substitute. In addition, when a member could not be persuaded to support the leadership position across the board, the task force worked for partial support. A participant explained: "Now, part of that, frankly, was sold on the basis of, 'If you're going to vote "no" on final passage of the budget resolution, help us out at this point by voting "no" on Holt-Regula or any other Republican substitute.' And that argument seemed to hold with a lot of people, that they were willing to help us out by voting 'no' on any Republican substitute, even if they were going to vote 'no' on the resolution. The case of Texas, as an example: every one of them voted 'no' on both Latta and Holt-Regula, and that really helped us out immensely."

On 14 May, by a vote of 220 to 184, the House adopted the budget resolution. Democrats split 211 to 50 in favor of the resolution; Republicans, 134 to 9 against. The resolution had been on the floor for nine days, and more than fifty amendments had been considered. As Jim Wright has said, "A budget is a devilishly difficult thing, not only to put together, but to keep together" (*Congressional Record,* 96th Cong., 1st sess., 9 May 1979, vol. 125, p. 2931). By virtue of hard work and organization, that was accomplished. The adopted resolution was close to the one that had been written by the HBC Democrats.

The leadership's problems, it turned out, were not yet over. The figures in the compromise reached by the conference committee were somewhat closer to the Senate figures than to those approved in the House; in the compromise there was more allotted for defense and less for social programs. Some liberals believed the HBC chairman, who they saw as a closet conservative, had "caved." Others attributed the conference outcome to the HBC members' exhaustion and to the Senate's intransigence on the defense figure. Even fairly liberal Senate Democrats supported the higher defense figure, it was said, because doing so would justify a later vote for the SALT treaty. David Obey, one of the conferees, believed he and Chairman Giaimo had an agreement that the House conferees would not go below $31 billion on function 500, which includes education, training, employment, and social services. When Giaimo and a majority of House conferees accepted a lower figure, Obey felt betrayed and refused to sign the conference report.

Obey immediately began to mobilize interest groups to oppose the budget conference report. The Democratic Study Group came out against the resolution, and when the vote was taken on 23 May, labor and education lobbyists were "six deep" outside the chamber. The conference report was defeated 260 to 144, with 152 Democrats defecting. The leadership had not realized the depth of the discontent until too late, and the last-minute lobbying it undertook was to no avail.

Attempts to work out a new compromise began immediately. The Senate refused to decrease the defense figure, but it did agree to add $350 million to function 500. The interest groups that had supported Obey agreed to go along, as eventually did Obey. The task force and the leadership set to work persuading members. One day after the rejection of the first conference report, the revised resolution was approved by a vote of 202 to 196.

Budget Politics 1980

▆▆▆▆▆▆▆▆▆▆▆▆▆ When, on 28 January, President Jimmy Carter sent Congress his budget, there was little indication that 1980 would be a watershed year for the congressional budget process. Continued congressional concern about inflation had led HBC Chairman Giaimo to conclude in early January that a balanced budget might prove to be a political necessity, and a series of informal bipartisan meetings among HBC members suggested that a bipartisan balanced budget might be possible. Carter's budget, however, proposed a deficit of $15.8 billion. In the absence of a galvanizing event it is unlikely that the HBC discussions would have borne fruit, but the 22 February announcement that the consumer price index had increased at an 18 percent annual rate in January created a crisis atmosphere. Administration officials met to plan a response and decided that further spending restraints were necessary. Spending cuts would, of course, require congressional action, and the administration consulted informally with congressional leaders.

In early March an unprecedented series of joint administration-congressional meetings took place for the purpose of discussing budget cuts. A senior HBC Democrat revealed the origins of these meetings:

> They got started because there was a very real crisis, an economic crisis. It's hard to describe, but it had a threat of doom like I haven't seen since I was a child. The markets were going to hell, the bond markets, the investment markets, everything was going to hell. There was real fear in the land. The CPI was somewhere around 18, 19 percent. And the president, apparently recognizing that he had to revise his budget, initiated some talks. I think what happened is that the president spoke to "Tip" and Byrd at a leadership meeting along the lines of "We've got to revise our budget." So out of that original meeting came a decision to meet informally, to see what we could do.

Chaired by Senate Majority Leader Byrd, the meetings included party and committee leaders from the House and the Senate and high-ranking administration officials. Secretary of the Treasury William Miller, OMB Director James MacIntyre, Stuart Eisenstat of the White House, and Charles Shultz, chairman of the Council of Economic Advisors, took part for the administration. The Speaker asked Majority Leader Wright to take the lead for the House; Wright, HBC Chairman Giaimo, and Richard Bolling, chairman of Rules, were the most active House participants. In eight days of meetings, the participants agreed on a package of spending cuts which would balance the budget and, the congressional leaders believed, could win congressional support.

Out of these meetings came what HBC Chairman Giaimo called his "pink sheet," which provided the guidelines for the chairman's mark. HBC Democrats discussed and partly approved the mark during two days of closed caucuses. Some committee liberals—Obey, Paul Simon (D.-Ill.), and Solarz, in particular—were unhappy with selected items but "wanted to stay on board." Jim Wright attempted to negotiate a compromise and came very close to succeeding. Worried that he would lose Republican support, Giaimo pulled out of the negotiations before an agreement was reached.

Despite the liberals' unhappiness, the mark-up was completed in only two days—a record. David Obey offered an amendment to add $500 million for local revenue sharing to cushion the effect of the elimination of state revenue sharing. Despite President Carter's support of it, Giaimo voted against the amendment, and it failed on a twelve to twelve vote. Giaimo believed that in the end big-city liberals would be unable politically to vote for the resolution and, consequently, that he had to maintain Republican support. Jim Wright, concerned about holding the party together, played the mediator role, but, aware that a split between the leadership and the HBC chairman would be fatal, he supported Giaimo when a choice had to be made. On 20 March the committee approved the fiscal 1981 budget resolution by a vote of eighteen to six. For the first time, committee Republicans supported the resolution; six liberal Democrats voted in opposition.

The resolution approved by the committee closely followed the agreement reached in the joint congressional-administration meetings; it proposed a $5.5 billion surplus and included reconciliation instructions to achieve it. Under the 1974 Congressional Budget Act reconciliation instructions that direct other committees to make spending cuts so as to bring spending in their areas into line with the budget resolution were to be included in the second resolution. The HBC realized, however, that only with this provision would the budget be enforceable. The resolution thus instructed eight House committees to prepare by 15 June legislation proposing specific dollar cuts in programs under their jurisdiction. The HBC would then package the proposals and send them to the floor as a single omnibus bill.

Although reconciliation occasioned little conflict in committee, its unprecedented inclusion in the first resolution activated strong opposition from most of the affected committee chairmen. Interpreting it as a serious threat to their committees' influence, sixteen chairmen wrote the Speaker a letter of protest which read, in part, "Invoking reconciliation in the first step of the congressional budget process undermines the committee system, reposing in the Budget Committee authority to legislate substantively with respect to the nature and scope of federal activities. Such a procedure, which infringes on the legitimate roles of authority and appropriations processes, is not required in achieving a balanced budget" (Clark and Cohen 1980, p. 593).

The substance of the resolution activated the opposition of a multitude of interest groups. A 147-member coalition of liberal groups organized by the AFL-CIO vowed to fight the cuts in social programs. Lane Kirkland, president of the AFL-CIO, attacked the resolution as representing "a misguided approach to fighting inflation that runs counter to the general welfare of the American people, especially the weak, the poor, the handicapped, minorities and the young and elderly of our society'' (Clark and Cohen 1980, p. 595). The Speaker, himself an old-line liberal, was unhappy with social program cuts, and particularly with HBC's defeat of the Obey amendment. It was not only liberals who were unhappy. The highway lobby, veterans groups, and federal employee organizations all believed that programs of interest to them had been singled out for an unfair share of the cuts. Under ordinary circumstances the array of forces in opposition would have doomed the resolution, but strong congressional sentiment that a balanced budget was a necessity both politically and economically counteracted the influence of the opposition interest groups. Nevertheless, success on the floor would require careful planning.

A consensus emerged early in the process that this budget resolution could not be sent to the floor under an open rule. At the first joint meeting Richard Bolling had suggested that a complex rule would be necessary. A Rules Committee staffer as well as staff representing the top party leadership figures monitored the entire budget mark-up. After the mark-up was concluded, a series of meetings at the staff level were held. Staff from the Rules and Budget committees and from the Speaker's and majority leader's offices came together and classified all the amendments that members wanted to offer. The purpose was "to get a really good idea of the range of major proposals.'' The last meeting included the principals—the Speaker, the majority leader, Bolling, Giaimo, Foley, and several other leadership figures—and was devoted to deciding which amendments should be allowed. There was also some discussion of limiting debate time on amendments, but it was decided that such a limitation might endanger the rule.

The rule agreed on allowed eight amendments and several specific amendments to those amendments. The amendments that were permitted reflected Bolling's belief that the budget resolution should be a macroeconomic document and that the function of complex rules is to "give members of the House the opportunity to make the big choices with adequate time and get away from the junk.'' Four major Republican amendments were allowed; in an attempt to soften liberal opposition, Obey's amendment was made in order; the committee chairmen were given the right to attempt to delete the reconciliation provisions.

The leadership decided that the greatest danger was presented by an amendment to be offered by Marjorie Holt (R-Md.), which proposed to shift $5.1 billion from domestic programs to defense. "If we can break the back of that, we've got it,'' a senior HBC Democrat said. The leaders, the appointed whips, and HBC Democrats attempted to persuade their colleagues to provide across-the-board support, but when they were unable to extract such a commitment they concentrated on the Holt amendment. "If you've got a choice,'' a participant said, "you get him on Holt and tell him he can do what he wants on the final vote." The Steering and Policy Committee voted to urge Democrats to oppose all four Republican amendments. Because the Speaker basically supported and Giaimo adamantly opposed the Obey amendment, the leadership as a collectivity side-stepped the issue. The Steering and Policy Committee was also split on the Obey amendment and so took no position regarding it.

Unlike in previous years, no budget task force was appointed. Because task forces had been used on highly partisan efforts, participants believed that setting up a task force might well drive away Republican votes. In addition, many of the Democrats who would have worked on this budget task force intended to support the Obey amendment, and, as a staffer said, "that would have been awkward."

On 23 April the rule for consideration of the budget resolution was approved by a vote of 261 to 143. The margin indicated that, despite their grumblings, members considered the rule to be fair. On 1 May the Holt amendment was rejected by a surprisingly large margin—246 to 164. The one-on-one persuasion efforts of HBC Democrats and party leaders as well as opposition letters from President Carter and Secretary of Defense Harold Brown had paid off. In addition, everyone knew that the Senate resolution would include higher defense figures and that adoption of the Holt amendment would thus severely decrease the House's bargaining room in conference. "We had a balanced budget," a HBC staffer explained. "What we were trying to sell was that you can't mess too much with it. On the Holt amendment, Giaimo was very effective because of his position on [the] defense appropriations [subcommittee]. We said leave it alone, we'll work that out in conference."

The House defeated the Obey amendment on a much narrower (201 to 213) vote, with Democrats splitting 165 to 96 in favor. Although O'Neill supported the amendment, he did not work for it actively, as that would have been interpreted as a slap at Giaimo. The amendment to strike reconciliation was easily defeated, 289 to 127. The only amendment adopted was one offered by Giaimo and backed by the leadership. On 7 May the House adopted the budget resolution by a vote of 225 to 193. Voting in favor were 203 Democrats and 22 Republicans; 131 Republicans and 62 Democrats opposed the resolution. Even though it provided for a balanced budget and, in contrast to previous years, the Republican Policy Committee took no position on it, the resolution received little support from Republicans—but because the vote was so close even that support was crucial. Obey and Simon, who had voted against the resolution in committee, supported it on final passage. Their disappointment with the product was outweighed by their commitment to the process.

For the House Democrats, the conference proved to be a disaster. The Senate, as it had been the previous year, was adamant on its much higher defense figure. Some close observers believe that Giaimo, who was sick during part of the conference and who had announced his retirement, simply did not have the necessary patience to bargain effectively. All of Jim Wright's attempts to negotiate among the House Democrats met with recalcitrance. A staff member said, "He tried to get the House conferees together but someone always thought he could get more, so it didn't work." A senior HBC Democrat explained the problem: "Given that we were in balance, if you added one place you had to find it someplace else. This was a first, and therefore you didn't have the flexibility that you had in earlier years of, 'What the hell, you compromise here, you compromise there, and you add it up and whatever it is, it is.' Well, you can't do that if you have a pie that you have got to divide up." At one point Giaimo believed he had procured an agreement that all of the House Democratic conferees could support. Five Democratic conferees, however, refused to extend their support. Giaimo ascertained that he had sufficient votes from Republicans and went ahead with the agreement. The refusal of the "gang of five" to sign the conference report, however, convinced most participants that it could not possibly pass on the House floor.

On 27 May President Carter expressed opposition to the budget resolution. O'Neill, who was genuinely distressed by the cuts in social programs and under pressure from House liberals, who are his natural constituency, came out against the resolution at the last moment. By then Wright, Brademas, Foley, and Bolling had already committed themselves to support. Thus not only the party but also the leadership group was badly split. Wright argued for the resolution on the House floor, but rather mildly. "This is not a perfect instrument," he said, "but I really believe that the criticism that has been leveled against it by the President and others has been somewhat overdrawn" (*Congressional Quarterly Weekly Report,* 31 May 1980, p. 1460). On 29 May the conference report was rejected on a 141 to 242 vote.

At that point the leadership lost control of the situation. Democrats got the word—how or from whom has never become clear—that they could go home. Delbert Latta, ranking Republican on the HBC, moved to instruct House conferees to stay with the high defense figures in future negotiations with the Senate. Chairman Giaimo's motion to table (that is, kill) the Latta motion was defeated 123 to 165. Giaimo was supported by 121 Democrats and 2 Republicans; 57 Democrats joined 108 Republicans in opposing him. Many Democrats had left the floor and did not vote. Giaimo next moved that the House adjourn; on a 141 to 145 vote, with 37 Democrats adding their support to 108 Republicans, the motion was defeated. The Latta motion to instruct was then adopted by voice vote.

Democrats, thus, had been outmaneuvered on the floor. Widespread absences and defections on procedural votes resulted in a situation Chairman

Giaimo called "ridiculous." "When you vote down one resolution because it's too high on defense and turn around and instruct the conferees to accept the Senate defense numbers, it's questionable," he said. "Now I've got two mandates" (*Congressional Quarterly Weekly Report,* 31 May 1980, p. 1459).

Attempts to reach a new agreement began immediately. Giaimo and Senator Ernest Hollings (D-S.C.), chairman of the Senate Budget Committee, held daily telephone bargaining sessions. On 3 June the two chairmen conferred with President Carter at the White House. House party leaders, Giaimo, and other HBC Democrats held a series of informal meetings. Progress was slow. Many House participants believed that Hollings would not "give an inch" on defense spending until after his primary election. On 11 June, the day after Hollings won his primary with 81 percent of the vote, agreement was reached. Domestic programs were increased by $1.3 billion; defense was decreased by $800 million.

Although the Speaker had opposed the first conference report, the events of 29 May, especially the defeat of the motion to adjourn, were a serious threat to his control. Defeat of the second conference report would be interpreted as a demonstration of Democratic inability not only to restrain spending but also to govern, and would seriously damage the Speaker's prestige. At this point the ambivalance that had characterized his involvement in the process gave way to strong determination to pass the compromise.

Because the first budget resolution should have been approved by 15 May, the leadership had to bring the conference report to the floor quickly. The leaders had begun to lay the groundwork soon after the disastrous floor session on 29 May. Both the Speaker and the majority leader, at the regular Thursday morning whip meetings, had made pointed comments about party loyalty; the Speaker had brought up the possibility that committee assignments might be used systematically to reward and punish.

On 11 June a Steering and Policy Committee meeting was convened. Chairman Giaimo briefed the members on the substance of the new conference report. The Speaker made it clear that he considered the vote a party matter and that he expected the support of Steering Committee members. A loss, he said, would play into the hands of Republicans in the upcoming elections. They would claim it showed that Democrats cannot govern.

As the Steering Committee meeting drew to a close at one o'clock the Speaker asked one of the HBC Democrats who attended to chair a task force. The vote was scheduled for three the next afternoon. A Steering and Policy staffer and a member of the task force chairman's staff immediately began to draw up a list of members. The Steering Committee staffer explained:

> On the phone, we talked through a list. Basically it was just a list of people we know, those who worked the budget, those who worked the debt limit. So you

go to people you know are approachable and willing to work and put together a list. For instance, there was a guy in _____ . . . who did such an outstanding job on the debt limit. I mean, you couldn't leave him off anything you really needed to pass because he just got every vote there was. Every vote he was asked to get, he got. Without exception. So, you ask him. So you have a series of people like that.

The task force met at four o'clock. According to the chairman, "We talked; we gave out the states to different people. We went over the numbers that we would need. We gave out the statistics of how people had voted on the prior two votes on the budget resolution. We gave out fact sheets on the settlement so that they knew what they were talking about, so they could explain it to people. And then we sent them forth to return the next day at noon to get their report on the members that they were to see."

Early the next morning the top leadership met with the deputy and the at-large whips, who were also working the vote, to review their efforts. At the regular whip meeting the leadership reiterated its expectation that Democrats would support the conference report. That morning Democrats received a strongly worded "Dear Colleague" letter signed by O'Neill, Wright, and Brademas. It read, in part,

Today you will be asked to decide the future of the Congressional budget process and at the same time resolve a fiscal crisis of dramatic proportions.
We urgently ask you to vote "yes" on the Giaimo motion. . . .
We have firm evidence that a large majority of Republicans have cast aside any sense of responsibility in an effort to block resolution of this fiscal issue and win votes in November. At stake is the ability of the Democratic party to govern the House. This danger crosses philosophical lines. Failure to adopt the first resolution would demonstrate clearly that the Democratic Congress cannot deal with the budget. It would discredit the party and the Congress.
All of your Democratic conferees have agreed on this compromise. . . .
This may be the most important vote you will cast both as a member of the 96th Congress and as a Democrat.

Several hours before the vote was scheduled, Budget Committee staff arrived on the House floor armed with bullets explaining the conference report, and they remained there until after the vote. The leaders and task force members continued to work on the Democrats assigned to them. One participant described the arguments used:

If their interest is higher defense spending, you point out the strong points in the budget in that regard. If they're interested in higher social-domestic spending and they're against higher defense spending, you confess, and you say that this is not a good budget for them, that you understand how they'd be upset about it, but you point out the importance of the budget process, you point out that this is just one step in the budget process, that they'll have another day in court, you point out that the process goes on year after year, and some years you win and some years you lose, but the important thing is that there be a process, and lastly you point out that the conferees did the best they could in a bad situation, and you point out that if the process falls apart, that the party of which they are a member will suffer. And so you really tie it to some kind of a party responsibility as well as an institutional responsibility.

At noon the task force met to assess the situation. Most members had completed their assignments. "We were within striking distance," the chairman said. The task force chairman and several other members then went to the floor. "[The task force chairman] and a few others stayed on the floor and worked the votes," a staffer explained. "When there were no people on the floor to talk to, they worked the telephones. And by the time the vote came on the floor, we had a hard count of about 200."

The first roll call came on Giaimo's motion to order the previous question, thus ending debate. The motion was agreed to by a 237 to 161 party-line vote; while only 12 Democrats voted against the leadership, not one Republican voted for the motion. The conference report was then approved on a 205 to 195 vote. Democrats split 195 to 55 in favor; Republicans, 140 to 10 opposed.

Because the budget resolution included reconciliation instructions, passage of the resolution was only one step in a highly complex and politically delicate process. Most committee chairmen had fought reconciliation on the floor. They saw it as HBC usurpation of their committees' powers, and many opposed the cuts required on substantive grounds as well. The Budget Committee lacked the clout to ensure compliance; the party leadership would have to play a central role in enforcing reconciliation. As Chairman Giaimo said, "Nothing is going to happen in legislative reform unless the leadership forces these committees to do it" (Clark and Cohen 1980, p. 592).

In mid-June the leadership, HBC Chairman Giaimo, and the affected committee chairmen met. Each chairman was asked to lay out his plans; each promised to comply. By then a series of meetings at the staff level had already taken place and negotiations were underway. Although still disgruntled, the committees, to a large extent, complied. According to a participant, "The reason that it wasn't more difficult was that Democrats were looking for a vehicle to demonstrate fiscal restraint. Many are getting hit over the head as big spenders in their campaigns." Not all the committees complied with good grace. An aide said, "If you read [the Education and Labor Committee's] report, you'll see they are really against all their own recommendations." Another participant said, "Some of the cuts made by committees seemed designed to draw a great deal of fire—the cut in child nutrition [programs] being one." Pressure from the leadership and the Democratic membership at large, however, was too strong for the committees to resist.

The various segments of the reconciliation bill were drafted by the legislative committees and packaged into a single bill by the Budget Committee.

On 21 July the HBC approved the bill and voted to ask the Rules Committee for a modified closed rule permitting only certain technical amendments. Considering the bill under an open rule, the participants agreed,
would doom it. Members would find the pressure to restore various cuts
irresistible, and most of the savings so painfully achieved would disappear.
"If you give them a free choice, there's no way that they'll ever vote for savings," a senior HBC Democrat explained. "The pressure around here on
the school lunches subsidies and on the postal subsidies was unreal, and if
they had had a straight up-or-down vote on either one of those, we would
never have voted to cut them. But when you're able to package it into a savings package, they're not going to go home and say they voted against saving six and a half billion dollars."

Most of the twenty-four witnesses who appeared before the Rules Committee asked to have an amendment made in order. After the witnesses were
heard, the point at which amendments to the rule were in order was
reached. Republican Bob Bauman offered an amendment to allow a floor
vote on an amendment reinstating the twice yearly cost of living adjustments for federal retirees. A committee roll call on the so-called "COLA
amendment" was requested and, when three Democrats joined all of the
Republicans, the motion passed on a vote of eight to seven. Chairman Bolling immediately adjourned the committee. The vote came as a complete surprise to Bolling and the leadership. Some observers speculated that the
Rules members voting for COLA had not expected it to pass. Bolling and
the Speaker talked with the defecting Democrats and found that none
would change his or her vote. The leadership then decided to postpone floor
consideration of the reconciliation bill until Congress returned from its
recess on 18 August.

A participant explained the problem: "Once COLA passed, it became
impossible to argue against other amendments, impossible to justify not
making other amendments in order. But [amendments allowed to come to a
vote] would all have passed on the floor and the savings accomplished by
reconciliation would have been minimal and the House would have demonstrated it couldn't be responsible." "It finally took the Speaker to get things
on track again," a senior aide said. O'Neill hosted a lunch for all Rules
Committee Democrats and told them they must not allow any other amendments. He said he would be Speaker again in the next Congress and everyone who wished to serve on Rules in the upcoming Congress should let him
know. When the Rules Committee reconvened on 28 August the meeting
went "quickly and smoothly." Voting as a bloc the Democrats turned down
all further amendments.

The campaign to pass the reconciliation bill began well before the rule
was granted. No whip count was taken because without a rule it was difficult to know what to count. Working the bill took the form of one-on-one

persuasion. "We kept a record of the people we talked to, and between myself, the Budget Committee, the Speaker, and the majority leader, we talked to 140 to 150 people [before the rule was reported]," a senior staffer said. "It was a low-publicity but not a low-keyed effort on purpose," another participant reported. "Essentially the legislative committees were being disciplined, so it shouldn't be rubbed in. We wanted to save face for the legislative committees and keep the Budget Committee from coming under any more fire than necessary." Lobbying in favor of COLA was intense—members were deluged with mail—so little effort was expended on the issue by the bill's supporters; their belief that defeating the amendment was impossible led them to concentrate their efforts elsewhere.

Everyone realized that the vote to order the previous question on the rule would be crucial. Losing that vote would result in a bill that was open to amendments. "We were working very hard to get people to treat the vote on the previous question as a leadership vote, a procedural vote," a participant said. "That was the sum and substance of Bolling's speech on the floor: Even if you don't like the rule, vote the rule down, not the previous question. If the previous question goes down, Republicans have the time and can make their own motion. Don't turn this over to the Republicans."

The reconciliation bill came to the floor on 4 September. The HBC staff and some of the members spent the entire day working the floor. Jim Wright was in evidence at the doors and in the well. During the previous question vote, the Speaker worked the whip's door until Brademas arrived; O'Neill then stood at the monitor—a signal to members of his interest in the vote. Chairman Bolling's motion to order the previous question was agreed to, 230 to 157; 230 Democrats voted yea; only 14 defected. All of the Republicans voted against the motion. The rule itself was adopted on a 206 to 182 vote; this time 39 Democrats defected, while the Republicans again were unanimous in opposition. The COLA amendment was overwhelmingly adopted by a 309 to 72 vote. The bill then passed on a bipartisan 294 to 91 vote.

Budget Politics 1981

███████████████ Ronald Reagan's electoral victory on a platform of deeply slashing federal spending transformed and raised the stakes of the battle over the budget. The Reagan administration decided to use the budget process as the primary mechanism not only for cutting funding but also for making substantive changes in law. To that end reconciliation, which first had been employed in 1980, would be used to instruct committees and, as in 1980, reconciliation would be ordered in the first, not the second, budget resolution.

The Democratic House leadership, although not convinced Reagan's program made economic sense, was prepared to cooperate with the administration. A large proportion of the Democratic membership interpreted Reagan's victory and the Republican takeover of the Senate as a mandate for spending restraint. Reagan was personally very popular with the public, and the leadership did not want the Democratic party to be labeled obstructionist. Furthermore, the loss of thirty-three Democratic House seats dangerously reduced the large Democratic margins of the previous congresses and suggested that a confrontationist strategy would not work. The Democratic leadership, thus, agreed to the use of reconciliation on the first budget resolution.

Jim Jones of Oklahoma, the new chairman of the Budget Committee, initially hoped to put together a bipartisan budget resolution. Because even Democratic liberals conceded that political necessity dictated giving Reagan much of what he wanted, bipartisanship on this previously intensely partisan committee seemed possible. Jones discussed his strategy with the Speaker, who expressed skepticism but did not discourage him. In making up the chairman's mark, Jones conferred exhaustively with a wide variety of House members and outsiders: HBC members (both Democrats and Republicans), committee chairmen, junior Democrats, and administration officials. "I think Jones's consultations were perhaps as broadly based as I've ever seen," a staffer reported.

Jones's refusal to convene the House Budget Committee Democratic caucus upset many moderate and liberal HBC members. Because of his reputation as a conservative, they feared Jones was selling them out in order to gain Republican support. But Jones did meet with these members singly and in small groups and did accede to some of their requests. Furthermore, his plan proved to be satisfactory to most of them. An aide said of eight liberal HBC Democrats who met with Jones on 2 April, "They emerged after three hours happy as clams when they found their package was fairly similar to Jones's proposed spending cuts. They agreed to support Jones in the end, though several reserved the right to try for amendments" (Cohen 1981a, p. 647). "It was a good bill considering the circumstances," said an aide to one of these members. "What developed was pretty much a consensus approach," a moderate HBC Democrat reported.

Communication between the leadership and the Budget Committee is constant, so the leaders were kept informed during the process. The majority leader, as a member of the committee, was directly involved in the negotiations. The Speaker's staff closely monitored the process, and both Wright and Jones periodically briefed O'Neill. A participant, describing the strategy behind the Jones mark, said, "The chairman tried to figure out a mark that would reflect the interests of the Democratic members of the committee and the key Democratic members of Congress. He tried to work out a mark that might have some bipartisan base; tried to work out a mark that was passable. And we tried to accommodate as much as possible of a popular president's program." The leadership generally agreed that this was the correct strategy and was pleased with the content of the Jones mark. "Everybody pitched in. We took some of every member's ideas," a leader commented. "And we thought that we had an amalgam that everybody could support. It had been the assumption from the beginning that that was what we were going to do."

When Jones presented his plan to the Budget Committee in early April, the administration responded with an attack. Secretary of the Treasury Donald Regan called the Jones plan "well intentioned but inadequate"; OMB Director David Stockman, architect of the Reagan budget, charged that Democrats were "changing their words but still singing the same old tune" of more taxes and spending (Cohen 1981a, p. 647). "Because it gave the administration at least 75 percent of what it wanted, Jones was very surprised the Republicans opposed his proposal so strongly," said the HBC's chief counsel. "But they apparently throught they could get more momentum for the later battles, especially taxes, from a total victory" (Cohen 1981b, pp. 888–89). Jones continued to urge the White House to help in devising a bipartisan plan, but the administration instructed the HBC Republicans not to compromise. Deeply angered by this recalcitrance, Jones accused Stockman of having a "bunker mentality stemming from a gargantuan sense of egotism." "The administration says it can accept no amendments; that its budget is untouchable. No administration has ever made such demands; and no Congress has ever accepted such demands," Jones said during the mark-up. "It is not the job of Congress not to think" (*Congressional Quarterly Weekly Report,* 11 April 1981, p. 610).

On 9 April, as the House Budget Committee was completing its mark-up, the Reagan-supported substitute—later to be known as Gramm-Latta—was unveiled. This substitute was very similar to the original Reagan plan except that it carried somewhat deeper cuts. Phil Gramm, an extremely conservative Texas Democrat and one of the forty-seven members of the Conservative Democratic Forum, had negotiated this alternative with OMB Director Stockman. Delbert Latta and other HBC Republicans who had been consistent supporters of the original Reagan plan were bypassed. Although they were furious, they had no choice but to go along (*Congressional Quarterly Weekly Report,* 18 April 1981, p. 672). House Budget Committee Democrats held together and rejected the Gramm-Latta substitute on a thirteen to seventeen vote with only Gramm voting with the Republicans. The Jones plan was approved by the committee on an identical vote.

The leadership knew that passing the resolution would be extremely difficult despite Democratic unity in committee. The 30 March attempt on the president's life made Reagan even more highly popular, and members were likely to be swayed by their constituents' pro-Reagan sentiments during the

Easter recess. Although many liberals were unhappy with the social program cuts in the Jones plan, conservative Democrats posed the major problem; a number of them were opposed to the defense spending figures in the HBC resolution. As a result of extensive meetings with the Speaker and conservative Democrats, Jones was persuaded to support the administration's higher military outlay figures. It was decided that Bill Hefner, an HBC Democrat from North Carolina, would offer a floor amendment changing the defense figures. "The feeling was that politically we couldn't hold any kind of Democratic coalition together, particularly southern conservatives, if we were cutting any amount from defense," a committee Democrat explained. "The Speaker felt that that was the case. And our hope was that if we gave everybody a vote for that kind of amendment restoring defense that we would then pick up the southern votes that we needed to try to win the resolution." At this point HBC Democrats were optimistic. "When we reported the resolution out of the committee and adopted it after a long battle in the committee we felt very good about what we had reported out," one of them said. "I felt we had a good shot at it."

Using a task force to work on the budget resolution had become standard operating procedure, but in this case no task force was appointed. A senior staffer said:

> Everybody knew how they were going to vote. You really weren't going to get votes with a task force. Not on something that was this salient. This was an issue that was as much political as any budget resolution has ever been. They've all been political but this was more political, more emotional, and less related to economics. This was a real political test of the president's popularity. A task force wouldn't have done any good. I mean a lot of times we've had task forces because a lot of members didn't know what the budget resolution did and didn't know its impact—if it either hurt them or helped them or what the alternatives were. And that was not relevant this time.

Although no task force was appointed, the Democrats did mount an extensive effort. "We wrote to all the Democratic mayors and governors—sent them a couple of letters," a participant explained. "Through the chairman and his staff, we activated every pressure group that we could. You know, in every sense of the word, there was an informal task force. The whips worked it; key people on the liberal side were consulted; key people on the conservative side were consulted; staff was encouraged to fan out; Foley and Wright really worked it hard."

This Democratic effort was no match, however, for the extensive and expensive campaign waged by the White House. A participant described the administration's effort:

> They called every campaign contributer that gave to Reagan and to a Democratic congressman in those districts. They had a very systematic effort—calling

key group leaders, chambers of commerce, bank presidents. In many of these districts they have conservative groups that go out and get petitions signed and so forth. I remember when I was in Fort Worth for a hearing on the budget, they were able to generate almost 875 names on a petition in less than three hours. They might even be a minority in the district, but they're so well organized they appear to be the majority. And that's the kind of pressure there was.

Another person who was deeply involved in the Democratic effort said, "The White House put on a full-court press. As my father used to say, they just took coal shovels full of money and threw them at it. And they went back into the districts of all these guys. They had banks of telephones. . . . So they put out a fantastic amount of money and got to the contributors."

While many of the Democrats whose votes would be key spent the recess in their districts on the receiving end of this well-orchestrated campaign, the Speaker was in Australia. An aide explained O'Neill's absence during this crucial phase of the legislative battle: "It wasn't just the Speaker's trip; it was a trip that was planned for two years by the legislature. The Australians had made rather elaborate preparations for it, so to cancel out would have been horrendous." On his return on 27 April the Speaker, tired from the trip and suffering from jet lag, made a statement at a press conference that the media interpreted as a concession of defeat.

The next day Ronald Reagan spoke to a joint session of Congress, making a plea for the approval of the Gramm-Latta substitute in his first speech following the assassination attempt. The White House's lobbying campaign continued unabated. "They used the president's personal popularity coupled with the polls showing that the public supported his program and they generated incidentally the most fantastic mail campaign that we've ever seen," a member recalled. "There was so much incoming mail the week before the Gramm-Latta vote that the House post office for the first time in its history literally was shut down and couldn't deliver mail without a three- or four-day delay to us." Some southern Democrats, it was reported, received promises that Reagan would not campaign against them if they supported him on the budget resolution.

Thus the administration threw all of its resources and those of its interest group allies into the campaign. Democrats found they had few allies. "The only groups that helped the Democrats were the groups that have no other place to go—labor and the minorities," a leader reported. Some groups that ordinarily would oppose spending cuts, at least in programs of interest to themselves, were immobilized by internal splits; in a number of cases the Washington staff of interest groups found themselves under attack by local affiliates who demanded support of Reagan. Other groups, convinced the Democrats could not win, were demoralized. The result was that Democrats received little effective help from interest groups.

Members involved in the persuasion effort began to see the results of this uneven balance of forces. One participant described how the balance tipped in favor of supporters of the White House: "I talked with a number of members and they thought [the Jones proposal] was a very sound mark, much more sound and much more realistic than the administration's position, which contained a lot of excessively optimistic economic assumptions, especially on interest rates. But there came a time when, . . . given the kind of constituent pressures they were under and given the fact that their voters were demanding the president be given his full opportunity, they didn't go with us."

Although the Democratic effort continued, the leadership knew before floor debate began that it would be defeated. The whip count, which was being conducted on a continuous basis, showed that the cause was lost. A senior staffer said, "We knew going in that there was no way that we could save the Jones bill and defeat Gramm-Latta." Because of the certainty of defeat, the leadership did not commit all its resources. "We were down all the way and we all knew it, so the kind of negotiations that would go on, if we were sitting there with two votes short, the whip count shows us within five votes, that's an entirely different kind of ball game," an aide reported. "A different kind of strategy, a different kind of arm-twisting, and a different kind of leverage on the part of the leadership would have occurred. But we were never really close after the recess. We were close before the recess, but we didn't vote then."

Floor debate on the budget resolution began on 30 April and continued for six working days. Republicans argued that the 1980 elections carried a mandate for the Reagan program, that a vote for Gramm-Latta was a vote for a freer and more prosperous America. Democrats disputed the content of the mandate, emphasized that the Budget Committee resolution made major cuts, and warned of the policy consequences of adopting Gramm-Latta. Majority Leader Jim Wright said when he addressed the House:

> Mr. Chairman, the consequences of the action we shall take in a few minutes here on this floor will cast a very long shadow. . . .
>
> I believe that we on the Democratic side of the aisle and in the Budget Committee have made an earnest effort to be responsible, to be constructive, and to be cooperative with the President of the United States. We introduced a budget which reduces spending dramatically. . . .
>
> As Mr. Gramm appropriately observed, we are shooting with real bullets, and that is correct in either case. . . .
>
> The question is, At whom are we shooting? Who are the targets of our gunnery? Do we aim mainly at waste and fat and fraud—or do we aim at health and feeding programs for the aged and the young? At training programs for the handicapped and the disadvantaged?
>
> I think the American people gave us a mandate to work together, though we may represent different parties in this Government. . . . They expect us to

cooperate with the President but not to be supine. To work with him does not mean to take orders from him.

Face the consequences of your vote. You shall have the opportunity in 60 days to vote on a reconciliation bill that will put into effect those changes that we vote for today. . . . Members should expect to vote later to carry out those changes for which they indicate a preference in their vote today. (*Congressional Record,* 97th Cong., 1st sess., 7 May 1981, vol. 127, p. 2047)

The Speaker of the House seldom gives a floor speech, but when he does a vote of overriding significance is indicated. O'Neill closed debate on the 1981 budget resolution:

Are we, with meat axes, now going to change the laws that made America as great as it is? I personally think we are wrong if we do that.

That is a judgment for you to make. I have talked with you one by one. There may be somewhere between 65 and 80 who may be leaving us. If you are leaving on the question of conscience, I have respect for you, but if you are leaving because not to leave may bring an opponent in an election against you or may cause you harm in the next election, then I have no sympathy for you whatsoever.

The difference in these bills is basically this. Do you want to meat ax the programs that have made America great or do you want to move slowly and say, if there has been a mistake, if we have been wrong in this program, we can come back. You close the door on America with the Latta bill. . . .

I want to say thanks to Jim Jones and the members of his committee. They worked hard. They worked diligently. They worked, in my opinion, in the best interests of America. (*Congressional Record,* 97th Cong., 1st sess., 7 May 1981, vol. 127, pp. 2053-55)

On the crucial vote, 63 Democrats joined all of the Republicans to approve the Gramm-Latta substitute, 253 to 176. Forty-nine of the defectors were from southern or border states; fourteen were from the North. A participant estimated that nineteen of the defectors would have voted for the Democratic alternative if their votes would have made the difference, but they "just bailed out" when Republican victory was assured. If that estimate is accepted, the firm vote for Gramm-Latta was sufficient to assure a comfortable victory for the administration. The budget resolution was then adopted on a 270 to 154 vote; Republicans voted 186 to 1 for the resolution, Democrats, 153 to 84 against.

Disappointed and embittered, many Democrats criticized the leadership, singling out Jim Wright's support of Phil Gramm for a Budget Committee position and the Speaker's trip to Australia and hi· "concession" statement. Yet few members believed that the vote could have been won, even if the leadership had acted differently. By and large the defectors had responded to what they perceived as strong, clear signals from their constituencies to support Reagan. When members perceive that a vote is likely to affect their chances of reelection, there is nothing the leadership can do. "Members were scared to death about their election," a Democrat explained. If a member has received 500 calls from his district, "there's no way 'Tip' can go into a member's district and promise he'll make it OK." Neither arguments about the merits of the legislation nor any of the favors the leaders have at their command are likely to have much effect. A participant described the hold constituency sentiment has on members: "You can't take a guy like [a southerner from a difficult district] and say, 'I'll give you such and such a public works project in your district; therefore, vote for my budget resolution,' because that won't work for _____ in this situation. You have to go to the people and get the people with you and then it will become possible for a guy like _____ to vote with you and then he'll be happy to do it." After discussing the administration's lobbying campaign, another participant said:

> I think its also a very serious mistake to assume that [the members who defected were] responding to that immediate pressure. The pressure was more one of what they perceive their districts to think. The specific efforts of the White House with the campaign contributers and so forth only broke down the commitments of a few Democrats—maybe ten or twelve votes. I think [the administration] would have gotten a good proportion of that conservative caucus anyway because that's the way they perceive the world; that's the way they perceive their districts.

The passage of Gramm-Latta presented Democrats with a dilemma. The House Budget Committee's reconciliation orders directed committees to cut $15.8 billion in authorizations and $23.6 billion in appropriations. Gramm-Latta directed $36.6 billion in authorization cuts. The Democratic plan would have cut spending but preserved programs; the Republican plan required changes in basic law that would wipe out whole programs. A substantial majority of Democrats violently opposed Gramm-Latta, yet if the party refused to comply with the budget resolution it would severely damage the budget process and probably lead others to brand Democrats as obstructionist and irresponsible.

The intraparty debate on the appropriate strategy to counter the Reagan program was intensified by the passage of Gramm-Latta. Most conservative Democrats and some other, electorally vulnerable, members argued for a bipartisan strategy; accommodate Reagan and take credit for it, they said. Many liberals advocated differentiating the Democrats' position from that of Reagan as clearly as possible. Given the numbers, such a strategy would, they realized, lead to Reagan's program passing largely intact. However, Reagan and the Republicans would then have to bear full responsibility for the consequences of the program. A participant committed to this strategy described his viewpoint: "To be honest about it, many of us were not all that concerned about winning. My worst fear has always been that we would pass a slightly better program that would mildly ameliorate the disaster that Reaganomics is going to bring and it would be enough so that he could claim it was our program rather than his that got us into trouble.

And given that we couldn't really get a good program through, the best solution seemed to be to create a good program, substantially better than the Reagan program, and get maximum publicity for it and then, if we lose, it's Reagan's responsibility." A third strategy, that advocated by the leadership, came to be called "damage control." Its object was to protect Democratic programs where possible, to limit the damage as much as possible. Its advocates contended that this was the most responsible course in terms of policy, and that it was politically wise because it is important for the party to be portrayed in the media as responsible. A leader talked about the three different strategies:

> [Developing a unified approach] has been very difficult because we have in our ranks some of those who will come into our huddle and hear us call our plays, then run over to the opposition and tell them what plays we're getting ready to run and help them tackle our running back. On the other hand, we have some on the other side, the liberal group, who are willing to battle but want to lose, don't want to win. There are some who want the president to prevail; they want the most severe, Draconian measures to go into effect. They want the public to bleed so that it will appreciate what it's doing when it calls and demands that we go along with Reagan. Well, I don't think either attitude is a very responsible one. You know, it seems to me that what we have to do is to try to perform what damage control we can and keep at least alive the framework of programs that may need to be brought into position if we get into a situation of high unemployment, for example.

Although obviously frustrating for the leadership, the split between the proponents of the clear differentiation and the damage control strategies had not had much effect on the effort to pass the first budget resolution—advocates of both strategies were satisfied with the HBC's resolution. Although the hard-line clear differentiationists did not commit their energies to passing the resolution, they voted the leadership position. Reconciliation would have been difficult in any case; the passage of Gramm-Latta, however, immensely compounded the problem.

Under pressure from the Budget Committee, the committees under instruction by Gramm-Latta largely adopted the damage control strategy. Although the budget resolution suggested specific cuts, the committees were only bound on the dollar figure. Budget Committee Democratic leaders, particularly Jones and Leon Panetta, chairman of the HBC's task force charged with overseeing reconciliation, threatened to make the cuts in the Budget Committee if a committee refused to do so. Commitment to the budget process and the protection of their own credibility dictated that these Democrats take a hard line. Both Jones and Panetta, in arguing against Gramm-Latta, had warned members not to regard the vote as symbolic; each had committed himself to enforcing whatever the House passed. Faced with the choice between deciding on the cuts themselves and having the Budget Committee do it for them, the committees largely complied.

Complying with the reconciliation orders was not easy. The committees had to make major substantive changes in law within a short time. Because the process was new, committee staffs and members had difficulty understanding what was required of them, what counted as a cut. The Budget Committee staff worked with the staffs of the authorizing committees on a continuing basis, but the technical aspects were nevertheless a problem. Much more serious problems were presented by the political and policy aspects. "We have to tromp on hallowed ground—kick old friends in the teeth to achieve some of these cuts," said Morris Udall, chairman of the House Interior Committee (*Congressional Quarterly Weekly Report*, 23 May 1981, p. 890). Given the magnitude of the issues and the number of committees involved, the leadership had to play a major role in the process. Shortly after Gramm-Latta passed the Speaker met with Panetta, the HBC Democrat overseeing the reconciliation process, and all of the affected committee chairmen to discuss what was expected of the committees and to lay out a schedule. Thereafter the Speaker had periodic lunches with the same participants to discuss progress and strategy. The leadership and Panetta "conferred on a continuing basis."

Reconciliation was especially difficult for the Education and Labor Committee. Traditionally the most liberal committee in the House, it was called on to make deep cuts in the social welfare programs under its jurisdiction. "We are meeting with a gun pointed at our heads," said Chairman Carl Perkins. "The majority of this committee does not want to make these drastic cutbacks" (*Congressional Quarterly Weekly Report*, 13 June 1981, p. 1030). The passage of Gramm-Latta and the reconciliation process put tremendous strains on the Democratic party as well. Deep and bitter antagonisms between members developed, and criticism of the leadership reached a crescendo. The leaders held meeting after meeting with groups of members in which they stroked members, persuaded hostile members to talk with one another, and tried to preserve some remnant of intraparty harmony.

By the 12 June deadline, fourteen of the fifteen instructed committees had sent their savings legislation to the Budget Committee. The Energy and Commerce Committee was deadlocked between Chairman John Dingell's proposal and that of James Broyhill, the ranking minority member. Dingell decided not to call for a formal vote; he sent his proposal to the Budget Commitee with a notation stating that it had the support of a majority of the committee's Democrats.

As soon as Gramm-Latta passed, the issue of how strictly to enforce the reconciliation orders arose, and the debate quickly came to center on the rule. The Speaker at an early point had committed himself to allowing votes on restoring some of the cuts in social welfare programs; the majority leader and the chairman of the Rules Committee agreed. The Education and Labor Committee had based its cuts on the Speaker's promise; during mark-up Perkins said that the committee was "only making these cutbacks because we have received an absolute guarantee from the Speaker and the chairman of the Rules Committee that we will be allowed several votes on the House floor in order to reverse some of the worst cuts" (*Congressional Quarterly Weekly Report,* 13 June 1981, p. 1029). The committee had made large cuts in the most popular programs in the belief that funds could be restored to them on the floor and that worthy but less popular programs could thus be spared massive cuts.

The argument for a rule allowing some amendments was twofold: funding for some important programs would be restored and Republicans would be placed in an uncomfortable position: to support the president, they would have to vote against some very popular programs. From the beginning, leading Budget Committee Democrats had argued for a closed rule. The survival of the budget process and the party's reputation for responsibility demanded that reconciliation be strictly enforced, and that required a closed rule, they argued. Furthermore, by allowing votes restoring funds for popular programs, "you allow," said Leon Panetta, "people who voted for these cuts to get off the hook by voting for the restoration" (*Congressional Quarterly Weekly Report,* 28 May 1981, p. 891). If a number of votes were allowed, Republicans would determine which restorations to make; they undoubtedly would vote to restore funds for programs such as impact aid and student loans which benefit their middle-class constituents, thus protecting themselves politically. "A lot of our people think that if you put up five or six amendments, the Republicans will be able to pick and choose which ones will pass," a staffer explained. "And then they'll go back to the electorate and say, 'See, we passed these two things. The Democrats would have cut the hell out of them but we saved them.' " Some Democrats, furious with their defecting colleagues, argued that they should not be "let off the hook" either. A staffer said, "They don't want these bastard Democrats who voted for Gramm-Latta to come in here and be able to vote for a couple of programs and be able to go home and say, 'See, I saved your impact aid.' They want to stick it right to them; that's what they want to do. Have a closed rule and say, 'OK, baby, this is your stuff, you just chew on it good and hard because that's yours.' "

As the likelihood that the Republicans would seek to offer an administration substitute to the reconciliation bill increased, sentiment within the Democratic party swung toward the closed rule alternative. Committee and subcommittee chairmen, who had made the painful cuts but at least had decided where those cuts would come, wanted to protect their committees' work. "[We] had managed to package cuts that met the dollar requirements of Gramm-Latta in ways that left us with very fragile preservation of programs," a committee chairman explained. Other members argued that a closed rule would limit the damage since it would be impossible to allow Democratic amendments without allowing Republican ones. On 16 June

Education and Labor Democrats met with the Speaker and Rules Committee Chairman Bolling and said that they now also supported a closed rule, and that they would revise their spending cuts by shifting funds to the popular programs they had cut for strategic reasons. A member of the committee explained the committee's change of mind:

> As we came close to the end of the process, it became apparent that the Republicans were trying to use this to put together an extraordinary package which I understand is now some 6,000 pages in length and offer that as a total substitute to all the work that the committees did. That would indeed be a total revolution and the epitome of irresponsible legislation. And so to consolidate our support, to consolidate the Democrats, we went back to the drawing board and made the changes, restored the popular programs to a great extent, cut other things, and now we'll have a single package coming, combined by the Budget Committee out of efforts of each of the individual committees.

Bolling reiterated his view that a closed rule was a major mistake, but the Speaker, believing party unity more important than the form of the rule, seems at about that time to have decided to go with a closed rule.

Later in the day the probability that the Republicans would offer a substitute increased when Reagan attacked the reconciliation bill during a press conference. The president claimed a mandate for his program, denounced the work of the House committees, and urged the Democratic leadership to revise the bill. In closing he said, "But if that proves impossible, let me be clear: My administration will have no other choice than to support the proposal of a number of Representatives in the House to offer a budget substitute on the floor that matches the resolution they voted for in May" (quoted in *Congressional Quarterly Weekly Report,* 20 June 1981, p. 1105).

Democratic leaders reacted angrily to Reagan's statement. "It's dictatorial," said the Speaker of Reagan's treatment of Congress. "They're trying to dictate to the House, not only dollar figures, but details of program reductions and program destructions that I think are quite beyond the presidential prerogative if one takes the Constitution seriously," the majority leader said. "He demands 101 percent. And not 101 percent of just the broad objectives that he announces, but 101 percent of the details that Mr. Stockman announces." The leaders' comments were not solely for public consumption; the leaders were genuinely dismayed at what they saw as a usurpation of congressional prerogatives.

The Democratic Caucus met on the morning of 17 June to discuss reconciliation. Leon Panetta summarized the bill, responded to some of the OMB criticisms, and explained why the Budget Committee would ask for what was essentially a closed rule. The choice was between adopting a bill that provides for damage control or implementing Reagan's cuts and his philosophy 100 percent, he contended. A vigorous debate centering on strategy followed. Most members knew the leadership had decided on a closed rule, but some advocates of the alternate rule strategy strongly argued their case.

One member argued that not making the Republicans go on record on individual cuts was bad politics; another, that with so many possible amendments certainly six to ten could be found which would present Republicans with a Hobson's choice. The Speaker responded that he had advocated allowing amendments all along but that the Democratic membership had talked him out of it. He had been meeting with members from eight in the morning until eight at night, and the overwhelming consensus was for a closed rule. "This is a democracy," he said. "We go by the will of the group." Several members expressed deep concern about the abuse of the budget process and urged the leadership to begin thinking about reforms. Some added that, given the substantive changes in law incorporated within the reconciliation bill, considering it under a closed rule was neither democratic nor responsible. Bolling said that, although he considered a closed rule a mistake in terms of both policy and politics, he would follow the will of the leadership and the caucus. Wright added that he too had advocated amendments but that now unity was more important than the form of the rule. A leader closed the debate by arguing for party unity:

> I plead with you, let us have enough confidence and enough faith in one another as members of this party that we can come together and present a program. Let us have enough faith in the committees of our House that they have the best judgment of how to preserve and protect the programs and maintain maximum damage control. . . . So whenever we come out with it, for God's sake, we are all going to have to have some confidence in somebody, or we haven't got a team. The word *disarray,* which has been so overly used, will be appropriately applicable to us. So let us have confidence in one another and when it finally comes down to it, let us stick together on a vote that will at least set the framework in which this bill can be considered in an orderly way.

The vigorous three-hour debate energized most of the participants, who began to feel that some semblance of party unity was reemerging.

Also on the seventeenth, the Education and Labor Committee met to make the changes in its section of the reconciliation bill. The committee restored funds for impact aid, student loans, Head Start, nutrition for the aged, and several other popular programs, taking the money from the CETA program.

Early the next morning, a Thursday, the whip's office was instructed to conduct a whip poll on a closed rule for the reconciliation bill—to ascertain the members' position on the previous question on the rule as well as their position on the rule itself. Republicans would try to defeat the previous question so as to make the substitute they almost certainly would present in order. The whips were informed about the poll at the regular Thursday morning whip meeting, and they were asked to do their count and get their results in quickly. A good and timely count was essential because if the votes for passing a closed rule were not attainable strategy would have to be revised. The leaders forcefully asked the whips to persuade members to vote for the rule. Because the vote was seen as so crucial, the leaders employed a "hard sell."

That afternoon the Budget Committee met to report the reconciliation bill and to vote on the type of rule to request. The committee voted to send the bill, with Chairman Dingell's recommendations for the Energy and Commerce section, to the floor on a straight party-line vote; Phil Gramm voted with the Democrats; one liberal voted "present." Democrats argued for a rule that only allowed a vote on substituting the Broyhill energy proposal for the Dingell proposal. Since that committee had been unable to muster a majority for either proposal, the HBC Democrats believed that fairness dictated allowing that floor vote. Republicans argued for allowing a vote on a Republican substitute. Democrats kept asking to see the substitute; they wanted to know, "What *is* the Republican proposal?" The Republicans had no reply because their substitute did not yet exist. Rumors that the Republicans were having major problems putting together a substitute seemed to be confirmed. Leon Panetta twitted the Republicans by reading from a letter sent to the Speaker by a number of Republicans, including several on the Budget Committee. The letter registered the Republicans' objections to the Speaker's earlier promise to allow votes on a number of amendments to the reconciliation bill. The Democrats' rule proposal was approved by the committee on a party-line vote, with only Phil Gramm defecting.

That evening Jones and Panetta were called to a meeting with David Stockman, who gave the Democrats a list of the further cuts he wanted made, which presumably would be included in a Republican substitute. The Democrats were dumbfounded; many of the cuts were politically very touchy, such as a large cut in social security and a further cut in student loans. Jones and Panetta informed the Speaker, who also was unable to understand the Republican rationale. Because these cuts would be very difficult to vote for, the Speaker began to reevaluate his strategy. Allowing votes on the cuts appeared to provide an excellent opportunity to embarrass the Republicans, to present them a Hobson's choice of their own making.

The next morning, Friday, 19 June, the leadership, Bolling, Jones, and Panetta met with Minority Leader Bob Michel and Minority Whip Trent Lott to discuss the rule; they were unable to reach an agreement. After the Republicans departed, the meeting continued into the afternoon. The prospect of allowing votes on some Republican amendments appeared more and more attractive; it would present Republicans with a difficult choice and would protect Democrats against charges of not allowing a vote on the president's program. Bolling, however, insisted on seeing the Republican amendments before committing himself to anything.

At an afternoon news conference Michel, accompanied by Phil Gramm and Delbert Latta, unveiled the administration proposal. It would change the work of seven of the fifteen House committees, would replace numerous programs by block grants, and (its proponents claimed) would save an extra $20 billion over three years. An even more sweeping substitute that the administration had been considering earlier had been dropped because of opposition among both Republicans and conservative Democrats. The Republican proposal that came to be called Gramm-Latta II included the politically delicate cuts that Stockman had outlined to Jones and Panetta on Thursday evening. Michel presented the proposal in general terms, as it had not yet been converted into legislative language.

Monday, 22 June, was a busy day for the Democratic leadership. Before a change in strategy on the rule could be made, the leaders had to confer with as many members as possible. Certainly all the committee chairmen had to be consulted; the whips who had been told to sell a closed rule had to be contacted. Because only a pro forma House session was scheduled, many members were out of town, and reaching them was difficult. "It may just be too late to change strategy," a leadership aide fretted. "Everyone understands the rationale of having a closed rule, and explaining the logic of allowing some Republican votes may not be possible in the time available." As the whip poll on a closed rule neared completion, it showed that passing such a rule was probably impossible. Approximately eighty Democrats were undecided as of Monday morning, and the leadershp considered the undecideds as likely "no" votes.

On Tuesday morning Reagan invited the sixty-three Democrats who had voted for the Republican budget resolution (now dubbed Gramm-Latta I) to breakfast at the White House. Reagan urged that his proposal be voted on as a package and revealed that he had called the Speaker asking for such a vote. The Republicans clearly knew they could not win if members had to vote on the cuts individually; if they could get a vote on a package, it could be portrayed as a pro- or anti-Reagan vote and their chances were much better.

The leadership met on Tuesday to make the final decision on the rule and on scheduling. It was agreed that votes would be allowed on the administration plan, but as a series of amendments, not as a package. Some advocated putting off a vote on the bill itself until after 4 July recess, arguing that members needed more time to understand the immensely complicated bill. Others said that putting the bill off would only leave the Democrats open to charges of obstructionism and that members might be bombarded with constituent requests to support Reagan as they had been over the Easter recess. The Speaker decided to take up the bill as scheduled later in the week and to finish it, even if that required staying through the weekend.

The Rules Committee opened its hearings at half past ten on Tuesday, 23 June. To accommodate the crowd of lobbyists and media representatives, the hearings were held in a large room in the Rayburn Building instead of the committee's small room in the Capitol. Even so, everyone who wanted to watch could not be accommodated. Both sides saw the meeting as an opportunity to sway public opinion. Chairman Bolling, in his opening statement, said it was the most extraordinary Rules Committee meeting he had attended in his years of service on the committee as well as the most complex bill it had ever considered. He had received the hefty Republican substitute at about ten o'clock the previous night. He called reconciliation as implemented this year, and especially the Republicans' attempt to bring up a massive administration substitute at the last moment, "a grave misuse of the [budget] process." It was, he said, "the most brutal imposition of executive will since Nixon's impoundments."

Jones and Panetta, appearing for the Budget Committee, requested a closed rule as instructed. Asked during the interrogation period why he opposed a vote on Gramm-Latta II, Jones replied tartly that he still had not been given a copy. In their questioning of Jones and Panetta, many committee Democrats echoed Bollings's concern about the abuse of the budget process. Gillis Long expressed doubt about substantive changes in law being made so quickly and with minimal public debate. "Many members don't know what's in it, the media don't know, and it's damn certain the public doesn't know," he said of the reconciliation bill. He declared that the substitute was understood even less, as there had been no hearings and no committee consideration. The Rules Republicans, knowing they would ultimately lose in committee, directed their comments to the television cameras. Not allowing a vote on the administration proposal as a package would be undemocratic, they claimed.

Opening statements and the questioning of Jones and Panetta lasted until half past twelve. When the committee reconvened at two, Jim Wright appeared first. The majority leader's appearance before the Rules Committee is unusual, signaling the importance the leadership placed on the rule. Wright argued against a closed rule and against allowing a vote on the substitute as a package. "It is entirely wrong to deny the House a clear choice. The changes are too big and consequential to use a 'gag' rule," he said. "The American people are entitled to know what we're voting on, who it will affect, and how much more it will save." When Republican Rules members objected to having separate votes, Wright asked deadpan, "Why don't you want separate votes on the pieces? Aren't you proud of them?" Minority Leader Bob Michel appeared next, arguing for the administration position. He attempted, rather testily, to refute the claim that the Republican substitute was really the work of David Stockman at OMB. Many Republicans were said to be annoyed by Stockman's dictation of the contents of the Republican substitute and consequently their own lack of a substantial role in devising it. It was also reported that Michel was furious with Stockman for his high-handed attitude toward the House Republican leadership. In response to Michel's continuing refrain that only a rule allowing a vote on the Republican substitute as a package would be fair, Bolling replied, "I've tried to cooperate with the administration but you might per-

suade me to open it up completely. You might want to check on how Stockman feels about that." The final witness of the day was Phil Gramm, who
received a chilly reception from the panel's Democrats. At shortly before six
o'clock the committee adjourned for the day.

On Wednesday, 24 June, the leadership hosted a breakfast for Rules
Committee Democrats. The Speaker had held a similar meeting several
weeks earlier at which he had stressed the importance of party unity. The
meeting on the day the committee would report the rule was labeled "rein-
forcement"; it was to be a forum for a "pep talk." "It never hurts for them
to sit across the table from the Speaker," a participant explained.

At his press conference held just before the House convened, the Speaker
announced the rule that would be granted. Six Republican amendments, a
motion to recommit without instructions, and a motion to recommit with
instructions on block grants would be allowed. One amendment was permitted in each of the following areas: social security and Aid to Families
with Dependent Children (AFDC), energy and commerce, school lunches
and student loans, food stamps, subsidized housing, and cost-of-living
adjustments in federal civilian and military pensions and a cap on federal
pay raises. The amendments could contain only cuts; no restorations would
be allowed. The Republican package was still being revised in order to
broaden its appeal. As the majority leader said during the press conference,
"Stockman's office had admitted they want to restore $9 or $10 billion to
pick up votes." The Democratic rule would be written so as to prevent the
addition of such sweeteners. The Speaker reiterated the primary argument
against the substitute: the committees of the House had followed the
instructions of Gramm-Latta I, and the decision on where to make the cuts,
as even President Reagan had emphasized during the first budget battle,
should be made by the legislature.

The leadership knew that winning the battle over the reconciliation bill
would be difficult, but grounds for optimism existed. Because a number of
committees had made their cuts on a bipartisan basis, the administration's
attempt to overturn the results grated on many Republicans and southern
Democrats. "Many of us are senior members of these committees and had a
major voice in making these cuts," said Bob Ginn of Georgia, a member of
the Conservative Democratic Forum. "We told Mr. Gramm that we were
tired of being manipulated by the White House" (*New York Times,* 18 June
1981). Many Republicans were reported to be resentful about David Stockman's dictatorial behavior. That the reconciliation bill made actual cuts
rather than just set forth targets was also expected to advantage the leadership. In addition, several polls showing a slip in Reagan's popularity might
influence Democrats who had voted for Gramm-Latta I out of fear of
electoral defeat.

After the press conference, the House convened and the majority leader
rose to announce the legislative program. The following morning, he said,

the first order of business would be the rule for the reconciliation bill. Members should be prepared to stay through Friday and possibly later, as the leadership hoped to complete the bill before the recess.

On Wednesday afternoon the leadership convened an extraordinary meeting in the whip's office. The whips, the members of the Steering and Policy Committee, and the Budget Committee Democrats were invited, and most of them attended. Some Democrats, particularly liberal ones, were still unhappy about the leadership's strategy. Some "couldn't—wouldn't because it's too painful—understand why Democrats couldn't offer restoration amendments" if the Republicans were given amendments. One member claimed he would not vote for any rule for reconciliation, which he deeply opposed. Another angrily charged that a closed rule had not been honestly counted; that the closed rule strategy that he favored had not been given a fair chance. Still another remarked acidly that if "the leadership agreed on this strategy for twenty-four hours, it must really be great."

The leaders explained the situation as they saw it and the rationale for their strategy. They reiterated that the votes needed to pass a closed rule were unattainable; that the rule they proposed would present the Republicans with a series of Hobson's choices as so many Democrats had been urging; and that, because it could not fairly be portrayed as a "gag" rule, their rule was much better for the image of the party. They pleaded for unity for the sake of the people who would be hurt by the deeper Reagan cuts and for the sake of the Democratic party. When the meeting ended some members were still unhappy, but most of them realized that not only voting with, but also working with, the leadership was imperative.

The majority leader and Jim Jones proceeded to a meeting with interest group representatives. The large Budget Committee hearing room, where the meeting was held, was filled to overflowing. Wright and Jones explained as well as they could what the Republican substitute would do. It was still being revised, though, so the only written information on the substitute available to Democrats—the one-page list of cuts that Stockman had given to Jones and Panetta and the package that had been delivered to the Rules Committee—was out of date. This information was sufficiently worrisome to a great many groups, and their lobbyists promised to do what they could.

Meanwhile, because of the number of members who wished to appear as witnesses and because of Republican delaying tactics, the Rules Committee was unable to take a vote on the rule during the day, although it held both a morning and an afternoon session. Bolling called an evening meeting to finish the committee's work. Republicans continued to insist that their substitute be voted on as a package and refused to write the six amendments allowed. Bolling responded to their stance by stating that he would have the staff draft the amendments and that the Republicans certainly did not have to offer them. The Democratic rule was adopted by the committe on a straight party-line vote.

It was clear that the roll call on the previous question on the rule would be the key. The Republicans knew they could not win on the amendments allowed by the rule; Michel had admitted that before the Rules Committee and the press and had said that if the Democratic rule passed, he would abandon the amendments. If the Republicans could defeat the previous question, however, they could propose their own rule and specify a vote on Gramm-Latta II as a package. The sixty-three Democrats who had defected on Gramm-Latta I were the target for persuasion from both sides. The whip count indicated that the key vote could be won.

On Thursday, 25 June, the day of the showdown, a mob of reporters attended the Speaker's press conference. "Today, we will see whether President Reagan's Republican robots are willing to match their budget-cutting rhetoric with their votes," O'Neill began. Replying to Republican attacks, he said: "In an effort to be fair, the House leadership has agreed to allow votes on the president's amendments. But the president does not want Congress to decide these issues on their merits. He wants to package them all together so people will not be able to tell how badly they are getting hurt and who is doing it to them." Asked whether the Democrats would win, the Speaker replied, "It will be extremely close. The president was up three-quarters of the night calling people and twisting arms. It's really close—and you know the frailties of human nature as well as I do." "Yesterday we had the vote easily won," he continued. "We only counted fifteen votes for them yesterday on this side of the aisle."

The Democratic leaders knew that one of their strongest arguments with conservatives was that the substitute represented dictation by the administration, and they took every opportunity to make that point. Told that Michel was furious about the rule, the Speaker responded, "We showed Mr. Michel the president's package, and that was the first knowledge he had of it. He hadn't been conferred with by the White House, by Stockman or Gramm, and neither was Latta. But when the White House twisted his arm, he caved in like the rest of them. Then he turns out to be so furious. What an act!" Richard Bolling added, "Late yesterday afternoon, they were still getting changes in Gramm-Latta II." Asked where the changes were coming from, Bolling replied, "The minority. I don't know which branch." Everyone laughed.

When the House convened at ten o'clock, one-minute speeches by members were in order. O'Neill was in the chair and the other leaders were on the floor, talking to doubtful Democrats, attempting to persuade them to vote for the previous question. It was expected that a large number of members would wish to make one-minute speeches on this occasion, but eventually it became clear that Republicans were using the one-minutes for delay. At one point the Speaker asked members who still wished to speak to raise their hands, and when he saw how many hands went up, he remarked, "Well, I guess the president will have time to make some more phone calls."

At noon the debate on the rule for the reconciliation bill formally began. The mood in the chamber, which had been highly charged during the one-minutes, became even more tense. Republicans argued that their package represented the will of the American people and the Democratic rule was unfair, a "gag rule." Democrats responded that the committees had complied with the Gramm-Latta I instructions, that calling the rule that allowed votes on the components of the administration package a "gag rule" was absurd, and that adoption of the Republican substitute would be an abdication of the rightful powers of Congress. Leon Panetta stated the issue this way:

> I recognize that this process is being stretched to the brink, it is being stretched to the breaking point. But in the very least we have had the committees of jurisdiction review the proposals that were before them and that is something we cannot say for a proposal that Mr. Stockman has come up with that is 350 pages and that was not even printed until 10 o'clock last night.
> I ask my colleagues from a reconciliation point of view, from a process point of view, but, most importantly, from an institutional point of view, that we not surrender the only power we have here, the power to check and balance the Executive. That line is going to have to be drawn sometime, and I urge my colleagues to draw it now by supporting the rule. (*Congressional Record,* 25 June 1981, p. 3372)

As speaker followed speaker, tension mounted. Increasingly, speeches were cheered and booed. At a quarter of one a whip call was sent out urging all Democrats to come to the floor immediately. At one o'clock Jim Wright spoke.

> Has the Congress of the United States—the last repository of the people's will—come to the point that we are willing to let an appointed official in the Office of Management and Budget dictate every last scintilla, every last phrase of law, to tell us what precise provisions we may and may not pass? . . .
> So I ask the Members: Vote for the rule, if you can. Give the Members choices among these significant proposals in order that we may go on record upon them individually and the public may know exactly what is being done. (*Congressional Record,* 25 June 1981, pp. 3377–78)

Minority Leader Michel closed debate for the Republicans. His remarks showed how deep the bitterness had become.

> I have got to vent my spleen over what you and your cohorts are proposing for us, the minority. We requested a rule giving us one clean vote on a comprehensive package of amendments to the committee bill. . . .
> Recognizing that in unity there is strength, you and your leadership group consciously decided that you had to cut us up in pieces, a sort of divide and conquer strategy. . . .
> This is not only a bad rule, it is a rotten rule. It is what you would expect to cram down the throats of a party of nincompoops. (*Congressional Record,* 25 June, 1981, p 3381)

Richard Bolling closed for the Democrats:

> The issue today is: Do we begin to accept the responsibility of members of the House of Representatives without regard to party, without regard to a popular President? De we have the guts to stand up for what we believe in? Do we have the guts to stand up for the people we represent? . . . . Or are we going to hide behind this parliamentary game, this attempt to gag the House?
>
> Mr. Speaker, I yield back the balance of my time, and I move the previous question on the resolution. (*Congressional Record,* 97th Cong., 1st sess., 25 June 1981, vol. 127, p. 3382)

Throughout the debate the Democratic effort to line up votes proceeded. The leaders, whips, Budget Committee Democrats, some members of Steering and Policy, and other willing members were involved in the persuasion effort that took place primarily on the floor. "Anybody who was interested was welcome. It was an expanded whip effort," a whip's staffer said. "Before the vote, we knew we were going to lose," a leadership aide said. "We would have won if the vote had been taken first thing in the morning, but the president was calling someone in the Democratic cloakroom every five minutes. Some are afraid of Reagan and others believe in him. We were losing someone else all morning long." A whip reported: "On Gramm-Latta II, right on the floor I was talking to somebody I knew was undecided. I was talking to him, Jim Wright was talking to him—I don't remember who the third guy was. There were three of us talking to this one person. The roll call was getting ready to start and Trent Lott came over, tapped the guy on the shoulder, says, 'The president wants to talk to you in the cloakroom.' They were good."

The previous question was defeated, 210 to 217; 29 Democrats, all but 4 of them from southern or border states, voted with the Republicans. Although fewer Democrats defected here than on the Gramm-Latta I vote, the number was large enough to give the Republicans a victory. (One Republican voted for the previous question but he claimed to have punched the wrong button.)

More than members' philosophical agreement with Reagan and fear of electoral reprisals accounted for the leadership's defeat. Reagan made numerous deals to obtain the necessary votes (*Washington Post,* 27 June 1981). John Breaux, a Louisiana Democrat who received a promise from Reagan to back higher sugar price supports, said, "I went with the best deal" (*Washington Post,* 27 June 1981). After the vote Jim Jones remarked, "The Democratic cloakroom had all the earmarks of a tobacco auction" (*Congressional Quarterly Weekly Report,* 27 June 1981, p. 1128). A Democrat involved in the leadership effort said, "I rate the president and the White House as very effective. You know all the stories about peanut prices and sugar prices and post offices and freeways and medical centers—they'll deal for anything—nothing is untouchable. A lot of things that were unacceptable to them all of a sudden became very easy to swallow because they wanted to win, and would expend any price. You've got to respect them. Most effective political hard-ball White House that I have seen.''

Democrats were again disappointed in the efforts of interest groups that had been opposed to the cuts. "Nothing happened, there was no mail, no push, no effort, no lobbying, no door-to-door effort at all," a HBC Democrat said. "It all kind of evaporated and the consequence was that there really was very little lobbying on our side. It was all coming from the White House."

Defeat of the previous question meant that the Republicans now controlled the time. Latta offered his rule as a substitute for the Rules Committee rule. It provided that only two amendments be allowed: the Broyhill substitute for the Energy and Commerce section, and Gramm-Latta II. The latter was to be "considered as having been read," although members still did not have copies of it.

Because of the closeness of the vote, the Democratic leadership continued to work. The Republicans had to win three more votes before the Latta rule would be adopted. Democrats forced roll calls to be taken on each of the votes so as to provide more time for persuasion. The Democrats lost the three votes, 219 to 208, 216 to 212, and 214 to 208 (see *Congressional Quarterly Weekly Report,* 27 June 1981, pp. 1160–61). Not a single Republican defected on any of the three votes, and although the leaders used all the persuasive talents at their command and talked to the defectors over and over again, they could not obtain enough Democratic votes. "We have nothing to give them," a participant in the persuasion effort explained.

The loss of these roll calls meant that the following day the House would vote on Gramm-Latta II, but no copy of the substitute was yet available. A copy was finally delivered to the House Budget Committee after eleven o'clock on Thursday night, and the staff frantically went to work analyzing it. About five hundred copies became available at half past eleven on Friday morning—after debate had begun. Gramm-Latta II was several inches thick, but it was not possible to tell exactly how long the document was because the pages were not sequentially numbered. It contained handwritten sentences, scratched-out numbers that had been replaced with others that had been written in by hand, and even a woman's name and phone number (scrawled in the margin). Clearly a number of last-minute changes had become necessary to keep various Republicans on board. A cursory examination of the document revealed that it made various significant changes in substantive law that were not directly related to budget cuts.

On Friday morning a letter from the majority leader was delivered to the Democratic defectors. After affirming every member's right to vote however he or she thinks best, it asked, "Do you know what's in Gramm-Latta II?" It then listed some of the provisions likely to be unpopular with most Democrats and asked the members to consider what other even worse provisions might be hidden in that thick document. A sheaf of pink papers was circulated to Democrats containing three sections entitled "Provisions Repealed in Gramm-Latta," "Increased Discretion to Executive Branch," and "I Bet You Didn't Know."

Because the leadership meeting consumed the time normally reserved for it, the Speaker's press conference was delayed until after the House had begun debate. In his opening statement, the Speaker previewed the arguments Democrats would use during the remainder of the struggle. No one in the House, not even its sponsor, Latta, really knew what the huge substitute contained, O'Neill claimed. A cursory examination revealed a "hidden agenda" of transferring wealth from the working people to the rich, the Speaker continued. The substitute would cut social security, student loans, and health programs; it would allow David Stockman to define poverty.

During the House floor debate, Democrats hit hard on the points made in the Speaker's statement. Members denounced the substance of the substitute; they placed their greatest emphasis, however, on process arguments. "This is an appalling proposal we are about to vote on," said Jonathan Bingham of New York. "The text of this amendment, which runs for hundreds of pages, was only distributed to Members of Congress this morning. It will take weeks for all of us to learn exactly what we are being asked to vote on this afternoon. This is a travesty" (*Congressional Record,* 26 June 1981, p. 3850). According to Ted Weiss of New York, if the substitute passed, "the Congress of the United States, this House of Representatives, will no longer be able to claim it is a legislative body. It is nothing more nor less than a rubber stamp. We do not even know what is printed on the stamp" (*Congressional Record,* 25 June 1981, p. 3540). And conservative Ed Jenkins of Georgia exclaimed, "There is only one book I have ever taken on blind faith and this is not it" (*Congressional Record,* 26 June 1981, p. 3896). The process arguments reflected a genuine concern. Democrats also believed that their conservative party colleagues were most likely to be swayed by such arguments. Several Democrats who had voted for Gramm-Latta I emphasized process arguments in explaining their opposition to Gramm-Latta II. "If this Congress ever loses the expertise of the committee system, then this Congress is in trouble and we are going to have chaos," said Tom Bevill of Alabama (*Congressional Record,* 26 June 1981, pp. 3920–22). "The authors of this amendment don't seem to know what's really in it either, having hatched it in the wee hours of last night," said Elliot Levitas of Georgia. "And now what we have before us is the most shoddily put together piece of legislation this body has ever seen" (*Congressional Record,* 26 June 1981, pp. 3920–21).

Even though they knew their chances were slim, the leaders did everything they could to defeat the substitute. The leaders, members of the expanded leadership circle, HBC Democrats, and anyone else who might have some influence talked with the defectors. Some of the defectors on the previous question vote had told the leadership they could not vote for the previous question because they could not be perceived as being unfair to the president, but that they could vote against the president on substance. Although it seemed likely that any gains among such members would be offset by those lost on substance, the effort had to be made. By mid-afternoon one of the participants in the persuasion effort had talked to twenty of the defectors. When he asked them "How can you vote for *this*?" too many replied, "We'll clean it up in conference." A leader remarked tiredly that he had been "twisting arms all day" and hadn't gotten anywhere. The majority leader closed debate for the Democrats:

> This is a document of reaction. This is a document which combines into one compendium all of the whims and prejudices of a little group of willful men who met in private, in a clandestine setting and undertook to arrogate to themselves the almighty wisdom to undo all of the decisions of all of the committees of the House, carefully arrived at in public session. . . . I know that the Members are not going to permit this travesty upon so many unsuspecting people and upon the integrity and the traditions of the House of Representatives. (*Congressional Record,* 97th Cong., 1st sess., 26 June 1981, vol. 127. p. 3926)

Gramm-Latta II was adopted by a 217 to 211 vote; 29 Democrats and 2 Republicans defected from their party's position. Five Democrats who had voted against the previous question switched and voted against the substitute, but five who had remained with their party on the previous question vote defected on the administration substitute.

Despite their best efforts, the Democratic leaders lost the battle of the budget. Given the reduced size of its majority, the leadership lacked the resources to defeat a still very popular president who was willing to use the resources of the presidency to bargain for votes. Nevertheless, the implications of the battle were not all negative. The number of defectors had been cut from sixty-three to twenty-nine. The growing resentment against Stockman on the Republican side suggested that the incredible unity Republicans had thus far displayed might prove to be temporary. Possibly most importantly, Reagan's clean win meant that the results of the budget cuts were now clearly his responsibility. The banner headlines trumpeting Reagan's victory would make it impossible for the Republicans to place the blame for the suffering the cuts would cause on the Democrats. After Gramm-Latta I had passed Democrats had realized they were faced with a dilemma. Some had advocated letting Reagan have everything he wanted so that the consequences would clearly be his responsibility. The leadership had opted for a damage control strategy, one that would minimize the inevitable pain of the cuts. If they had won the reconciliation battle, however, the Democrats would have had to share the responsibility for the results with the Republicans. The legislative loss, many Democrats believed, would prove to be politically beneficial.

CHAPTER 7

THE

LEADERSHIP

IN ACTION:

OTHER

CASES

Panama Canal Treaty
Implementation Legislation

██████████████ The Panama Canal Treaty—actually two treaties that gradually transferred full responsibility for running the waterway to Panama—was negotiated by both Republican and Democratic presidents. It nevertheless became a highly emotional right-wing cause, and a massive administration lobbying campaign had been necessary to obtain Senate ratification. The implementing legislation required House as well as Senate approval, and House passage promised to be difficult. Intense right-wing lobbying against the bill was not countered by pressure from any supportive groups. Furthermore, many House members believed that because the treaty disposed of property that belonged to the United States, the House should have been involved in the ratification process. John Dingell, a mainstream Democrat, expressed the resentment of members at what they considered the administration's "extraordinary arrogance" in ignoring the House: "We in the House are tired of you people in the State Department going over to your tea-sipping friends in the Senate," he said. "Now you good folks come up here and you say you need legislation, after you ignored the House. If you expect me to vote for this travesty you're sorely in error" (*Congressional Quarterly Weekly Report,* 17 February 1979, p. 306).

In 1978 the Carter administration informed the House leadership that it. wanted the Panama Canal Treaty implementation legislation passed early in the 96th Congress. The treaties were scheduled to go into effect 1 October 1979, and a variety of preparations that depended upon the legislation needed to be made prior to that date. Speaker O'Neill believes that aiding a

Democratic president in passing his program is a duty of the Democratic leadership. The Speaker, however, is personally much more interested in domestic than foreign affairs. Furthermore, very much aware of his limited resources, O'Neill did not want to put his prestige on the line any more than necessary given the unpopularity of the bill and the doubtful prospect of victory. He thus made it clear that, while he would help, he expected the administration to take the lead role.

In November 1978 the Speaker assigned a Steering and Policy Committee staff member the task of riding herd on the bill. The staffer perceived the situation this way: "When the implementing legislation came along [the administration] had already built some enemies [who], number one, were opposed to the canal treaties and, number two, [whose] noses were turned because they had been left out of the ratification process. So we knew we had a big problem with this bill." During November the staffer took part in a series of meetings which included several people from the State Department, a White House representative, and staff from the Merchant Marine Committee, which would have primary legislative jurisdiction over the bill. These meetings served to clarify the wide disparity between what the administration wanted and what the committee was likely to approve. John Murphy (D-N.Y.), chairman of the Merchant Marine Committee, was clearly hostile to the administration approach.

Information gleaned from these meetings provided the basis for some early decisions on strategy. By the time the bill was introduced in January, the Speaker had decided to use his multiple referral powers. Although Merchant Marine was given primary legislative jurisdiction, parts of the bill were also referred to the Committees on Foreign Affairs, Post Office and Civil Service, and Judiciary. "We wanted the other three involved because they were sympathetic to the administration," the Steering Committee staffer explained. "And we needed their help, their votes, and their people."

When the Speaker refers a bill to more than one committee, he has the power to set a deadline for reporting. This was another reason for multiple referral on the Panama legislation; a deadline meant Merchant Marine "couldn't sit on it." The date for reporting was negotiated by the Steering and Policy Committee staffer. The Merchant Marine Committee wanted a date in June; the administration, no later than early March. The tenth of April was agreed on.

The staffer monitored the lengthy Merchant Marine Committee hearings on the bill. As the Speaker's representative, he sat in on the caucuses of the committee Democrats and on committee staff meetings on the bill. "As we went through the hearings, we got some of the Murphy strategy, where he would give, where he was firm and would not give," the staffer said. "And the [die-hard opponents], their strategy, what they might focus on, what they thought was the weakest point of the bill." Simultaneously, the staffer was meeting regularly with a small group of State Department lobbyists.

"We were mainly counting," he explained. "We started counting votes very early to find out where we had to start working on whom. And we had this constant comparing of notes: 'Well, I talked to Joe Blow, and he's starting to waiver' and 'This guy's just got his feet in cement and you can't change him.' And it was a constant checking of names and shifting a name from this to that category."

By the time the committee mark-up began, it was clear the administration bill would not pass. The decision was made to scuttle it, but to attempt to extract some concessions from Chairman Murphy. In a series of meetings before the mark-up Murphy compromised on a few points, but not on any of the major ones. Although the administration was unhappy with the Murphy bill, it agreed to support the bill in the mark-up and to concentrate on defeating amendments designed to kill it—particularly the Hansen amendments.

Although he was not on the Merchant Marine Committee, George Hansen (R-Idaho) had already established himself as the most vocal House opponent of the treaties and the legislation. His amendments, which the White House asserted were clearly treaty violations and consequently completely unacceptable, were offered in committee but were defeated. According to a staffer, the administration "hated" the bill that came out of committee but had no choice other than to support it.

Although the administration had made no serious attempt to defeat Chairman Murphy and win approval of its bill in committee, the relationship between Murphy and State Department representatives was strained at best. Yet, if the bill was to have any chance of passing the House, they would have to work together. According to the Steering and Policy staffer:

> This is where a guy in my position is helpful. As a Speaker's guy I was able to be the spokesman between Murphy and the administration, knowing that you need them both to get a bill out, that they hate each other, and that they need someone to go to and let off steam. I brought them together after the committee mark-up, after the committee bill came out and we knew what was going to go to the floor, and I said, "OK, now everybody's got problems, let's get it all ironed out." We had a pretty good meeting on floor strategy, deciding which amendments we would oppose. It brought them together for the first time. They were speaking to each other as a team: "We have a bill, we're going to get behind it." And so in that sense a job like mine serves a good purpose.

Throughout the process the Steering and Policy Committee staffer kept the Speaker informed. On several occasions the Speaker talked with key participants to encourage greater flexibility. O'Neill's attention was primarily focused on other matters, however. That fact, and administration pressure to pass the bill quickly, led to a miscalculation. A vote on the rule for considering the bill was scheduled for 17 May. When the rule barely passed (by a vote of 200 to 198), it became clear that the necessary work had not been done. The leadership immediately postponed action on the bill itself. The near-loss activated the proponents. "I was surprised, as badly as Carter said he wanted this bill, there was very little really big effort by the White House, until the damn rule almost lost," a participant said. "Then Carter really got involved. He personally got involved. He had his dinners [for members of the House] on this and his telephone calls and all the heavy stuff the White House can do with members."

The White House geared up a major campaign. Under the direction of presidential advisor Anne Wexler, those who had been involved in the ratification of the treaties in the Senate were reactivated. A letter to 5,000 of these proponents of the administration's view was sent out under the signatures of Democratic and Republican party elders Sol Linowitz, Hugh Scott, and Averill Harriman. Theodore Roosevelt IV, Gerald Ford, Henry Kissinger, and John Wayne were induced to make statements or sign letters. Lobbyists for a variety of religious, labor, and business groups were brought into the effort. Carter and members of his cabinet made dozens of calls to members of the House.

Some of the White House representatives involved in the effort wanted the Speaker to appoint a task force to pass the bill, and they suggested to the president that he ask the Speaker to do so. Carter, however, declined, and O'Neill decided to put John Brademas, the whip, in charge of the effort. Some participants interpreted this as an indication that the Speaker did not want to risk his prestige; others believed that because task forces in the past had been used on highly partisan matters, using the device on the Panama legislation might make getting Republican votes more difficult.

The Panama working group held its first formal meeting in the whip's office on 1 June. Members in attendance included Brademas, one of the deputy whips, two senior Democrats from the Foreign Affairs Committee, John Murphy of Merchant Marine, and two Democrats from the subcommittee on the Panama Canal. (Carroll Hubbard, chairman of that subcommittee, opposed the legislation and thus was not involved.) Each member of the leadership was represented by a senior aide; O'Neill's representative was the Steering and Policy staffer who had been working on the bill since November.

After a general discussion of the situation, the members reviewed the crippling amendments that were expected. All the participants were in accord that defeating the Hansen amendments was the top priority, but many other troubling amendments could also be expected. Information would have to be produced and disseminated to members of the House explaining which amendments were crippling and why.

Next on the agenda was the whip count. One poll had already been taken and another was planned. A decision on the question's wording had to be made. "Will you support the chairman of the committee?" was suggested. An expert from the whip's office objected, saying that question produces "a very soft count." After further discussion it was agreed that they would retain the question asked in the first count: "Will you vote against crippling amendments?'' House members would be told to listen to the chairman to determine which amendments were crippling.

The working group then went through the results of the first whip poll, which indicated much work still needed to be done. Members reported, and further assignments were made. In a few cases it was decided that representatives of outside groups (labor, for example) or prominent individuals (Father Hesburgh, president of Notre Dame, in one case) would be asked to talk with particular members. John Brademas closed the meeting by asking the participants to have their results in by early the following week. At that point the legislation was tentatively scheduled for floor consideration on 12 June.

In addition to this working group, a staff task force was also working on the bill. Made up of forty to fifty staffers of members committed to passing the legislation, this bipartisan group met a number of times in May and early June. Its members were attempting to educate congressmen via their staff. According to the Steering and Policy staffer who had helped form and who worked with this group, ''They did a lot of legwork. They talked to the legislative aides—the most influential staff people—and they did some good selling. I'm convinced they helped us to win votes.'' This staff group conducted its own count, and because it was a bipartisan group, it was able to count Republicans as well as Democrats.

Ordinarily the Democrats get information on Republican voting intentions from friendly interest groups. The dearth of interest groups strongly committed to this legislation plagued the effort throughout. ''It was a lonesome bill,'' a participant said. ''That was our problem, we couldn't get the shipper excited, they wouldn't do anything. The port people wouldn't do anything. There was this very effective right-wing operation. The mail that was pouring into this joint was 1,000 percent against the bill and you couldn't get one letter in favor of it.'' The administration eventually involved a number of outside groups in their lobbying effort, but many of the groups that participated did so primarily as a favor to the White House.

The Democratic leadership was also employing the regular Thursday morning whip meetings to educate its membership and to attempt to sell the bill. At the 17 May meeting John Murphy was brought in to explain why the Hansen amendments would kill the bill. The legislation was mentioned at each of the next few meetings, and the leaders emphasized the dire consequences of its defeat. At the 7 June meeting one of the leaders said, ''This one will separate the men from the boys. The whips are supposed to have some spine and help others have some spine.'' Another told the whips they should remember that a great deal of oil is shipped through the canal to the Northeast and that the shipments might be cut off if the bill was not passed. He said the constituency problem with voting for the legislation has been exaggerated, and that the repercussions of defeating the bill would require extensive explanations.

The regular White House leadership breakfast on 6 June was devoted to only two topics—energy and Panama. The president reviewed the extensive administration lobbying effort and promised the House leadership he would do whatever they asked. Although both the whip count and the administration's own count showed that the votes to defeat crippling amendments were not in hand and that even a majority for passage was doubtful, the president asked that the vote be held on for 12 June and not be delayed. The White House effort was geared to that date, with a series of endorsements to take place in the days immediately preceding, and large newspaper ads to appear on the day of, the vote.

Reports that Panama was involved in smuggling guns to the Sandinista guerrillas attempting to overthrow the Somoza regime in Nicaragua gave opponents of the legislation new ammunition. At the request of George Hansen and Robert Bauman, another vocal opponent and a member of the Merchant Marine Committee, the Panama Canal Subcommittee held two days of hearings on the charges.

Taking a careful look at its whip poll results, the leadership concluded it did not have the votes and decided to pull the bill off the schedule. The White House, determined to go ahead, persuaded O'Neill to put it back on for 12 June. According to a Hill participant, "The White House seems to be looking at this from the perspective of what Anne Wexler's operation is going to do rather than from whether the vote count is there" *(Washington Post,* 8 June). By 11 June, however, the White House concluded that the votes necessary to pass the bill were not yet in hand. Vice President Mondale was sent to the Capitol to ask the Speaker to postpone action. O'Neill agreed to do so but refused to make a commitment to reschedule the bill before the 4 July recess as the White House had requested.

House proponents of the legislation expected the bill to be rescheduled soon if they could offer a reasonable prospect of victory. They and the administration redoubled their efforts. Because of the unpopularity of the bill and the number of floor amendments expected, a major informational effort was necessary. The White House, the whip's office, and the Merchant Marine Committee produced and disseminated succinct descriptions of the amendments expected and what their effects would be. The committee sent to every member a port-by-port breakdown of the tonnage shipped through the canal.

The effort to build a majority now concentrated on intensive one-on-one persuasion. A participant explained:

> The problem with the Panama bill was essentially a political problem. It wasn't so much a substance problem. I think there was wide private agreement in the House that (a) the Panama Treaty wasn't all that bad, (b) in any event the treaty had been concluded, that (c) if there was going to be an orderly transfer of the canal and one that protected the interests of the United States we had to have a bill something like that. . . . It was a question of political perception at

home, and members were afraid that their constituents who opposed the canal treaty for good or bad or even irrational reasons would consider a vote for this bill as a vote to approve the treaty, which it was not really at all. And so what you had to do really was to persuade members that the only responsible thing to do was to vote for the thing. Was to bite the bullet and vote for it, and per- suade them that indeed it wouldn't turn out to be that big a deal at home any- way. And that just involves a lot of talking to people.

Departments of State and Defense and White House liaison people made the rounds of member offices. Members of the working group and those at-large whips who supported the legislation took more names, talked to their assignees, and reported back to the whip's office. The leaders undertook to persuade those with whom the lower echelon had had no luck. The arguments emphasized were simple. One of the information sheets outlined them thus:

> The 1977 Treaties are now the law of the land.
> Only technical legislation is needed to carry out the mechanics of the Treaties.
> The Treaties will still go into effect October 1, 1979, with or without legislation.
> Without legislation, however, chaos will result and closing of the canal could result.
> Canal closure would impact seriously on U.S. economy and defense needs.
> U.S. honor and its integrity as a treaty partner are at stake.

The effort began to show results and, when the count indicated that some form of the bill would pass, floor consideration was scheduled for 20 June. On the nineteenth a final shakedown meeting of the working group was held, which the majority leader attended. Also present was a senior Republican who was actively supporting the legislation. John Brademas reported that the whip count indicated that defeat of the Hansen amendments was still not a certainty and distributed further rebuttal material on each of the amendments for use on the floor. Chairman Murphy outlined the floor strategy. The "nuts and bolts" amendments from the Post Office and Civil Service Committee would be taken up first. These were not controversial, and taking them up first was designed to convey that this was basically an administrative bill. Then the Hansen amendments would be considered. Instead of attempting to defeat Hansen on an up-or-down vote, Murphy would offer "a Zablocki–Foreign Affairs type substitute"—one keeping much of the Hansen language but leaving its implementation to the president's discretion.

Brademas estimated that about twenty Republican votes would ensure victory, and the Republican participant said his whip count showed nineteen Republican votes. "Not getting the Republicans mad so they close ranks" was, all agreed, crucial to success. Attacks on Hansen were not likely to coalesce the Republicans. When Ken Kramer, a Republican freshman, offered his amendment, the Democrats would have to be careful. It was decided that the Republican proponent who was present should be "the heavy" on the Kramer amendment.

Majority Leader Jim Wright, Clem Zablocki, chairman of the Foreign Affairs Committee, and a senior Republican proponent, it was decided, should speak on the floor. "The real liberal guys on Foreign Affairs could be a problem [in scaring away moderates and conservatives]," one member observed, and there was general agreement that those members should be discouraged from speaking if possible.

On the morning of the twentieth the opponents made a dramatic move in their campaign to defeat the legislation. Robert Bauman demanded a secret House session to hear classified government material about Panamanian gunrunning. The Democratic leadership decided to accede to his request because, according to Jim Wright, "We thought it might have a beneficial effect. We got everything out on the table and proved there were no secrets anybody didn't know all along" (*Washington Post*, 21 June, 1979). The opponents' tactic seems, in fact, to have backfired. Wright, the premier orator in the House, took the opportunity presented by the secret session to give his floor speech for the legislation; in view of the rarity of a secret session, he had an unusually attentive audience.

Later in the day and into the night, the House in open session considered the Panama legislation. A horde of State and Defense departments lobbyists camped out in the majority leader's office; the White House liaison people did the same in the Speaker's rooms. They were present to analyze new amendments that might be offered, to negotiate on the wording of such amendments if necessary, and to produce information sheets on them. Mostly they simply sat and waited, watching proceedings on the House televison. They had done what they could.

As expected, the showdown came on the Murphy substitute to the Hansen amendment. When the Murphy substitute was adopted on a 220 to 200 vote, the most severe test had been passed. Voting for the substitute were 195 Democrats and 25 Republicans; 68 Democrats and 132 Republicans opposed it.

The bill was finally passed, however, only after another close call. On the evening of 20 June the Democratic leadership worked out a time agreement with the Republicans; the House was to finish the bill by one o'clock the next day. When the House resumed work on the twenty-first, Sonny Montgomery, a conservative but well-liked Democrat from Mississippi, offered a somewhat milder version of the Hansen amendment. Many members did not understand that Montgomery's amendment would also kill the bill, and many believed they had voted with the leadership on this unpopular bill as often as they could politically afford. The amendment was rejected 213 to 210, but only after O'Neill and Wright, standing in the well, managed to change a number of votes during the last moments. That near-disaster averted, the bill passed on a vote of 224 to 202.

Even then the struggle was not over. The president stated that he was gratified the legislation has passed but hoped it would be improved in conference. It had been anticipated that the administration, unhappy with the Murphy bill but forced to support it in the House, would try to get some of its objectionable features removed in conference. Both the die-hard opponents and John Murphy were determined to resist a weakening of the bill.

On 27 July the House leadership attempted to send the bill to conference using the usual unanimous consent procedure. Robert Bauman rose to ask whether conferees from the Foreign Affairs, Post Office, and Judiciary committees would be restricted to the jurisdiction of the committees they represented or would have authority to negotiate on the entire bill. When the Speaker indicated that the latter procedure would apply, Bauman objected to the unanimous consent request. Bauman's objections to, and the Speaker's support for, allowing the conferees from committees other than Merchant Marine to vote on all sections of the bill were, of course, due to these conferees' friendliness to the administration position.

The Speaker then went to the Rules Committee and got a rule sending the bill to conference. Bauman, a member of Rules, attempted to amend the rule in committee so as to restrict the range of issues the conferees from Foreign Affairs, Post Office, and Judiciary could vote on, but the committee Democrats defeated that move. Aware that he could not defeat the rule on the floor, Bauman, when the rule was brought up on 30 July, moved to instruct the conferees to insist on certain House provisions. He argued that administration strategy all along had been to "squeak the bill through the House in any form you can get it" and then "to undermine the stand taken by the House" in conference (*Congressional Record,* 96th Cong., 1st sess., 30 July 1979, vol. 125, p. 6855). Stripped of its sensational innuendos, that was, in fact, the administration plan. Conscious of this, Murphy, who had opposed the administration approach from the beginning, supported the motion to instruct, and it passed on a 308 to 98 vote. Instructions are not binding on conferees, but they do serve notice of what the House is likely to accept.

The conference committee reached an agreement that satisfied Murphy on the points he was most interested in as well as President Carter to the extent that all provisions believed by the administration to violate the treaties were deleted. Die-hard opponents, led by Robert Bauman, were deeply dissatisfied and claimed that House conferees had "caved-in" to the Senate.

This continuing opposition, new concern about Soviet troops in Cuba and other threats to United States security in the Caribbean, and scheduling miscalculations led to defeat when the conference report was brought up in the House on 20 September. The leadership had scheduled a number of highly controversial bills for consideration in the same week, and as a consequence there was insufficient time to "work" any one of them as thoroughly as necessary, and a series of defeats followed. On a 203 to 192 vote, the House sent the Panama Canal bill back to conference.

The treaties were due to go into effect on 1 October—time was running out. On 24 September the conference committee agreed on several revisions, which allowed Bauman, an extreme conservative but also a realist, to claim that many of his demands had been met and to give a backhanded tacit endorsement to the bill. Although he voted against the bill, he admitted it had to pass. The administration was pleased that the bill contained not one of the House provisions it believed to be treaty violations.

Both the White House and the House leadership worked hard to reverse the previous week's vote. The administration enlisted Henry Kissinger and other influential figures to warn members of the effects of another rejection. Carter personally called more than a dozen congressmen. The president's signing of a controversial bill ordering completion of the Tellico Dam may have swayed some members. Many conservatives and southerners strongly supported construction of the dam which had been delayed because of environmental problems. A White House aide who was working to reverse the vote on the Panama legislation said Carter's signing the bill "contributed to the favorable mix of votes" (*Los Angeles Times,* 27 September 1979).

Majority Leader Jim Wright sent out a "Dear Colleague" letter strongly urging support. O'Neill and Wright personally asked a number of members to change their votes. They made sure that a few supporters who had been absent from the first vote be present. On 26 September, when the conference report was again considered, both Wright and O'Neill gave the floor speeches appealing to members' sense of responsibility. When the vote was taken, 25 members switched their position, and the conference report was approved on a 232 to 188 vote. Voting in favor were 196 Democrats and 36 Republicans; 70 Democrats and 118 Republicans voted in opposition.

Synfuels

■■■■■■■■■■■■■■ Jim Wright's interest in synthetic fuels—oil and gas made from coal and other materials—long predates his tenure as majority leader. In 1968 he attempted to interest Stuart Udall, who was Secretary of the Interior at the time, in a synthetic fuels program, but, as a senior aide explained, "This was in the dying days of the Johnson administration and the idea died with it." In the mid-1970s a synthetic fuels bill out of the Science and Technology Committee was killed on the House floor by one vote. Wright's interest continued, and a member of the majority leader's staff was assigned the task of thoroughly familiarizing himself with the issue so as to be prepared when the opportunity arose.

In January 1979 Wright decided the time to "do something positive" in the energy area was at hand. As a first step he asked a number of his aides to begin drafting a major energy speech. According to a participant, "In that speech we included some paragraphs about synfuels but didn't advocate a big program for building synthetic fuel plants. We mentioned synthetic fuels as an option that should be explored and deplored the fact that the president cut funds for synfuels out of his '80 budget." As work on the speech proceeded, the majority leader received a letter from William Moorhead (D-Pa.), chairman of the Economic Stabilization Subcommittee of the Banking Committee. Moorhead requested Wright's cosponsorship of synthetic fuels legislation upon which his subcommittee was working. Although they responded with a strong affirmative, the participants in the majority leader's office at this point did not view the Moorhead bill as a vehicle. The Moorhead bill was an amendment to the Defense Production Act; Wright desired legislation on a broader scale.

On 8 May the Banking Committee reported HR3930. Among its other provisions, the bill authorized $2 billion in price and loan guarantees for synthetic fuels to produce the equivalent of 500,000 barrels of oil a day. The proposed program was modest, and the bill, to this point, had received no media coverage. It seemed destined to be just another of the multitude of minor bills which pass with little controversy and no fanfare.

On 10 May, by a vote of 159 to 246, the House rejected Carter's standby gas rationing plan. Long lines at gas stations, a national phenomenon, helped to sink the rationing plan but also convinced Jim Wright that something had to, and could, be done. The defeat of the rationing plan had put Congress in a bad light, he believed; it had made the Democratic majority appear to be incapable of constructive action. He believed the House needed to act promptly to show that it could indeed address the energy problem.

Wright's energy aide set up a series of meetings to discuss the possibility of moving ahead on a synfuels program. Experts from the Department of Energy and from industry and high-ranking staffers from the Science and Technology Committee and from Moorhead's subcommittee participated. After exploring a variety of alternatives, the aide became convinced that the Moorhead bill was the ideal vehicle. The approach of the bill was one Wright favored and, because it had already been reported by the committee, expeditious action was possible. Committee consideration of a new bill would consume a great deal of time, and the conditions favoring its passage might fade. Jim Wright thus tentatively decided to offer an amendment to the Moorhead bill greatly expanding the synfuels program. According to one participant, "We were a little worried that we were taking a little bill that was perceived as not controversial and, by enlarging it, might be making it controversial and might endanger its passage." The opportunity provided by the long gas lines, however, was too good to miss. Members were receiving heaps of mail from irritated constituents and consequently were much more inclined than usual to act swiftly.

Wright believed that passage required an education campaign. The staff prepared a series of charts which Wright could use in presentations to his colleagues and on 31 May Wright made his presentation at a leadership meeting attended by the Speaker, John Brademas, Dan Rostenkowski, and Tom Foley. The response was enthusiastic, and the Speaker decided to put the full weight of the leadership behind the Moorhead bill and the Wright amendment.

Wright then initiated a series of lunches and meetings with his House colleagues on the legislation. The chairmen of committees and subcommittees with energy jurisdiction as well as other influential members, Republicans as well as Democrats, were invited. Because the bill might be interpreted as intrusive on the jurisdiction of the Commerce Committee's Subcomittee on Energy and Power, Chairman Dingell was given special attention. Both Wright and Moorhead, and then Wright alone, met with Dingell. Dingell expressed general support for the measure but also concern about some of the language.

On 5 June the Speaker called a special meeting of the Steering and Policy Committee. The committee unanimously endorsed the Moorhead bill and instructed the leadership to expand it. That afternoon Jim Wright held a briefing for all interested members at which he again made his presentation, and then he, Moorhead, and various experts answered members' questions.

Aware that energy would be discussed there and of John Dingell's apprehension concerning the intrusion of the Moorhead bill into his committee's jurisidiction, the Speaker "promoted" the White House to invite Dingell to the regularly scheduled White House leadership breakfast on 6 June. Morris Udall and Henry Jackson, chairman of the Senate Energy Committee, were also present. A broad discussion of the energy problem resulted. The congressional participants expressed support for the synfuels program, and the president appeared, at least, not to be opposed. On the seventh a joint House-Senate leadership meeting again discussed the proposal.

On 15 June, Jim Wright, William Moorhead, Secretary of Energy James Schlesinger, Stuart Eisenstat (representing the White House), and several congressional aides met in the majority leader's office. Schlesinger seemed strongly favorable to the proposal, but Eisenstat was somewhat hesitant. He said that, while the president was willing to support the Moorhead bill, he (Eisenstat) could not give the president's blessing to the expanded version. The White House, in addition, wanted the program funded from the energy trust fund, which would be set up once the windfall profits tax passed. Wright, knowing that passage of the tax was still uncertain, opposed such funding. In the words of a participant, "the meeting was not a love fest." Nevertheless, later in the process "the White House finally did get on board. The strong consensus in the House and the gas lines did it."

During June, while Jim Wright proselytized his colleagues, his staff worked to activate outside groups. One aide devoted himself to identifying groups that should have an interest in the legislation, providing them with information, and suggesting that they express their support to members of Congress. Other staffers got in touch with lobbyists they happened to know and attempted to get them actively involved.

The major remaining problem was the continued disagreement between the Banking Committee and the Energy and Power Subcommittee. John Dingell had said that he supported the program in principle but wanted to draft a perfecting amendment. Wright was agreeable so long as it did not hold up the process or make the plan unworkable. After Dingell sent Moorhead a lengthy memo expressing his concerns, Wright assigned his aide the task of negotiating a compromise between the two committees. The passage of energy legislation in the White House has long been made more difficult by jurisdictional problems. Committee and subcommittee chairmen quite naturally protect their "turf." Such jurisdictional considerations made the aide's task more difficult. A long series of meetings ensued; compromises on a number of points were worked out, but some differences remained.

On the nineteenth of June the Speaker convened a meeting of the party leadership and the committee and subcommittee chairmen who had energy jurisdiction. Its purpose was to discuss possible components of a major energy program. That the expanded Moorhead bill should be the first element found general agreement. As the meeting ended, the Speaker remarked pointedly, "I hope no one will oppose this." Said a participant, "the only trouble is that they didn't get into specifics, where there still is disagreement."

HR3930 came before the Rules Committee on 21 June. William Moorhead and Stewart McKinney of Connecticut, ranking minority member of the Economic Stabilization Subcommittee, testified on its behalf. Jim Wright explained that, under instruction from the Steering and Policy Committee, he would be offering an amendment to increase the figure to 2 million barrels of oil a day. Asked if he would need a waiver in the rule, Wright assured the committee that he had checked the amendment with the parliamentarian and that it would be germane and thus would require no waiver. The final language had not yet been decided on, he explained, because he was attempting to accommodate some technical amendments offered by Dingell. The tenor of the questions asked by Rules Committee members indicated strong support for the bill. Testimony by several Commerce Committee members provided the only discordant note. "Dingell testified before Rules that he was for synfuels but that this was a badly drafted bill that needed to be fixed and he was prepared with all kinds of amendments and that he wanted to be sure that bill had an open rule—no gimmicks," a participant commented. "We had already assured him of that." The Rules Committee granted the one-hour open rule that Moorhead had requested.

Attempts to resolve the problems between the Banking Committee and the Energy and Power Subcommittee continued. One "long and painful" meeting between the staffs ended in failure. Shortly before the bill was scheduled for floor consideration, a strategy meeting between majority leader's staff and high-ranking Banking Committee members and their staff was held. "We were going over the various amendments we had in hand that Dingell was proposing," a participant reported. "Even in those areas where I saw the possibility of compromise, the members didn't want to, they were willing to fight it out on the floor. One thing after another fell in that category. That worried me because I thought 'My god, this is going to take forever.' Anyway, we went through all the amendments and devised a strategy for each."

Originally the majority leader's office had scheduled HR3930 for Friday, 29 June, the last day before the 4 July recess. A mass of major legislation was awaiting consideration, and that seemed to be the only possible day to take up the synfuels bill. But as a senior staffer explained, that late date would have worked to the advantage of the bill's opponents. By some judicious juggling of the schedule, HR3930 was moved up to Tuesday 26 June. It was clear, however, that if the bill was not finished on that day, it could not be finished before the recess. The Labor-HEW appropriations bill was scheduled for Wednesday, and the remainder of the week would be consumed by that and other high-priority measures.

The proponents were convinced they had more than enough votes to pass the bill. The danger lay in the long series of amendments which Energy and Power Subcommittee members intended to offer. A participant explained the origins of the strategy to counter this threat:

> I thought about it all night. At 4 A.M. it occurred to me. Looking at the apparent level of support we had managed to build with the luncheons and all the other things we'd done to promote this—I think there were 170-some-odd cosponsors. With that kind of support what we might be able to do was move to cut off amendments at a certain hour and thus we wouldn't have to worry about running out of time. We could finish it. Granted, it would be a gamble because cutting off debate is always something members are reluctant to do. Nevertheless, I felt the mood of the country is such, the mood of Congress is such, that we could probably do that and it would save us.

In the days preceding floor consideration, the majority leader's office had been coordinating the mailing of a series of targeted "Dear Colleague" letters urging support for the legislation. Thus, all members of the Coal Caucus received such a letter from Nick Rahall of West Virginia. Dan Rostenkowski signed a letter to all Democrats; Fernand St. Germain (D-R.I.) and Edward Boland (D-Mass.) to members of the New England

Caucus; Gunn McKay (D-Utah) to the Steel Caucus, the Rural Caucus, and the United Democrats of Congress, a group of moderate and conservative members. Letters to selected groups of members went out under Wright's signature.

On the morning of the twenty-sixth all members received a letter signed by Wright, Majority Whip John Brademas, Minority Whip Robert Michel, Republican Conference Chairman John Anderson, and Stewart McKinney and William Moorhead of the Banking Committee. The letter briefly explained the bill and pointed out its broad support:

> To date 170 Members have co-sponsored the bill.
> The bill now is supported by the White House; the Department of Energy; the Department of Defense; the House Leadership on both sides; the Chairmen and Ranking Minority Members of the House Interstate and Foreign Commerce Committee, the House Banking, Finance and Urban Affairs Committee, the House Education and Labor Committee, the House Agriculture Committee, the House Appropriations Committee, the House Small Business Committee; and 155 other Members of both parties, reflecting every committee in the House.
> In addition, the bill is backed by the AFL-CIO, the UAW, the United Mine Workers, the Steel Caucus, the United Democrats of Congress, and the Rural Caucus.

After further justifying the bill, the letter continued: "We urge our colleagues to defeat every effort—no matter how sweetly phrased or reasonable it may sound—to encumber H.R. 3930 with language that would slow down or retard the growth of a synthetic fuel industry in our country. Those same voices that will attempt to hamstring and encumber this synfuels production bill were those same people who three years ago defeated consideration of a similar bill by one vote." A "Dear Colleague" letter sent to all Democrats with the signatures of the Speaker, Wright, and Brademas pointed out that "the bill and the Wright amendment have the strong support of the Democratic Steering and Policy Committee, the House Leadership and the Carter Administration."

The House began consideration of HR3930 at about one o'clock on 26 June. To a large extent general debate was a bipartisan love fest as member after member spoke in support of the bill and congratulated the authors on their fine work. Even members of the Energy and Power Subcommittee were guarded in their criticism. Only a few very conservative Republicans expressed opposition, claiming the bill was just another example of government interference with private enterprise.

When the time allotted for general debate expired, the House proceeded to consider amendments to the bill. The first Dingell amendment was easily defeated on a 60 to 351 vote. Soon thereafter Jim Wright's amendment was adopted on a voice vote. At four o'clock William Moorhead moved that debate cease at 6:40 P.M. When the motion carried on a 209 to 183 vote, the proponents knew they had won. A proponent explained why limiting debate was necessary: "Otherwise we wouldn't have finished it that week. We probably would have passed it anyway, but probably encumbered with some amendments. It would have given opponents time to crank up a lot of crazy arguments against it."

The rest was anticlimactic. Another Dingell amendment was defeated by a vote of 94 to 291. Because the House rules provide debate time for certain amendments even when the House is working under a time limitation, the vote on passage did not come until almost ten o'clock. HR3930, as expanded by the Wright amendment, was approved by the House on a vote of 368 to 25. Eager to take home to their constituents an accomplishment in energy legislation, members had put aside jurisdictional and partisan wrangling and overwhelmingly passed a major energy bill.

The production of synthetic fuels was a major component of the new energy program President Carter announced to the nation on 15 July. Thus the administration, which had been so reluctant in early summer to support the expanded version of HR3930 had, one month later, made a similar proposal the center of its energy program.

Increasing the Debt Limit

███████████████████████ In January of 1981 it became clear that the debt ceiling would have to be raised by mid-February. Higher than expected inflation and unemployment were increasing the federal deficit much beyond the forecasts of September 1980, when the debt ceiling had been set for the fiscal year. During the Carter presidency debt ceiling votes had been extremely difficult for the Democratic leadership. Few Republicans voted in favor, and many Democrats, fearful of being branded big spenders, were inclined to vote in opposition. The election of Ronald Reagan to the presidency altered the political calculus; now a conservative Republican administration was requesting a debt limit increase.

During the 1980 campaign many incumbent Democrats had been excoriated as irresponsible big spenders on the basis of their previous votes to increase the debt ceiling. The issue had figured prominently in the campaign of John Brademas, who was defeated, and of the newly appointed whip, Tom Foley. The temptation for Democrats to "pay back" the Republicans by voting against the increase was great. As a senior Democratic aide said, "A lot of Democrats have been savaged on this issue over the years, and they'd like to let the Republicans twist slowly in the wind" (*Washington Post*, 5 Feb. 1981).

Throughout its tenure, however, the leadership had argued that support for debt limit increases was the only responsible course on the grounds that such increases are necessary to allow the federal government to meet its obligations. Also, Reagan's honeymoon with the press was in full swing, and as a result the media would likely label House Democrats obstructionist if they were to defeat the president's requested increase. Conseqently, the leadership decided that House Democrats should support the increase. The Republicans, however, would also have to demonstrate responsibility; passage would be contingent upon Republican support.

To make it clear that this time passage of a debt limit increase was a shared responsibility, Secretary of the Treasury Regan and OMB Director David Stockman were called to testify in favor of the increase before the Ways and Means Committee. Many Democrats enjoyed forcing Stockman to testify because as a House member he had never voted for a debt limit increase. The committee approved the increase by voice vote without audible dissent. Most of the committee Republicans indicated that they would support the increase, but John Rousselot, a very conservative Ways and Means member, said after the meeting that he would vote in opposition. It was rumored that some Republicans were angry because they believed the Speaker had "sandbagged" the new president into requesting an inadequate increase. O'Neill, according to the story, had greatly exaggerated the difficulty of passing even a moderate increase. These members believed that Reagan would be forced to ask for another increase when its necessity could no longer be blamed on the Carter administration.

The Democratic leaders spread the word that they wanted their membership to support the increase. A junior liberal Democrat who, it was rumored, was beginning to organize an opposition bloc was told by leaders to "cut it out." At the same time, however, the leadership was quietly letting Democratic freshmen know that they were not expected to place themselves in political jeopardy on the vote. A freshman described the leaders' attitude: "The leadership said, 'This is our first big economic vote and we really don't think you freshmen ought to have to hang yourselves out on it if you don't want to.' So I was putting the message out, saying, 'Look, we don't really have to vote for this if we didn't want to.' " The leadership simply wanted a majority of Democrats to support the bill; it did not go after every vote as it had during the Carter administration.

A whip count was begun, but because many members were out of town it proceeded slowly. Many Democrats still wanted to oppose the increase. The leadership informed the White House that if the administration wished to see the bill passed the first time, the president had better write every Democrat a personal letter requesting support. On 4 February, the day before floor consideration, every member of the House received a letter from the president. For Democrats the letter provided an explanation for their vote to satisfy even their most conservative constituents.

The Republicans knew that the House Democrats would not alone take responsibility for passage and let Republicans, most of whom had a long history of opposing debt limit increases, off the hook. Secretary of the

Treasury Regan and Max Friedersdorf, head of congressional liaison, actively lobbied House Republicans. At a closed Republican conference, Minority Leader Michel made a strong plea for support, pointing out how embarrassing to the new administration a loss would be. Barber Conable of New York, ranking Republican on Ways and Means, sent a letter to every House Republican urging support. Several days before the vote Republican leaders assured the Speaker that at least one hundred Republicans would vote in favor.

At the regular Thursday morning whip meeting on the day the vote was scheduled, the Speaker again urged Democrats to support the increase. He argued that the Democratic party has not been, and should not become, obstructionist. Quoting Sam Rayburn he said, "Any jackass can kick down the barn door, but it takes a carpenter to build one." He told the whips that the party should pick its shots, and that the debt limit increase was the wrong target. During the meeting a member suggested that the debt limit be approved on a voice vote, but the Speaker immediately rejected that suggestion. He had no intention of letting the Republicans shirk their responsibility.

At his press conference just before the House went into session, the Speaker was asked if he expected a majority of Democrats to oppose the bill. "No," he replied. "I think it will depend a great deal on how many Republicans vote for it. There are [between] 100 and 125 Democrats who will support it." Tom Foley, the whip, added, "We have over 100 firms and another 40 or so who are strongly leaning." O'Neill then said, "The leadership has been urging our membership to go along, realizing it is hard in some areas, while the Republicans are still voting against it. I anticipate that it will be passed."

The debt limit increase was brought to the floor under a closed rule, which was quickly approved on a 333 to 67 vote. Debate on the bill itself was characterized by a series of Republicans explaining why they were voting in favor when they had consistently opposed debt limit increases in the past. Democrats who spoke in favor emphasized that political temptation should be rejected, that a "yes" vote was the responsible course. James Shannon, a junior Democrat from Massachusetts, said, "Now, I must admit that the visceral Democratic reaction is to look to the Republican side and say, 'This is a political opportunity.' It is very satisfying to all of us to see so many of you, who have become so expert at throwing stones, find yourselves living in glass houses. But I do not think it is in the best interest of the country, of my party, or of your party to demagog this issue" (*Congressional Record*, 5 February 1981, p. 385). Ed Jenkins of Georgia explicitly warned the Republicans that conservative as well as liberal Democrats expected the president's party to support the increase. If Republicans voted against the bill, "I shall never, never again ask conservative Democrats to give President Reagan any assistance on this troublesome issue," he said

(*Congressional Record,* 5 February 1981, p. 383). Majority Leader Jim Wright summed up for the Democrats.

> Some of the Members on my side of the aisle have raised questions. "Why," some of them asked, "must I vote for this today when my opponent in the last election excoriated me publicly and tried to portray my votes for the debt ceiling erroneously as big spending votes?"
>
> Well, the only answer to that is: "Because it is the responsible thing to do."
>
> Another Member asked, "Well, since the Members on the Republican side did not give a majority vote to support the extension of the debt ceiling on any of those occasions when our President, President Carter, was in office, why should we bail out their President?"
>
> Well, I think the answer to that is quite simple, too: Because he is not just their President, he is our President, he is the President of all of us, and this is our first and best opportunity to demonstrate that we have the capacity to be responsible, to join ranks, and to give to the new President every opportunity and every chance that the American people desire for him to have.
>
> (*Congressional Record,* 97th Cong., 1st sess., 5 February 1981, vol. 127, pp. 389–90)

The recorded vote began. Many Democrats held back, waiting to see if the Republicans would actually vote in favor. With two minutes remaining, less than half of the Democrats had voted. When more than half of the Republicans had voted "yea," the Democratic holdouts cast their votes in favor of the increase. The bill passed on a 305 to 104 vote; 150 Republicans and 155 Democrats voted for the bill; 36 Republicans and 68 Democrats voted against it.

Conclusion

These case studies illustrate the variety of techniques the leadership employs in coalition building; they illustrate more concretely the strategy of inclusion. These points have been discussed previously, however, and need not be belabored here. The cases also make clearer than the more analytic previous chapters the tenuousness of leadership control and the extent to which leadership success depends on factors beyond the leaders' control.

On major legislation, the leadership's discretion in deciding whether to get involved is severely limited. Of the cases examined, only on synfuels did the leadership have a free choice: in that instance a leader's personal policy interests and the current political context interacted to produce leadership involvement. The other cases are more typical. Satisfying the legislative output expectations of their membership and guarding their own reputations and that of the party require leaders to be actively involved in the budget process; intense leadership activity is a prerequisite to passing a budget resolution that is a majority party document. In 1980 the Speaker attempted to keep his distance with the result that his reputation was damaged because he was perceived as indecisive; he was eventually forced to commit himself fully. The Speaker at first had hoped to limit the leadership's involvement in the battle over the Panama legislation, but this too proved to be impossible. The bill was a major priority of a Democratic president. Defeat of the bill, a certainty without leadership involvement, would have damaged the reputations of a Democratic president, the Democratic party in the House, and the leadership itself. Under different conditions the leadership might have separated itself from the effort to raise the debt limit at the beginning of Reagan's presidency, and in fact involvement in the effort was on a much smaller scale than it had been during the Carter years. A hands-off leadership attitude, in this case, however, would probably have resulted in defeat of the debt ceiling increase and a black eye for the party.

When the president is of the opposition party, the leadership tends to have somewhat greater feedom in choosing when to get involved. The leaders do not owe an opposition-party president support—nor do they need to oppose him across the board. They must continue to satisfy their members' expectations and those of allied groups. Consequently, the leaders' discretion depends on the extent to which such expectations are lowered by opposition party occupancy of the White House.

Because the leadership has limited discretion to pick and choose and must involve itself in so many battles, its problem of limited resources is especially acute. These case studies demonstrate that the leadership possesses considerable resources that can be used to structure the situation. The Panama legislation exemplifies the usefulness of the new multiple referral rules, the creative use of which enabled the Speaker to bring into the process committees that were friendly to the administration position to counter the basically hostile Merchant Marine Committee; the use of a reporting deadline forced Merchant Marine to report the bill out in a timely fashion. Both the Panama and the synfuels case studies illustrate the significance of control over the floor schedule: the leadership was able to postpone the Panama legislation until the votes to pass it were in hand, and consideration of synthetic fuels legislation was moved up so that a possible delaying tactic by the opposition would stand little chance of success. The Speaker's control of the Rules Committee provides an immensely important resource because it makes possible the use of carefully constructed rules to structure floor choices. The closed rule under which the 1980 reconciliation bill was considered is an especially notable example because all of the participants questioned agreed that the rule was vital to the sucess of the bill; if it had been considered under an open rule, the bill would have been emasculated on the floor.

Structuring the situation is an indirect way of influencing members' behavior. Under the right circumstances it can be very effective in altering the results of members' voting calculus and, consequently, the outcome. Because the 1980 reconciliation bill was considered under a closed rule the choice facing members was whether to vote for or against savings; if amendments had been allowed the choice would have been between voting for or against cutting a number of popular programs. The tools the leadership possesses for structuring the situation are not, however, sufficiently powerful and flexible to create an ideal choice situation on most legislation. Usually creative use of the tools will increase the probability of, but not ensure, success. Furthermore, the use of the tools is subject to member approval. The rule for the 1981 reconciliation bill was constructed so as to present leadership opponents with a Hobson's choice, but the leadership was unable to pass the rule.

Given that even structuring the choice situation is seldom sufficient, the leaders must often influence members' behavior directly in order to prevail on a difficult roll call. But the leaders' resources for directly influencing members' behavior are severely limited. The leaders can and do perform a great many favors for their members, but by and large the favors are not critical for member goal achievement, especially the reelection goal. If the reelection goal dictates a vote contrary to that which the leadership wants, nothing the leaders can give a member is sufficiently valuable to ensure a vote on behalf of the leadership. The leaders may be able to persuade the member that he has misperceived and exaggerated the electoral risk or that the national interest, the good of the party, or personal friendship outweigh the electoral risks. They cannot decrease the risk involved in the vote or compensate him for taking it.

A skillful use of resources affects leadership success, as these case studies show. Yet the House environment militates against truly optimum resource allocation. The leaders work under tremendous time pressures. Often several battles are proceeding almost simultaneously. In 1979, for example, the Panama legislation was on the floor on 20 and 21 June, the synthetic fuels bill was on the floor on 26 June, and the budget resolution conference report had been completed on 24 May. Immediately prior to floor consideration of the 1981 reconciliation bill, extension of the Legal Services Corporation was on the House floor. Although Legal Services was important, the leadership simply lacked the time to work on it. A Steering and Policy Committee staff member did work on the bill but largely on his own initiative. Wide participation and high uncertainty exacerbate the difficulty of optimum resource allocation. The 1979 budget resolution battle is a case in point. During floor consideration a junior Democrat, a moderate from the the majority leader's own state, offered an amendment that could have destroyed the coalition backing the resolution, and it was unexpectedly accepted. Furthermore, a usually loyal Democrat organized an interest group campaign to defeat the conference report on the budget resolution. Both outcomes were later reversed; the case studies include a number of other instances of reversals. The frequency with which this occurs is an indication of the highly unpredictable environment in which the leaders operate.

The leadership's success, however, depends not only on a skillful use of resources, but, even more, on factors outside the leadership's control. Given the leadership's limited effect on member goal achievement, the leadership's influence on coalitions is always at the margins. Because their resources are limited, the leaders cannot construct a majority from scatch; a core of support must exist. Consequently, the level and breadth of intraparty agreement on policy are critical determinants of leadership success. During the mid and late 1970s the Democratic core consensus was shrinking under the impact of continuing high inflation combined with generally sluggish economic growth. During the 95th and 96th congresses Democratic majorities in the House were large enough to compensate to a considerable extent for the effects of the shrinking consensus, and the leadership won most of the major legislative battles. The 1980 election not only significantly decreased the size of the Democratic majority but further damaged the fragile and narrow Democratic core consensus. Many Democratic House members read the election returns as a signal that their constituents demanded support for the Reagan program and consequently were receptive to administration persuasion. Most House Republicans also interpreted the election as a Reagan mandate, and the result was incredibly high Republican cohesion on key elements of Reagan's economic program in 1981. Under those circumstances, there was no way in which the Democratic leadership could defeat Reagan. The broader political context overwhelmingly favored the Republicans; the leadership's resources, no matter how skillfully used, are insufficient to overcome an advantage of this magnitude.

CHAPTER 8

MAJORITY

PARTY

LEADERSHIP IN

THE POSTREFORM

HOUSE:

PROBLEMS AND

PROSPECTS

Leadership Problems and
Coping Strategies

Successful leadership always requires satisfying the expectations of followers. For leaders who do not control entry into the organization and who are directly dependent on their followers for their leadership positions, developing strategies consonant with member expectations is certainly a prerequisite to success.

Members of the postreform House expect to pursue their goals of reelection, influence, and policy with little restraint. They expect to participate broadly in the legislative process and to engage freely in other reelection-directed activities. Party maintenance requires that leaders facilitate rather than hinder members' high level of activity and broad participation; it dictates that they do so for all their members, not just for those whose participation is likely to be helpful to them. Yet extensive participation results in an unpredictable legislative process, which makes coalition building more difficult.

While members expect their leaders to pass legislation that satisfies members' reelection needs and policy goals, no member expects the leaders to tailor their legislative priority list to his or her individual preferences; members realize that the leadership must be responsive to the diversity of inter-

237

ests within the House Democratic membership and to significant actors out-side the chamber. Yet the leadership is expected to be reasonably successful at coalition building on legislation of importance to its members.

When an intraparty policy consensus does not exist, building a winning coalition requires persuading some members to support a position other than their preferred position. The leadership cannot use direct rewards and punishments as a primary means of persuasion because its stock of them is limited and because party maintenance needs constrain the use of them. Highly desirable committee assignments and appointments to the Steering and Policy Committee, for example, cannot effectively be used as a quid pro quo simply because the number of such positions is too small. Further-more, such use would contravene fairness norms and participation expecta-tions and, consequently, would be costly in terms of party maintenance. Similarly, the leadership cannot systematically use its control over legisla-tive scheduling and floor procedure to reward or punish, because doing so would have a highly negative impact on party maintenance.

The leaders thus must balance the often conflicting dictates of party maintenance and coalition building. The current leaders lack both a strong intraparty policy consensus and resources sufficient to affect decisively members' goal attainment. They cannot count on members' goal-directed behavior being conducive to party maintenance or coalition-building suc-cess; nor can they assure desirable member behavior by the use of rewards and punishments.

In their attempts to cope with these problems, the current leaders have developed a three-pronged strategy: they are heavily engaged in the provi-sion of services to members; they make use of their formal powers and in-fluence to structure choice situations; and they attempt to involve as many Democrats as possible in the coalition-building process.

By providing services to members collectively and individually, the lead-ers help their members play the active role they desire in the chamber and facilitate their goal achievement. Leadership information dissemination helps members play an active role in the House. Legislative scheduling that is sensitive to members' needs conserves members' limited time and can contribute to the attainment of reelection, policy, and power goals. The many favors leaders do for individual members (such as making personal appearances in their districts) also furthers those members' goal attainment.

The leadership expects the collective services it provides to contribute to party maintenance and to produce a favorable climate for coalition build-ing. Doing favors for individuals is expected to have the same effect; no direct quid pro quo is involved. Furthermore, the leadership will seldom withhold favors as a punishment. Members who have been helpful to the leadership will receive more and faster attention; the few members who almost never support the leadership do not ask for favors. The leaders will, however, do favors for members who freqently defect from the party posi-tion. Withholding favors from such members, the leaders believe, is likely to alienate them rather than produce leadership-desired behavior. Favors, then, are used to build up a psychological credit balance, a sense of obligation in the benefited members. So long as the resources the leadership commands are insufficient to affect decisively members' goal achievement, punishment, and even the withholding of rewards, is likely to be counterproductive. Party maintenance would be harmed without a commensurate gain in coalition-building success. Furthermore, coalition building is a continuing enterprise; to achieve success over the long run, the leadership needs to maintain ties to all sections of the party. In the process of doing favors, the leadership picks up information vital to effective coalition building. And even a frequent defector may occasionally provide an essential pro-leadership vote from a sense of obligation.

Most leadership favors—attending members' fund-raisers, helping a member obtain a district project—can be dispensed in a nondiscriminatory manner. Like representatives' casework, they may do some good and cannot do any harm. Some favors, however, have a direct effect upon coalition-building success; consequently, decisions about their distribution are considerably more complicated. In using its influence over committee assignments, especially assignments to the most important committees, the leadership must balance the need to accommodate all sections of the party against the need for a reliable committee majority. Sometimes by helping a frequent defector obtain such an assignment the leadership can co-opt him, thus contributing to coalition-building success. The majority leader's support of Phil Gramm for a Budget Committee seat was in part thus motivated. As that case shows, attempted co-optation is a risky strategy but its occasional success complicates decision making on committee assignments. The current leadership has been reasonably successful in balancing the dictates of the two functions: even in the 97th Congress the key committees had reliable majorities.

In its relationships with the committees, the leadership is again faced with a delicate balancing act. Frequent or heavy-handed intervention into committee deliberations would violate old norms of committee autonomy and new participation norms; yet the form in which a bill emerges from committee strongly affects the probability of coalition-building success. The weakening of the committee autonomy norm allows the leadership to intervene, but it intervenes as discretely as possible and on an ad hoc basis. When intervention fails, the leadership seldom opposes a Democratic committee majority on the floor. Using its resources against a committee would be too expensive in terms of party maintenance. Yet the leadership does exercise discretion over the amount of help it gives committees on the floor.

Because members and significant outside actors expect legislative results, party maintenance needs cannot be allowed to lead to immobility. Yet, lacking resources sufficient to affect decisively members' goal attainment, the leadership cannot base its coalition-building efforts on the employment of direct rewards and punishments. The reforms of the 1970s have augmented leadership resources for structuring members' choice situation. The Speaker's powers as presiding officer, leadership control over floor scheduling, and the leadership's decisive influence over the Rules Committee often make it possible for the leadership to advantage the party position.

Structuring the choice situation, through the use of a complex rule, for example, is a means of coercing members collectively. The strategy is limited by the requirement of overt or tacit member approval. When the strategy is skillfully used, members will acquiesce because what they gain is greater than what they lose by having their choices constrained. If, for example, members' policy goals dictate a proleadership vote but their reelection goal a contrary vote, leadership structuring of the choice situation so that the key roll call occurs on a procedural motion may allow members to vote their policy preferences.

From the leadership's point of view, the requirement of member acquiescence in the strategy of structuring the choice situation is both a disadvantage and an advantage. It limits the use of the strategy. Yet, coercion to which one has consented tends to be perceived as not unreasonably coercive. Because of the uncertain environment, leaders do not always know what their members will consider acceptable. Misjudgment may lead to a legislative defeat; members may, for example, vote down a rule. But, for the leadership, losing almost any particular legislative battle is preferable to creating serious dissatisfaction among the membership. Few legislative battles are worth winning if the price is a severe reduction in the probability of future coalition-building success.

The attempt to involve as many Democrats as possible in the coalition-building process is the third element of the current leadership's strategy. As rules and norms changes dispersed influence more widely in the chamber, more extensive vote mobilization efforts became necessary. The leadership could not rely on the traditional whip system for the help it needed because of the problematic loyalty of the elected zone whips. In response to these problems, Speaker Carl Albert began to enlist other members in specific coalition-building efforts. The current leadership's strategy of inclusion differs significantly from its predecessor's approach, though. It is a sustained, multifaceted strategy rather than an ad hoc response to a specific legislative battle, and its scale is much broader.

The current leaders' use of task forces, and of less formal ad hoc groups to work on specific legislation, and their use of the expanded whip system, the Steering and Policy Committee, and the Rules Committee are all elements of the strategy of inclusion. The leaders' regular interactions with members of the extended leadership circle provide them with information that is vital to successful coalition building in the unpredictable postreform House. By enlisting a large number and broad variety of Democrats in leadership efforts, the leaders acquire the help they so badly need. The large number involved makes one-on-one persuasion with a large proportion of the membership possible. The broad variety ensures that the group as a whole will have ties to all sections of the party. The strategy of inclusion, thus, contributes to coalition-building success.

The leaders believe that the strategy of inclusion also contributes to "keeping peace in the family." In the postreform House rules allow and norms dictate high rank-and-file participation. The leadership either channels such participation in directions that are helpful to the party effort or it will find itself by-passed and, consequently, will lose influence. Involvement in the extended leadership circle and in specific coalition-building efforts gives a large number of members the opportunity to participate actively, but in a way that helps rather than hurts the leadership.

The contrast between Speaker Rayburn's relationship to the Democratic Caucus and that of the current leadership illustrates how the transformation of the House has required changes in leadership strategies. Rayburn did not use the caucus because he believed that providing a forum in which the warring party factions could confront each other directly would only exacerbate intraparty conflicts. Instead, he acted as a negotiator among factional leaders. In contrast, the current leaders reacted to the intensified intraparty conflict in the 97th Congress by making much greater use of the caucus. All members now expect to be able to express their views to the leadership; all have considerable capacity to act upon their beliefs and, in so doing, can harm leadership efforts. Because leadership attempts to reduce the level of member participation would have severe negative consequences on party maintenance and would probably be unsuccessful, the leaders endeavor to satisfy members' desires for participation by providing forums in which members can attempt to influence leadership decisions and by including members directly in leadership coalition-building efforts. Doing so, the leaders believe, not only meets members' expectations about their roles in the chamber but also has a positive socializing effect, especially on junior members. The strategy of inclusion, the leadership believe, teaches junior members the value of joint action under the aegis of the party and may result in some identification with the leadership.

Although the strategy of inclusion contributes to both party maintenance and coalition-building success, it does not completely resolve the conflict between the dictates of the two functions. Party maintenance requires accommodating all sections of the party; it dictates drawing a broad cross section of the Democratic membership into contact with the leadership and giving a diversity of members a voice in party decisions. The consequent heterogeneity of the group involved can hinder coalition-building efforts.

When constructing task forces and less formal vote mobilization groups, the leadership will attempt to enlist a diverse group of members, but support for the legislation at issue is a prerequisite to involvement. In its relationship with the structures of the extended leadership circle, the leadership must balance the need for loyalty and the need for diversity. The optimal balance is not obvious, and the leadership's solutions have been varied and ad hoc. In making appointments to the Rules Committee, O'Neill has emphasized the dictates of the coalition-building function. By refusing to appoint state delegation–endorsed members, the Speaker has sacrificed party maintenance objectives. He has been willing to do so because a loyal Rules Committee is essential to coalition building; the leadership's ability to structure the choice situation is dependent upon the Rules Committee being a true arm of the party leadership. Since O'Neill served on the committee during the period of conservative dominance, he is starkly aware of the dangers to the leadership of an unreliable Rules Committee.

The expansion of the whip system and the division of labor between elected and appointed whips were attempts to balance the dictates of the two functions. The leaders' interactions with the elected whips contribute to party maintenance. Because the zone whips are a diverse group, the whip meetings provide the leadership with information about the sentiments of most segments of its membership and provide a cross section of the party with regular access to the leadership. The zone whips' heterogeneity precludes their effective use in coalition building, however; they take the initial count, but for persuasion the leadership relies on the whips it appoints.

A comparison between the Steering and Policy Commitee of the 95th (1977–78) and the Steering and Policy Committee of the 97th Congress (1981–82) shows that the broader political environment strongly affects the extent to which party maintenance and coalition building can be successfully reconciled. Because twelve members of the Steering and Policy Committee are elected by Democrats from twelve geographical zones, the committee's membership is diverse. In the 95th Congress the Speaker sought to balance party maintenance and coalition-building needs by appointing a relatively heterogeneous but nevertheless reliable group to fill the remaining slots. From the more conservative regions the Speaker chose members who had previous ties to the leadership. Partly as a result of his selections but even more because of a conducive political atmosphere, the committee was able to play an effective role in the coalition-building process. The Democrats had just won a presidential election and had maintained their large House majority. The Speaker received every legislative endorsement he requested; even such intensely controversial measures as Carter's energy program and common situs picketing legislation were endorsed without public dissent.

During the 97th Congress the changed political environment made balancing the functions more difficult. Not only had Democrats lost the presidency and thirty-three House seats, but many members read the election as a mandate for Reagan's program. Party maintenance needs required that the Speaker accede to conservatives' demands for greater representation on Steering and Policy. Although the three conservative members appointed by the Speaker were carefully chosen from among members the leadership considered responsible, the highly charged political climate prevented the more heterogeneous committee from playing a meaningful role in coalition building. Neither the appointed nor the elected conservatives were willing to go along with leadership wishes as similar members had done in previous congresses. Doing so, such members believed, might be costly in terms of re-election. Aware that requesting endorsements on the key economic measures would only exacerbate intraparty conflicts, the Speaker did not bring such matters to Steering and Policy.

The extent to which the leadership's two primary functions can be successfully reconciled is highly dependent on the broader political environment, over which the leadership has little control. The size of the majority, which itself is determined by broader political forces, is one important factor. When the Democratic majority is large, accommodating all segments of the party without endangering coalition-building success is easier. In that case some unreliable members can be given desirable committee assignments; the size of the Democratic committee majority will assure that such members do not adversely affect outcomes. Floor success requires persuading fewer members to vote contrary to their preferences because, with a large majority, winning does not require high cohesion.

Successful reconciliation of the two functions depends even more on the extent of intraparty policy agreement. When a consensus exists, there is little conflict between the dictates of party maintenance and coalition-building success. In contrast, when the party is badly split, both functions are difficult to perform and reconciling the two is nearly impossible. Accommodating one section of the party is likely to embitter others, with a consequent negative impact on future coalition-building success. Floor success requires persuading a considerable number of members to vote contrary to strongly held preferences, which, if it can be accomplished at all, is costly in terms of party maintenance. Discussing leadership efforts in 1981, a perceptive junior member of the leadership explicated the costs involved in coalition building when the party is fragmented:

There's a penalty for doing this, and the penalty is that the position taken is a very low common denominator that displeases everybody. You wind up with everybody feeling that he or she was overcompromised in order to come to that position, and if you continue to create that feeling, you're going to have people dissatisfied with themselves and ultimately with their party and their leadership. So there's a limit to the number of times you can take people through that. And the natural result of that is that people are going to feel badly not only that they lost, but that they wound up in a position they didn't really feel comfortable with, and that they gave up too much of their own true feeling to the group in order to conform to the group, and so leadership is going to get the bad rap. That's, I think, what's being expressed when people say the leadership stinks. Part of what they're saying is, "They made me adopt a position that is one-tenth of what I believe and nine-tenths things I don't believe in and what kind of leadership is that? If they were any good, they would have given me a position that's totally mine." And so that compromise process is a tough one, and the leadership loses a lot in terms of its own credibility driving people to those positions.

The current leaders' coalition-building strategies depend for success on some core intraparty policy consensus. Structuring the choice situation requires member acquiescence; the strategy of inclusion depends on members being willing to participate in leadership efforts. Because its resources are limited, the leadership's effect on coalitions is always at the margins. When the party is badly fragmented, leadership resources, no matter how skillfully they are used, will be insufficient to produce success.

An Assessment of Party Maintenance and Coalition-Building Success

Evaluating the leadership's coalition-building success would seem to be an easy task. The fate of bills in the House, after all, is a matter of the public record. Any assessment, however, must take into account the great variation in leadership interest and involvement. For the following analysis, two categories are used. The first includes the major bills that the president or a core party constituency declared top priority. The second category consists of measures that were less visible outside of Washington but that were important to the leadership's reputation within the Washington community and especially with the House membership. The choice of legislation is based primarily on interviews with House leaders and their staff, which skews the selection toward the tough issues. Some important measures that never became controversial, such as the multilateral trade agreements, are not included.

Table 8.1 is a list of the legislation included in the first category for the 95th Congress, the 96th Congress, and the first session of the 97th Congress. A rating of leadership success and an indication of the final disposition are included. In the 95th Congress the leadership scored nine successes and two defeats on top-priority legislation; results in three other cases were mixed. When the minimum wage bill was on the House floor the indexing of the minimum wage was deleted by amendment, but an amendment providing for a subminimum for youths, a provision strongly opposed by labor, was defeated. The Senate version was more generous than that passed by the House, and the conference agreement leaned toward the Senate provisions. To increase its chances on the House floor, the original concept of the Humphrey-Hawkins full employment bill was severely weakened by the

PROBLEMS AND PROSPECTS

Table 8.1

HOUSE LEADERSHIP RECORD ON TOP-PRIORITY LEGISLATION, 1977–1981

Congress	Legislation	Result for House Leadership	Final Disposition
95th	Economic stimulus program	successful	enacted
	Hatch Act revision	successful	died in Senate
	Strip mining bill	successful	enacted
	Labor law reform	successful	died in Senate
	New York City aid	successful	enacted
	Social security bill	successful	enacted
	Lifting of Turkish arms embargo	successful	enacted
	Suspension of B-1 production	successful	enacted
	Energy program	successful	radically changed in Senate, then enacted
	Minimum wage bill	mixed	strengthened in Senate, then enacted
	Humphrey-Hawkins full employment bill	mixed	weakened in Senate, then enacted
	1978 tax bill	mixed	enacted
	Common situs picketing bill	unsuccessful	died
	Consumer protection agency	unsuccessful	died
96th	Chrysler loan guarantees	successful	enacted
	Synthetic fuels bill	successful	enacted
	Windfall profits tax	successful	enacted
	Busing constitutional amendment	successful	killed by House's action
	Taiwan Relations Act	successful	enacted
	Panama Canal implementation legislation	successful	enacted
	Fair housing bill	successful	died in Senate
	Welfare reform	successful	died in Senate
	Standby gas rationing bill	mixed	enacted
	Energy mobilization board	unsuccessful	died
	Hospital cost control	unsuccessful	died
	Oil import fee	unsuccessful	died
97th	First budget resolution	unsuccessful	enacted
	Reconciliation bill	unsuccessful	enacted
	Tax bill	unsuccessful	enacted

committee. Although the bill sustained no further damage on the House floor, it was further weakened by the Senate. Neither the Speaker nor President Carter liked the form in which the tax bill emerged from the Ways and Means Committee. The leadership's primary effort on the floor was to defeat an amendment embodying the Kemp-Roth 30 percent tax cut, and on this it was successful.

In the 96th Congress the leadership scored eight successes and three defeats; results in one case were mixed. Neither the Taiwan Relations Act nor the Panama Canal treaty implementation bill emerged from the House in a form totally satisfactory to the administration but they are counted as successes because the House leaders accomplished what they set out to do, which was prevent the adoption of "killer" amendments. The House vetoed Carter's standby gas rationing plan in the spring of 1979. A new bill providing for rationing authority and for a different congressional review process passed several months later. That bill, however, emerged from committee weaker than the president or the leadership wanted it to be, and it passed the House only after the leaders reversed the vote on what they believed to be a killer amendment.

In 1981 the new Reagan administration decided to use the congressional budget process to accomplish its priority objective of cutting spending. The three most critical measures that came to a House vote were the first budget resolution, the reconciliation bill, and the tax bill. In each case House Republicans offered administration substitutes for the committee versions that the leadership backed, and in each case the leadership was defeated.

On the big bills, then, the House majority party leadership was at least reasonably successful in the 95th and 96th congresses. The leadership won approximately 65 percent of its legislative battles in the two congresses and suffered defeats in 20 percent. In 1981, however, the decreased size of the Democratic House membership, a popular Republican president, and a change in the national political mood combined to hand the Democratic leadership three successive major defeats.

The second category of roll calls includes votes on budget resolutions (in the 95th and 96th congresses), debt limit increases, and measures of special personal interest to members of the House. Eighteen key budget resolution roll calls were identified in the 95th Congress. The leadership lost on four of the votes. During consideration of the first budget resolution in 1977, an amendment to increase defense spending—helped along by some covert lobbying from the administration—passed. Liberals retaliated by voting against passage of the resolution, which failed by a large margin. When a slightly revised resolution was brought to the floor, the defense spending amendment was defeated and the resolution passed. In 1978 a Republican amendment cutting HEW funds passed, but the vote was reversed before the first resolution was passed. During consideration of the second resolution in 1978 one amendment (which cut CETA and counter-cyclical aid) was adopted over the objections of the party leadership and the committee majority. Thus, only one of the eighteen roll calls resulted in a permanent defeat for the leadership. A loss that is later reversed is not, however, cost free. Resources must be expended to reverse the initial defeat, and every defeat tarnishes, at least temporarily, the leadership's reputation. For these reasons, debt limit votes have been a recurrent problem for the leadership. Every member knows the ceiling must be raised periodically, yet, especially in a time of high inflation, few like to vote for an increase. During the 95th Congress the need to increase the debt ceiling arose three times; in each case, the bill failed the first time it came to the floor and then, after heavy leadership lobbying, passed on the second attempt.

Four other measures in the 95th Congress fall into the second category. The Speaker staked his reputation on passage of a strong ethics code and of a substantial congressional pay increase; both were successfully enacted. The leadership also supported a bill providing for public financing of congressional elections and a measure recommended by the Obey Commission reforming the administration of the House. In both cases the rule for consideration of these measures was defeated. The leadership, then, won on only two of these four measures, though it was successful on the two most critical to the Speaker's reputation.

In the 96th Congress the leadership lost six of twenty-four key budget resolution roll calls, but all these defeats were reversed. During consideration of the first resolution in 1979, the Mattox amendment cutting countercyclical aid was adopted. Had that decision been allowed to stand, liberal Democrats would almost certainly have voted against the resolution, ensuring its defeat. The amendment was, however, largely nullified by the subsequent adoption of another amendment. Both the conference report on the first resolution and the second resolution were initially defeated but subsequently approved. In 1980 the conference report on the first resolution was again defeated, and in the aftermath the leadership lost two important procedural votes (see chapter 6). These losses were particularly embarrassing, but a somewhat revised budget resolution was subsequently approved.

There were seven votes related to increasing the debt limit during the 96th Congress, of which the leadership lost two (both of the losses were, of course, reversed). Two of the wins were especially important. In early 1979 conservatives twice tried to defeat the previous question on the rule for consideration of the debt limit increases; their aim was to attach to the bill a provision requiring a balanced budget. The leadership's success on the previous question votes prevented the proposal (which, given the political climate, was almost irresistible) from coming to a vote.

Seven other roll calls in the 96th Congress fall into this category. The leadership twice successfully prevented the expulsion of Congressman Charles Diggs. Members of the Black Caucus were very much concerned that Diggs not be expelled before his appeals were exhausted; the leadership, by preventing such a move, built up credits with an important internal constituency. The leadership position also prevailed on the Obey-Railsback bill to limit political action committee (PAC) contributions in House races, but this measure died in the Senate. Of considerable importance to the leaders themselves was approval in 1979 of a change in the procedure for increasing the debt limit; under the new procedure, debt limit increases are included in the budget resolution, thus usually making a separate bill unnecessary and reducing the visibility of the decision. The leadership twice failed to win approval of a congressional pay increase but finally succeeded in late 1979.

From the leaders' point of view, winning is what is critical; the size of the margin and the sources of their support are of secondary importance. An analysis of such factors, however, contributes to our understanding of leadership coalition building. In the following analysis, voting patterns are examined within issue areas. The roll calls used are the key votes on the bills and other measures that were identified earlier. In the foreign and defense policy area, these have been supplemented by some additional votes that, although they were not taken on bills qualifying as top priority, were of unquestioned importance. Most of these additional roll calls represent attempts by congressional hard-liners to restrict President Carter's discretion in the foreign and defense policy area. During the 95th Congress, for example, an amendment expressing congressional opposition to Carter's plan to reduce ground troops in Korea came to a vote; a vote was taken on overriding the president's veto of a weapons procurement bill; and there were votes on two amendments restricting the nations to which foreign aid may go. During the 96th Congress there were a number of attempts to prohibit aid to Nicaragua and several to lift sanctions from Rhodesia. In all these cases the leadership took an active part in upholding President Carter's position.

Although the leadership won much more frequently than it lost in the 95th and 96th congresses, its winning margins tended to be slim (see tables 8.2 and 8.3). On the sixty-nine key roll calls identified in the 95th Congress, the mean percentage of members supporting the leadership position was 53.2; in the 96th Congress on seventy-nine roll calls, the mean support percentage was 52.0. In the 95th Congress the leadership position was defeated on 21.7 percent of the roll calls; in the 96th, on 25.4 percent. Because many of the defeats were later reversed, these figures do not provide a true indication of leadership success, but they do indicate that coalition building in these congresses was no easy task. Of the roll calls won in the 95th Congress, 74 percent were won by less than 60 percent of the vote; in the 96th, 83 percent were won by less than 60 percent.

Examining support by issue area, one finds that only in the "other government management" area in the 95th Congress did mean leadership support reach a comfortable level. Included in this category are a number of roll calls on the 1977 economic stimulus program on which Democrats did agree. The other issue areas were much more difficult; a mean leadership support level of greater than 55 percent is unusual. In both congresses,

Table 8.2

SUPPORT FOR THE LEADERSHIP POSITION IN THE 95TH CONGRESS
(In Percentages)

Group	Budget	Debt Limit	Energy	Other Government Management	Issue Area Foreign and Defense	Labor	Social Security	Internal	All Issues
All	50.7	48.1	53.8	59.6	51.1	53.9	55.6	52.8	53.2
Democrats	72.8	67.6	74.8	81.2	64.1	74.1	77.4	74.5	73.6
Northern Democrats	79.7	74.3	82.3	89.1	71.6	87.3	86.3	80.1	80.6
Southern Democrats	53.1	48.3	53.4	57.9	42.8	36.5	52.9	58.7	50.6
Republicans	8.5	10.3	11.6	17.3	25.8	14.2	13.7	10.1	13.7
Number of roll calls	18	6	7	12	8	9	4	5	69

249

Table 8.3

SUPPORT FOR THE LEADERSHIP POSITION IN THE 96TH CONGRESS
(In Percentages)

Group	Budget	Debt Limit	Energy	Other Government Management	Foreign and Defense	Social Welfare	Civil Liberties	Internal	All Issues
				Issue Area					
All	51.8	50.6	46.5	54.0	54.0	52.6	50.5	56.0	52.0
Democrats	74.6	78.7	62.2	71.4	73.4	77.1	67.6	74.6	72.6
Northern Democrats	76.8	84.7	62.7	80.1	81.3	88.6	77.9	79.4	77.3
Southern Democrats	68.1	61.7	60.9	46.2	51.4	43.5	39.7	61.6	59.2
Republicans	13.0	1.5	19.6	23.5	20.7	9.9	21.2	23.7	16.6
Number of roll calls	24	7	12	2	22	2	2	8	79

mean support on budget resolution roll calls barely surpassed the 50 percent mark.

As can be seen in tables 8.2 and 8.3 southern Democrats are clearly the most troublesome segment of the party for the leadership. In three issue areas in each congress, the leadership received on the average less than one-half of southern Democratic votes. In the 95th Congress the mean leadership support percentage of southern Democrats on the total set of key roll calls was barely over 50; in the 96th, this increases to 59.2. Although northern Democrats as a group are much more supportive of leadership positions than their southern party colleagues, their support is far from unanimous. During the 95th Congress slightly less than 20 percent of northern Democrats defected on the average; during the 96th, slightly more than 20 percent defected. High cohesion among Republicans made the leadership's task even more difficult. During the 95th Congress, the leadership received on the average only 13.7 percent of Republican votes, and during the 96th, only 16.6 percent. Only on foreign policy votes during the 95th did as many as 25 percent of Republicans typically support the Democratic position. However, given the narrow victory margins characteristic of these congresses, gaining even a small number of Republican votes was often essential to victory.

In the 95th and 96th congresses a highly but not totally cohesive Republican party faced a large but much less cohesive Democratic party. The leadership managed to corral enough votes from its members to win a substantial majority of the key votes, often with the help of a few Republican defectors. The victory margins, however, tended to be narrow. Given this situation, the losses in the 97th Congress are hardly surprising. The size of the Democratic party decreased and Republican cohesion increased. Democratic cohesion on the first of the key votes was about the same as the average for the 95th and 96th congresses; on the other two, Democratic cohesion was much higher than the average of the previous congresses (see table 8.4). Thus in the 97th Congress the leadership was at least as successful in mobilizing Democratic votes as it had been in the two preceding congresses. However, winning would have required much higher Democratic cohesion than had prevailed in the previous congresses. Given the popularity of the president and the mandate interpretation of the 1980 election to which many Democrats subscribed, the leadership with its limited resources was incapable of engineering such extraordinary cohesion.

Assessing the leadership's success at party maintenance is considerably more difficult than assessing coalition-building success, but members evaluations of their leaders provide one basis for assessment. The Democrats interviewed do not constitute a random sample; as a group they are, however, representative of the Democratic House membership in terms of region, ideology, and seniority.

Table 8.4

SUPPORT FOR THE LEADERSHIP POSITION ON KEY VOTES
IN THE 97TH CONGRESS
(In Percentages)

Roll Call	All	Republicans	Democrats	Northern Democrats	Southern Democrats
First budget resolution—Gramm-Latta substitute	41.0	0	73.6	87.4	35.9
Reconcilation—previous question on rule	49.2	.5	87.8	97.1	62.5
Tax Bill—Republican substitute	45.0	.5	80.2	88.7	56.9

Asked what the membership wanted of its leadership, a top leader replied wryly, "A very strong leadership that pressures everyone else into doing what they want done." During interviews in 1979, 1980, and 1981, a number of Democrats expressed a desire for stronger leadership and complained that the current leaders were not tough enough. Asked if the leadership possessed sufficient resources to lead effectively, a senior member said, "The tools are there; I'm not sure the carpenter is. 'Tip' is such a nice man. I believe in using rewards and punishments. If you never help out, you shouldn't get the good committee assignments," But, while one group of members called for greater discipline, another complained that the leadership was insufficiently tolerant. These members believe the leaders discriminate against them in the awarding of committee assignments and other desirable positions. Ideology perfectly distinguishes the two groups. All the members who advocated more discipline are mainstream Democrats; all of those advocating greater tolerance are conservatives.

Clearly the leadership cannot fully satisfy both groups, and the smaller the size of their majority, the greater the problem the groups' conflicting expectations create for the leaders. When the majority is small, the minority conservatives have much greater bargaining power. Using negative sanctions against them is likely to be counterproductive; using inducements tends to breed resentment among the mainstream majority, especially if the inducements do not produce legislative victories. Peter Peyser's floor speech on the day after Democrats lost the key vote on the 1981 reconciliation bill provides some indication of mainstream Democrats' resentment toward the conservative defectors. "Rank and file Democrats in the House have had it," he said. "We have been abused and betrayed by those who have accepted and benefited by this party's support. We are really mad as hell, Mr. Speaker, and we are not going to roll over and play dead any more" (*Congressional Record*, 97th Cong., 1st sess., 26 June 1981, vol. 127, p. 3611).

Members' evaluations of their leadership are strongly related to whether the most recent major legislative battle was won or lost. This was evident throughout the interviews; sentiment sometimes altered massively almost overnight. The leaders are at least temporarily blamed for an important loss, regardless of whether their actions were a contributing factor. "They tend to fire the manager after the baseball team loses the pennant," a member said. "It's not unusual in America. Firing the manager doesn't make a 220-hitter hit 300, but there's always going to be dissatisfaction when you don't emerge successful." Legislative losses clearly have a negative impact on party maintenance.

Member dissatisfaction, if it is deep enough, can be politically fatal to the party leadership. A syndrome can develop in which intraparty splits lead to legislative defeats that in turn increase intraparty animosity that further decreases the probability of legislative victories. At some point the leaders' very positions as leaders become endangered. Yet even the mauling House Democrats took in 1981 did not lead to that syndrome. Certainly dissatisfaction was lessened by the improvement in Democratic political prospects by the fall of 1981. The leadership's strategy of inclusion also worked to keep dissatisfaction in check. The wide consultation and broad involvement that the strategy of inclusion entails results in a large proportion of Democrats being participants, rather than just followers, in leadership efforts. Because members of the postreform House want to participate actively and broadly in the legislative process, the opportunity to do so given them by the leadership mitigates dissatisfaction, even when the legislative battles in which they are involved do not end in success. Furthermore, although members blame the leadership when important legislative fights are lost, those members who have participated in the development and implementation of strategy tend to be somewhat more understanding after the initial disappointment has worn off. When the political environment imposes unusual stress on the House Democratic party, the strategy of inclusion cannot prevent, but does serve to mitigate, destructive intraparty dissatisfaction.

The Future of Leadership

■■■■■■■■■■■■■■ During the 95th and 96th congresses the House majority party leadership was reasonably successful at building winning coalitions; but in 1981 it lost the major legislative battles. "Keeping peace in the family" was also much more difficult in the 97th Congress. A change in the broader political environment accounts for the leadership's decline in success. The 1980 election diminished the size of the Democratic majority, demoralized the membership, and further decreased the already shrinking intraparty policy consensus. The result was a series of legislative defeats which then further demoralized Democrats and exacerbated intraparty conflicts.

The political climate and, with it, the leadership's likelihood of success has since changed. The size of the majority tends to be cyclical; an increase makes the successful performance of leadership functions easier directly and, by alleviating members' reelection-related fears, indirectly. The reestablishment of a core intraparty policy consensus of some breadth would significantly increase leadership success; when such a consensus exists, members contribute to leadership success while pursuing their individual goals. Even the reestablishment of a narrower intraparty consensus when accompanied with the likely decline in Republican cohesiveness would increase leadership success. The cyclical character of national party politics assures cyclical variations in leadership success.

Leadership success and leadership influence are not, however, synonymous. A significant increase in leadership resources depends on members' perceiving such an increase to be conducive to their goal attainment. In the late 1970s and early 1980s a growing number of members were concluding that the reforms had gone too far. Many members believe that some subcommittees' lack of expertise, committee chairmen's inability to perform a quality control function, and the increased tendency to mark-up legislation on the floor have seriously impaired the House's capacity to legislate responsibly. Members for whom good public policy is an important goal seem increasingly willing to let the leadership assume a greater role in setting priorities and controlling quality.

Members are also beginning to believe that the attainment of their other goals is hampered by some of the effects of the reforms. The high rate of amending activity on the floor forces members repeatedly to go on the record on politically perilous issues. It also results in extremely lengthy floor sessions that impinge on the time members have for other tasks. In late 1979 a number of Democrats, including junior as well as senior members, sent the Speaker a letter requesting that he make more use of restrictive rules so as to decrease the length of floor sessions, and the Speaker has responded to this request by using restrictive rules more frequently.

To the extent that members become convinced that leadership-strengthening changes are necessary for the attainment of their individual goals, such changes will be made. However, given that impetus for change, it is extremely unlikely that members will alter fundamentally the participatory character of the postreform House. They may be willing to place some restraints on themselves and thereby give the leadership additional tools, but a return to anything approaching the Speakership of the 1890–1910 period is unimaginable.

As Cooper and Brady (1981) have pointed out, the powerful Speakership of the 1890–1910 period depended on the existence of a strong party system in the country and on the member norms attendant on such a system. Turn-of-the-century Speakers had powers that gave them significant influence over member goal attainment. Members supported the strong Speakership because, within a strong party system, the attainment of individual goals is dependent on party success. As the strong party system and its attendant norms began to erode and the Republican party split, more and more members perceived the strong Speakership as a barrier to their goal attainment. Speaker Cannon's spectacular failure to understand that the dictates of party maintenance had changed led to the revolt that stripped the Speaker of much of his power. Barring the reestablishment of a strong party system, members will not again vest such extraordinary powers in their Speaker.

Consequently, the majority party leadership in the foreseeable future will continue to be faced with the tasks of building winning coalitions and "keeping peace in the family" with limited resources and within an environment characterized by wide participation and thus high uncertainty. Leadership success will continue to require accommodating and making use of members' expectations of participation as well as employing limited resources as effectively as possible.

Yet the most important determinants of leaderships success will remain beyond the leaders' control. So long as the majority party leaders have little influence over members' individual goal achievement—and particularly over the reelection goal—their influence over members' behavior within the chamber will remain tenuous. On issues of some saliency, the perceived preferences of constituents and of other political actors who do affect the reelection goal will carry greater weight than the wishes of the leadership. The success of the majority party leadership, consequently, is highly dependent on the content of those perceived preferences. To large extent, the post-Cannon House receives its policy dynamics from the outside. When members perceive strong, clear signals favoring policy change from their constituencies, they respond with policy change. When signals are muted, confused, or contradictory, the House of Representative's capacity to make policy departures of any significance is extremely limited.

REFERENCES

Bach, Stanley. 1980. "The Structure of Choice in the House of Representatives: Recent Uses of Special Rules." Presented at the Annual Meetings of the American Political Science Association, Washington, D.C.

Bibby, John F.; Mann, Thomas E.; and Ornstein, Norman J. 1980. *Vital Statistics on Congress, 1980*. Washington, D.C.: American Enterprise Institute.

Clark, Timothy B., and Cohen, Richard E. 1980. "Balancing the Budget: A Test for Congress—Can It Resist the Pressure to Spend?" *National Journal* 12 (12 April): 588-94.

Clausen, Aage. 1973. *How Congressmen Decide: A Policy Focus*. New York: St. Martin's Press.

Clausen, Aage, and Van Horn, Carl E. 1977. "The Congressional Response to a Decade of Change." *Journal of Politics* 39 (August): 624-66.

Cohen, Richard E. 1978a. "They Won't Take Jim Wright for Granted This Time." *National Journal* 10 (6 May): 712-14.

———. 1978b. "Tip O'Neill: He Gets By with a Little Help from His Friends." *National Journal* 10 (2 September): 1384-88.

———. 1981a. "Budget Battle Takes to the Trenches—But Who Ever Said It Would Be Easy?" *National Journal* 13 (18 April): 645-48.

———. 1981b. "The 'Fun and Games' Are Over—Now Congress Has to Enact the Cuts." *National Journal* 13 (16 May): 888-90.

Congressional Quarterly Weekly Report. Washington, D.C.: Congressional Quarterly. 1976-1981

Congressional Record. 1972-81, daily edition. Washington, D.C.

Cooper, Joseph, and Brady, David W. 1981. "Institutional Context and Leadership Style: The House from Cannon to Rayburn." *American Political Science Review* 75 (June): 411-25.

CQ Guide to the Congress of the United States. 1971. Washington, D.C.: Congressional Quarterly Press.

Davidson, Roger H., and Oleszek, Walter J. 1981. *Congress and Its Members*. Washington, D.C.: Congressional Quarterly Press.

Deering, Christopher, and Smith, Steven. 1980. "Majority Party Leadership and the New House Subcommittee System." Presented at "Understanding Congressional Leadership: The State of the Art," conference sponsored by the Dirksen Center and the Sam Rayburn Library, June, Washington, D.C.

Dodd, Lawrence C. 1979. "The Expanded Roles of the House Democratic Whip System: The 93rd and 94th Congresses." *Congressional Studies* 7 (Spring): 27–56.

Dodd, Lawrence C., and Oppenheimer, Bruce I. 1977. *Congress Reconsidered.* New York: Praeger.

Dodd, Lawrence C., and Sullivan, Terry. 1981. "Majority Party Leadership and Partisan Vote Gathering: The House Democratic Whip System." In *Understanding Congressional Leadership*, ed. Frank H. Mackaman, pp. 227–60. Washington, D.C.: Congressional Quarterly Press.

Ehrenhalt, Alan, ed. 1981. *Politics in America.* Washington, D.C.: Congressional Quarterly Press.

Ellwood, John W., and Thurber, James A. 1981. "The Politics of the Congressional Budget Process Re-examined." In *Congress Reconsidered*, ed. Lawrence C. Dodd and Bruce I. Oppenheimer, 2d ed., pp. 246–71. Washington, D.C.: Congressional Quarterly Press.

Fenno, Richard F. 1965. "The Internal Distribution of Influence: The House." In *The Congress and America's Future*, ed. David B. Truman, pp. 52–76. Englewood Cliffs, N.J.: Prentice-Hall.

_____. 1973. *Congressmen in Committees.* Boston: Little, Brown.

_____. 1978. *Home Style.* Boston: Little, Brown.

_____. 1981. "What's He Like? What's She Like? What Are They Like?" Presented at the Thomas P. O'Neill Conference on the United States Congress, February, Boston College.

Follett, Mary Parker. 1896. Reprint 1974. *The Speaker of the House of Representatives.* New York: Bert Franklin Reprints.

Galloway, George B. 1961. *History of the House of Representatives.* New York: Thomas Y. Crowell.

Gertzog, Irwin N. 1976. "The Routinization of Committee Assignments in the U.S. House of Representatives." *American Journal of Political Science* 29 (November): 693–712.

Harris, Louis. 1973. *The Anguish of Change.* New York: W. W. Norton.

Hinckley, Barbara. 1980. "The American Voter in Congressional Elections." *American Political Science Review* 74 (September): 641–50.

Jacobson, Gary C., and Kernell, Samuel. 1981. *Strategy and Choice in Congressional Elections.* New Haven: Yale University Press.

Johnson, Haynes. 1980. *In the Absence of Power.* New York: Viking Press.

Jones, Charles O. 1981. "House Leadership in an Age of Reform." In *Understanding Congressional Leadership,* ed. Frank H. Mackaman, pp. 117–34. Washington, D.C.: Congressional Quarterly Press.

Kingdon, John. 1973. *Congressmen's Voting Decisions.* New York: Harper & Row.

_____. 1977. "Models of Legislative Voting." *Journal of Politics* 39 (August): 563–95.

LeLoup, Lance T. 1979. "Process vs. Policy: The U.S. House Budget Committee." *Legislative Studies Quarterly* 4 (May): 227–54.

Loomis, Burdett A. 1982. "Congressional Careers, Legislative Behavior and Policy Outcomes." Presented at the Annual Meeting of the Midwest Political Science Association, April–May, Milwaukee.

Malbin, Michael J. 1977. House Democrats Are Playing with a Strong Leadership Lineup." *National Journal* 9 (18 June): 940–46.

_____. 1981. "Remember the Caucus." *National Journal* 13 (12 September): 1642.

Mann, Thomas E., and Wolfinger, Raymond E. 1980. "Candidates and Parties in Congressional Elections." *American Political Science Review* 74 (September): 617–32.

Oleszek, Walter, J. 1978. *Congressional Procedures and the Policy Process.* Washington, D.C.: Congressional Quarterly Press.

_____. 1980. "Multiple Referral of Legislation in the House." Presented at the Annual Meeting of the American Political Science Association, September, Washington, D.C.

Oppenheimer, Bruce I., and Peabody, Robert L. 1977. "How the Race for House Majority Leader Was Won—By One Vote." *The Washington Monthly,* November, pp. 47–56.

Oppenheimer, Bruce I. 1977. "The Rules Committee: New Arm of Leadership in a Decentralized House." In *Congress Reconsidered,* ed. Lawrence C. Dodd and Bruce I. Oppenheimer, pp. 96–116. New York: Praeger.

_____. 1981. "The Changing Relationship between House Leadership and the Committee on Rules." In *Understanding Congressional Leadership,* ed. Frank H. Mackaman, pp. 207–26. Washington, D.C.: Congressional Quarterly Press.

Ornstein, Norman J., ed. 1975. *Congress in Change.* New York: Praeger.

Peabody, Robert L. 1976. *Leadership in Congress.* Boston: Little, Brown.

Ripley, Randall B. 1967. *Party Leaders in the House of Representatives.* Washington, D.C.: Brookings Institute.

_____. 1969. "The Party Whip Organization in the United States House of Representatives." In *New Perspectives on the House of Representatives,* ed. Robert Peabody and Nelson Polsby, 2d ed., pp. 197–226. Chicago: Rand McNally.

Schick, Allen, 1980. *Congress and Money: Budgeting, Spending and Taxing.* Washington, D.C.: Urban Institute.

Shepsle, Kenneth. 1978. *The Giant Jigsaw Puzzle: Democratic Committee Assignments in the Modern House.* Chicago: University of Chicago Press.

Sinclair, Barbara. 1977. "Party Realignment and the Transformation of the Political Agenda: The House of Representatives, 1925–1938. *American Political Science Review* 71 (September): 940–53.

_____. 1981. "Coping with Uncertainty: Building Coalitions in the House and Senate." In *The New Congress,* ed. Thomas Mann and Norman

Ornstein, pp. 178-220. Washington, D.C.: American Enterprise Institute.

_____. 1982. *Congressional Realignment, 1925-1978*. Austin: University of Texas Press.

Volger, David J. 1978. "The Rise of the Ad Hoc Committees in the House of Representatives." Presented at the Annual Meeting of the American Political Science Association, September, New York.

Waldman, Sidney. 1980. "Majority Leadership in the House of Representatives." *Political Science Quarterly* 95 (Fall): 373-93.

Wright, Jim. 1976. "The Responsibilities of the Majority Leader as I View Them." Mimeo.

INDEX

BARBARA SINCLAIR is professor of political science at the University of California, Riverside. She is the author of *The Women's Movement: Political, Socio-Economic and Psychological Issues* and *Congressional Realignment, 1925–1978.*

THE JOHNS HOPKINS UNIVERSITY PRESS

MAJORITY LEADERSHIP IN THE U.S. HOUSE

This book was composed in Times Roman text
and display by Illustrations Unlimited
from a design by Gerard A. Valerio.

It was printed on 50-lb. BookText paper
and bound by Book Crafters, Inc.